TAKING BOOKS
TO THE WORLD

A VOLUME IN THE SERIES
Studies in Print Culture and the History of the Book
EDITED BY
GREG BARNHISEL
ROBERT A. GROSS
JOAN SHELLEY RUBIN
MICHAEL WINSHIP

Taking Books to the World

AMERICAN PUBLISHERS AND THE CULTURAL COLD WAR

Amanda Laugesen

University of Massachusetts Press
Amherst & Boston

Copyright © 2017 by University of Massachusetts Press
All rights reserved
Printed in the United States of America

ISBN 978-1-62534-309-3 (paper); 308-6 (hardcover)

Designed by Jack Harrison
Set in Adobe Garamond Pro with Linotype Centennial display
Printed and bound by Maple Press, Inc.
Cover art: A Cairo exhibit of Franklin's publications, 1958.

Library of Congress Cataloging-in-Publication Data
A catalog record for this book is available from the Library of Congress.

British Library Cataloguing-in-Publication Data
A catalog record for this book is available from the British Library.

All illustrations are from Franklin Book Programs Records, 1920–1978, Public Policy Papers, Department of Rare Books and Special Collections, Princeton University Library.

For Damien

Contents

Acknowledgments ix

Introduction. American Cold War Book Empires 1

Chapter 1. Books for a New War 9

Chapter 2. Book Diplomacy in the Middle East 39

Chapter 3. A World of Books, an Empire of Books 58

Chapter 4. Book Work as Modernization 89

Chapter 5. Book Modernization in Africa and Latin America 113

Chapter 6. The Decline and End of Franklin Book Programs 130

Conclusion. Assessing the Legacy 155

Abbreviations 159

Notes 161

Index 189

Acknowledgments

I began this book while teaching in the Department of American Studies and the Department of History at Flinders University in Adelaide, and I particularly acknowledge the encouragement of Don DeBats during my early research for it. After moving back to Canberra, I worked sporadically on the manuscript for several years while finishing a number of other projects. The School of History at the Australian National University gave me a space to continue my work on the book as well as the opportunity to present some of my ideas in the school's seminar program. Since 2012, I have been working in the School of Literature, Languages, and Linguistics at the university, which gave me the institutional support that allowed me to complete the book. As I was finishing up the manuscript, my colleagues at the Australian National Dictionary Centre tolerated my frequent trips over the lake to the National Library of Australia to read *Publishers Weekly,* for which I am grateful.

The scholarly community, especially the international community of book historians, has been inspiring—especially Greg Barnhisel, Cathy Turner, Trysh Travis, Erin Smith, and John Hench, as well as the broader community of the Society for the History of Authorship, Reading, and Publishing. While I have only occasionally been able to attend their wonderful annual conferences, they have always been a stimulating forum for sharing my work and for learning from the work of my colleagues in book and publishing history. I also thank Louise Robbins, who generously passed on her collection of materials on Franklin Book Programs in 2007; her work on Franklin was an early inspiration for this project, as was her work in book and library history more generally. Bruce Wilcox, the former director of the University of Massachusetts Press and a former employee of Franklin Book Programs, generously shared with me his views on his time at Franklin.

The anonymous readers of my manuscript provided useful and valuable feedback, and their enthusiasm helped me complete the book despite the difficulties I was facing at the time. I am grateful to Doug Craig for reading the entire manuscript and to Damien Browne, who not only read the manuscript but also gave me much detailed feedback and criticism. I also thank Brian Halley of the University of Massachusetts Press, who expressed an interest in the project a few years ago and was very encouraging when I finally submitted the proposal. I greatly appreciate his ongoing assistance in bringing this book to publication. I would also like to thank Dawn Potter for her copyediting work on the manuscript.

Several grants enabled me to complete crucial archival research in the United States. In 2007, I received both a Faculty Establishment Grant from Flinders University and a Friends of the Princeton University Library Research Grant, which allowed me to consult the Franklin Book Programs papers at Princeton's Seeley G. Mudd Manuscript Library. In 2011, I received an Alfred A. and Blanche W. Knopf Fellowship to conduct research in the Knopf papers at the Harry Ransom Center at the University of Texas, Austin. In 2014, I was awarded the Reese Fellowship for American Bibliography and the History of the Book in the Americas from the Bibliographical Society of America, which allowed me to complete my archival research.

I particularly thank the staff at the Mudd Library and the Ransom Center, both wonderful and welcoming places to do research. I also thank the staff at the National Library of Australia (which holds an almost complete run of *Publishers Weekly*) and the National Archives and Record Administration in College Park, Maryland. All of these institutions are vital centers of humanities research and should be supported and preserved. The Franklin bookmen who are the subject of this book had their flaws and their blind spots, but they valued the importance and significance of books and knowledge. In a world in which rational thought, complex ideas, and the beauties of art and culture are increasingly devalued, there is much to be gained from their vision of a world united and inspired by the magic of books.

TAKING BOOKS
TO THE WORLD

INTRODUCTION
American Cold War Book Empires

In 1957, Ghana became an independent nation, and the United States, through Vice-President Richard Nixon, presented the new country with 2,000 technical books to mark the occasion. The American book industry's periodical *Publishers Weekly* noted that this was "as useful a gift as could have been selected," one that demonstrated the U.S. government's recognition of the "importance and influence of books" and thus the American book industry. The gift was, the periodical declared, an embodiment of the slogan "Books Make Friends" and a sign of America's efforts at cultural diplomacy and its desire to help new nations move ahead.[1] This moment in "book diplomacy" offers insight into many of the themes I will explore in this book: the role of books and the book industry in cultural diplomacy and modernization; the desire of American publishers to actively aid Cold War and American foreign policy work while also promoting their product globally and domestically; and the belief that books could help stakeholders achieve a range of lofty goals, from making friends to creating new nations.

There were many different Cold War book programs. The United States Information Agency (USIA) engaged in book translation and publication programs, gave books to institutions and individuals abroad, and set up libraries and reading rooms around the world to promote American culture and values. With government and book industry sponsorship, American book shops were established in countries such as Indonesia and Pakistan not only to promote American books but also to demonstrate commercial bookselling practices. Government-funded organizations translated American books into

Arabic, Hindi, Swahili, and other languages, and they trained publishers and developed book industry practices in the countries in which they operated. The result was a kind of American Cold War book empire, one that brought American books and the publishing industry to all corners of the globe.

This book focuses on one of these Cold War book operations: Franklin Publications, later known as Franklin Book Programs, which was established in 1952 and shut down in 1978. Franklin's history has yet to be fully told, yet a study of its twenty-six years of existence reveals much about the currents within American Cold War publishing.[2] Franklin was established with government money, but it was run by publishers and bookmen and was later supported by private donations, foundation money, and foreign government support. Thus, it brought together public and private motivations for engaging in book work abroad. Because it also worked through local offices and hired local staff, its story allows us to see how people engaged with and regarded this kind of American cultural activity. In 1960, *Publishers Weekly* described Franklin as "the most conspicuously successful piece of book industry foreign relations in the postwar period."[3]

Franklin operated in a variety of countries around the globe, among them Egypt, Iran, Afghanistan, Indonesia, Nigeria, and Pakistan. All of these countries were seeking to modernize, and all were strategically important in America's Cold War with the Soviet Union. To date, most scholarship on the American cultural Cold War has focused on Europe, but Franklin's story takes place in areas of the world that are now considered part of the global south.[4] Examination of its activities expands our understanding of America's cultural Cold War because it allows us to explore how cultural programs worked in countries with less developed cultural industry infrastructure.

Franklin's annual report for 1963 declared that the program was "the unofficial representative of the entire American book world to the book worlds of the other countries and . . . provides liaison among all the interested groups making up the book complex, including educators, editors, writers, illustrators, layout specialists, printers and distributors."[5] This expansive vision is what makes Franklin's story so interesting and important. The organization imagined a world in which an American-style publishing industry stretched across the globe, with books readily available for populations that were moving confidently into the future. Its belief in its own impact was clear: it frequently released statements asserting that Franklin's books were appreciated in many places, even when American power was not. Franklin told an apocryphal tale of a college library in Beirut, where a student sat surrounded by Franklin-sponsored political science texts. A classmate tried to persuade him to come and watch an American movie. The student looked up, pointed at his books, and told his friend, "No, thanks; *this* is the America I want to see."[6]

In its work, Franklin sought to offer a particular image of the United States, one that highlighted the best elements of the nation and of what it had to offer to the world. The organization thus focused on translating serious literature and nonfiction rather than popular fiction. According to Thomas J. Wilson, a director of Harvard University Press and a publisher who worked with Franklin for a number of years, one of the organization's most important goals was to substitute "the image of a book for the image of a soulless machine which America's enemies have tried to fasten on us."[7] Franklin's battle was a Cold War one—the need to combat communism—but it was also about projecting an image of the United States that would improve the world's opinion of the country, its culture, and its ideas, and perhaps promote this particular view of the United States at home as well.

In this book, I concentrate more on the functioning of American book programs than on the texts themselves. Although Franklin translated and promoted specific types of books and authors, the heart of its story was its vision of developing book industries and book cultures abroad. Franklin bookmen placed great value on the object of the book and all it represented in culture and society. Hence, they took a holistic view in promoting and building the book industry, including bookselling, distribution, paper supply and printing, and library and literacy programs. They wove these ideas into the framework of modernization and development that was popular in American foreign policy and aid programs during the 1950s and 1960s.[8] Franklin's work thus came to encompass book modernization as well as book diplomacy, and my exploration of this aspect of its work adds a new perspective to how cultural and modernization programs came together.

As I have mentioned, Franklin was supported through its life by a mix of public and private funding, notably from the USIA, the United States Agency for International Development (AID), and the Ford Foundation. It also received money and support from the governments of countries in which its programs operated. Institutional and corporate support came through donations and through the participation of key individuals on Franklin's board of directors. Government and foundation money helped to put American books into circulation around the globe, and assisted the American commercial publishing industry to find its way into (if only fitfully) new foreign markets.

Franklin was a good example of the complex state and private networks that were crucial to America's Cold War operations.[9] Writing about the importance of examining "non-state actors" in Cold War cultural diplomacy, Andrew J. Falk notes that it is possible to see cultural diplomacy as a "messy and mutable process of collaboration and adaptation."[10] It is also possible to trace the continuing presence of cultural internationalism—which largely disappears from state-run cultural work—in private initiatives such as Franklin's. The organization's story is a testament to the complexities, tensions, and fissures in state-private networks. Franklin and the book industry would eventually become disillusioned with the way in which American government book diplomacy worked, dissatisfaction that echoes the questioning of American foreign policy that became mainstream by the 1970s but also reflects the failure of the state-private network to function as effectively as it could have.

In his study of the British publisher Allen Lane of Penguin Books, Alistair McCleery has highlighted the importance of considering publishers as individuals as much as corporate entities.[11] The Franklin story spotlights the story of American publishers at an important time in publishing history, and several key figures played an important role in the program, notably Datus Smith, formerly of Princeton University Press. Franklin's bookmen had a particular vision of publishing and of the world that they sought to export, and they had a significant impact on publishing and the book industry both at home and abroad. Yet like other empires, the U.S. Cold War book empire was fraught with tensions and complications. The people who ran the empire did so for a variety of reasons. The empire itself was made up of many different types of programs and outposts, which achieved varying degrees of success and acceptance among local populations. Some of the people in the empire's outposts cooperated because they believed in the empire; others cooperated for reasons of self-interest. Moreover, the ideology of the empire was not always consistent.

An imperial analogy works well for thinking about American book diplomacy, even though American publishers would never have considered themselves imperialist. Nonetheless, today it is hard to avoid seeing that America's cultural Cold War functioned as a type of imperialism—subtle and complex at times, and certainly soft power—in its dimensions and ambitions. The United States became heavily involved in many countries during and beyond the Cold War. It directly intervened in some cases; it had more subtle influence in others. Its involvement can be defined as imperialism because it undoubtedly desired to control and influence, yet American imperialism varied from place to place and was also laden with a rhetoric that presented the United States as determinedly *anti*-imperial. Imperialist thinking helped to structure the engagements of American programs on the ground and was often underpinned by preexisting assumptions about the nature of what were considered to be traditional or underdeveloped societies. Often this engagement was also underpinned by racial assumptions.

American imperialism was not simply met with anti-Americanism. It is important not to generalize about the nature of local opposition to programs such as Franklin's, for responses were often complex and tied to a range of locally driven factors. Max Paul Friedman's study of anti-Americanism suggests that it is important to understand criticism of American policy, activities, and programs in a nuanced way.[12] Many of the countries in which Franklin operated had or would develop strong opposition to the United States, but they also exhibited considerable support for American assistance and involvement. The developing world embraced what it wanted from programs such as Franklin's, using what worked and rejecting what did not. Books and culture became important means for promoting cultural nationalism in the face of cultural imperialism, but it is possible to discern a variety of motives for embracing elements of American culture as well as the multiple uses to which such culture was put.[13]

Undoubtedly, book diplomacy and book modernization programs worked to fashion a kind of imperial culture. Book professionals sought to transfer American culture and know-how to other countries, in part because that transfer would help to fashion a world that was more familiar and more manageable. In so doing, they posited American culture and values as superior and desirable. While there were disagreements over just what version of America was being exported by cultural diplomacy efforts (a highbrow culture? American popular culture? art, music, or engineering?), the bookmen were united in believing that the United States offered the best possible model for others to follow.[14] This fundamental assumption structured American understandings of and engagements with other countries.

Imperialism provides one framework for understanding Franklin's book work; another is globalization. The term has become a buzzword in recent scholarship, but it does have some applicability to understanding the Franklin story—not so much in the government's book diplomacy efforts (texts had a limited effect in transmitting American ideas to the world, especially when compared to, for example, Hollywood films) but in some of the attempts to develop book trade and publishing industries.[15] Book historians have been calling for a greater focus on the international dimensions of the history of publishing as a way to illuminate networks of power, influence, and trade across the globe; and in this book's conclusion I discuss some of the lasting legacies of Franklin, including the training of national and international book industry professionals.[16] Franklin functioned as a national organization, focusing on American concerns and the commercial interests of American publishers. At the same time it envisioned and wanted to create a global publishing industry. Publishers abroad were seen as part of a common global network, an imagined community of bookmen interested in the publication of serious intellectual and cultural works. In this aspect of its work, Franklin had an impact on the globalization of publishing and so, perhaps, helped to promote some version of international understanding.

Franklin Publications was very much a creature of its time. Its bookmen fervently believed in the power of the book to transform lives and societies; they saw it as a way to win the Cold War and thus spread the American versions of freedom and democracy. These men looked to a future in which American books would help to bring prosperity to both the United States and the world. Their work was underpinned by many assumptions: that literacy and education were necessary and desirable, that American-style modernity should be embraced, and that the American book industry was the best model for all nations to follow. In her study of jazz ambassadors during the Cold War, Penny Von Eschen writes that cultural programs, although initiated as exercises in cultural diplomacy, could be used by participants in a variety of ways, some of which significantly reworked the official image of the United States promoted by the state.[17] In other words, those who participated in Cold War government programs rarely replicated the government line without modification. There was always agency and resistance. Franklin operated in ways that reflected official cultural diplomacy and modernization efforts, but it also developed its own ideas, frameworks, and programs that made its work in book diplomacy and modernization different from the government's.

Franklin's commercial ambitions were fundamental to the work it tried to do, and understanding those ambitions is key to understanding the organization's rise and fall. Franklin saw itself as an advocate for the publishing industry's role in world affairs, not least because it hoped that trade would follow diplomacy. It wanted to show the U.S. government and the people of the world that American publishers were fully supportive of the Cold War and of general social and political progress and welfare. By so doing, they demonstrated their corporate citizenship on an international stage. Yet they kept their focus on expanding the American book trade to new areas of the globe, and these commercial aspirations shaped all that they did.

My goal in this book is to contribute to our understanding of how American publishers participated in the cultural Cold War and how they used their participation to further their own interests at home and abroad, primarily by emphasizing the book's importance in American society and culture and by working to expand their industry into overseas markets.[18] In the age of mass media, Franklin's bookmen sought every opportunity to promote the importance of books and reading at home and abroad. They fervently believed that books could improve lives. Thus, they were patriots and philanthropists as well as businessmen, for they saw their work as both a profession and a vocation. These roles sometimes came together effectively; at other times, they were less easy to reconcile.

Taking Books to the World is structured chronologically. Chapter 1 explores the founding of Franklin at the beginning of the Cold War. It examines earlier efforts in American book diplomacy and in particular considers the Council Books in Wartime, a World War II operation, as a model for how Franklin would operate. The chapter also considers the broader contexts of the early cultural Cold War and early development thought as well as the concerns of the American publishing industry.

Chapter 2 is a case study of Franklin's operations in the Middle East. The organization's first office (established in 1953) was in Cairo and was intended to produce American books translated into Arabic. It laid the foundations for Franklin's subsequent operations and provided a model that the organization then tried to replicate in other offices.

Chapter 3 focuses on Franklin's expansion into other areas around the globe, including East and West Pakistan, Southeast Asia, and Iran—all of them places of geopolitical importance as the U.S. government ramped up its cultural diplomacy efforts in regions it believed were threatened by communism. This chapter also examines Franklin's relationship with the USIA and examines some of the texts it produced and helped to put into circulation.

Chapter 4 explores Franklin's work during the 1960s as a book industry modernizer and focuses on how Franklin incorporated and put into practice modernization ideas in its work. Chapter 5 explores two case studies from that decade, Africa and Latin America, demonstrating that the offices founded during those years were explicitly conceived within a modernization framework.

Chapter 6 considers Franklin's demise in the 1970s. The Iranian office was the last to close its doors: already an independent organization, it came to an end with the 1979 Iranian Revolution. Franklin as a whole failed to survive for many reasons, the most basic of which was its lack of funding. But its demise also signaled a change in attitudes toward American foreign policy, fundamental shifts in the publishing industry, and the passing of a generation of publishers who had committed to helping the government fight its international battles.

In 1958, Datus Smith, the president of Franklin Publications, delivered the eighteenth Bowker Lecture on Book Publishing at the New York Public Library. In that prestigious forum, he identified what he considered to be the moral responsibility of the American book industry to the rest of the world. Commercial interests should not be paramount in book work abroad, he argued. If American publishers were to stop the translation of American books into other languages to preserve English language book sales, they would do a "grave disservice to Asia." U.S. publishers should support the translation of American books into other languages; they should also support the development of book industries abroad. "The imperialist approach to book publishing is no longer good enough," he argued. "The whole cultural and political temper of the times rejects as outdated the condescending idea that smaller or less developed countries will be content to remain in cultural tutelage forever." Smith went on to condemn American cultural provincialism and called for more books in translation to be published in the United States "for the good of our own souls."[19]

Smith's lecture was addressed to the American book industry, an attempt to convince it to support the work of Franklin, then barely five years old. His words are admirable and suggest the importance that cultural internationalism and morality played in the Franklin project, but they also disguise the much more complicated, and political, story of American publishers abroad. By working to understand the complex politics of American book diplomacy and book modernization during the nation's cultural Cold War, we can learn much about the exercise of American power, the nature of the Cold War, and the role that American publishers played in it.

1

Books for a New War

On June 5, 1952, a group of men gathered in a room on Fifth Avenue in Manhattan to incorporate Franklin Publications. Malcolm Johnson, the head of the publishing company D. Van Nostrand, was named its temporary chairman, and George P. Brett of Macmillan Publishing became its temporary secretary.[1] A who's who of figures from the worlds of American publishing, education, and libraries were present that day, and many would play roles at Franklin over the years. They included Robert L. Crowell (of Thomas Y. Crowell), Cass Canfield (of Harper and Brothers), Leon Shimkin (of Simon and Schuster), Douglas M. Black (of Doubleday), Victor Weybright (of the New American Library), Robie D. Marriner (of the American Book Company), Curtis W. McGraw (of McGraw-Hill), John O'Connor (of Bantam), Datus Smith (of Princeton University Press), Arthur S. Adams (the president of the American Council on Education), Carl H. Kraeling (a Yale University professor and an expert in Near Eastern archaeology), Harold D. Lasswell (a political scientist and communications expert), Luther H. Evans (the librarian of Congress and later the director-general of the United Nations Educational, Scientific, and Cultural Organization), Francis R. St. John (the director of the Brooklyn Public Library), and Norman Armour (a diplomat).[2]

Franklin's lengthy certificate of incorporation included an idealistic statement of purpose in a postwar world, one that promised,

> through the publication and dissemination of the printed word to the peoples of the world outside the United States of America and its territories, to stimulate interest in and to promote the freedom, dignity and welfare of mankind; and to convey to them knowledge and information relating to

the people of the United States, and to stimulate interest in the history, government, culture, economy, technology, science and learning of the people of the United States.

To achieve these aims, it would translate and assist in the publication of books, magazines, and other printed material in languages other than English; commission publications in languages other than English; secure translation rights with American publishers; help develop publishing and manufacturing operations; and work to establish effective book marketing and distribution channels.[3] Franklin's board of directors would consult and guide its work and decisions, and a president would oversee its day-to-day operations. A chairman would head the board, which would consist of members with some "technical knowledge in the publishing field and its problems" (in other words, industry figures) and a slightly smaller number with "experience in the fields of education, literature or public affairs, and [who] shall represent the public interest."[4] Two weeks later, a public announcement described the founding of Franklin Publications and declared that Datus Smith would be its first president.

Established with a $500,000 grant from the U.S. Department of State, Franklin was initially intended to be a Middle East operation with the task of translating and publishing American books into Arabic.[5] A brief November 1952 article in *Publishers Weekly* described it as a "private and independent organization" established "because . . . the need for books in other countries could not be met either by the direct activities of government or by straight commercial operations."[6] It was an offspring of the American Book Publishers Council (ABPC), the industry's representative body, and an attempt to support U.S. government work by making American books available around the world.[7] Dan Lacy, a notable figure in the ABPC, was convinced that the publishing industry would be better at this work than the government.[8]

Franklin's establishment demonstrated the publishing industry's support for Cold War activity and served to assert the importance of the book and the publishing industry and its expertise in American life. But it was also an attempt to gain a foothold for American publishers in areas of the world in which they had not previously operated. In the early 1950s, optimism about global American commercial expansion was high, and the developing world and areas that had formerly been part of European empires seemed to offer potential new markets for U.S. publishers. Franklin could help publishers survey possible commercial opportunities and lay the foundations for a future commercial trade in American books.

Franklin drew on World War II precedents, especially the work of the Council Books in Wartime. It hoped to replicate the council's success in asserting the value of books and reading to American society as well as the achievements of the council's Overseas Editions program in bringing American books to liberated Europe. In addition, several key contexts shaped Franklin's early formation and work: the early cultural Cold War as formulated and waged through the 1950s; the publishing industry's desire to explore commercial opportunities abroad while supporting the Cold War; and the idealism of Franklin's members and supporters, who were committed to spreading American-style publishing, books, and education to other parts of the world. Yet before discussing these contexts, we need to consider the longer history of American book diplomacy.

The Beginnings of U.S. Book Diplomacy

Before and during World War II, the U.S. government engaged in several cultural relations programs in which books played a small but significant part. By relying on the support of private industry and private organizations and institutions, it began to form the state-private network that would become an important dimension of cultural diplomacy after the war. There were advantages for private industry in engaging with government initiatives. During the war, for instance, the book industry worked with the government in book programs that not only served the war effort but also helped American publishers establish themselves more effectively in the European market. This focus on globalizing the American book market continued after the war, albeit with greater complications.

Emily Rosenberg writes about an ideology of "liberal developmentalism" that shaped America's relationship with the world from 1890 to the end of World War II and identifies a number of major features that characterized this ideology. These included a belief that other nations could and should replicate America's own developmental experience; faith in private free enterprise and support for free or open access for trade and investment; the promotion of the free flow of information and culture; and a growing acceptance of governmental activity to protect private enterprise and stimulate and regulate American participation in international economic and cultural exchange. Rosenberg points to Americans' faith in their own country's history as a universal model as well as a new sense of America's mission in the world that was developing through this period.[9] Frank Ninkovich similarly hypothesizes the development of what he calls "liberal internationalism" by the end of the nineteenth century. Liberal internationalists imagined a global economy organized by free trade, envisioned a common humankind, and assumed the eventual triumph of liberal democracy.[10]

These scholars' ideas provide a useful starting point for understanding the way in which Americans approached global engagement in the twentieth century. For many Americans, the United States offered the ideal model for others to replicate, one fundamentally based on free enterprise. Some felt a duty to bring their ideas, culture, and industry to the world. Tied to this interest was a desire to take American technology and ingenuity to the world, especially to places they saw as less developed. Well before the Cold War, Americans were convinced of their capacity to offer the world a model of progress based on the U.S. experience, and their convictions sometimes extended to active intervention. For example, efforts at development and social engineering were very much in evidence during the U.S. occupation of the Philippines after the Spanish-American War.[11]

Before World War I, there was no formal governmental program to oversee cultural diplomacy or to engage in technical aid or intervention but the United States had many informal global encounters. Alongside America's state-led activities, such as the Spanish-American War and the subsequent occupation of the Philippines, were a range of private initiatives and involvements, such as American missionary activity in China and elsewhere and increased American investment in a range of countries, particularly in Latin America and the Caribbean. Technical missions to countries such as Japan and Persia (now known as Iran) aimed to help them modernize, usually along American lines.[12] All of these early engagements were marked by a U.S. belief in itself as a model society and were often motivated in part by the desire to establish connections that benefited U.S. commercial interests. At the same time, this global engagement allowed Americans to encounter others and opened them to new ideas and cultures. Some Americans began to envision a world made up of people who had more commonalities than differences, and the seeds of a liberal vision of one world were sown.

Government-sponsored cultural diplomacy was first practiced during World War I. President Woodrow Wilson created the Committee for Public Information (CPI) for the duration of U.S. involvement in the war, and it engaged in a range of informational, cultural, and propaganda activities. The CPI was headed by George Creel, a former journalist who was keen to use the agency to make an impact at home and abroad. It set an important precedent, producing a wide array of governmental propaganda, including pamphlets and films that extolled the United States and its way of life. The material sought to convey America's image "as a powerful, industrialized, free, and just society that others should emulate." This image was also tied to a desire to promote an American vision of a new international order, which Wilson imagined might develop after the end of the war.[13]

World War I marked an important stage in U.S. engagement with the world, particularly in its demonstration of a new desire to actively promote American principles, ideas, and values abroad.[14] The period also saw the formation of some of the mechanisms of this promotional activity. The CPI opened several overseas outposts, including some in Latin America. It also engaged in book-related activity, establishing a few reading rooms abroad, among them one in Mexico City. When the war ended, the CPI's work ceased, but Creel and the agency had proven that the United States could be successfully advertised through mass media.[15] This lesson would be useful when World War II began.

Although the U.S. government took part in few official cultural activities abroad during the interwar period, American industry and private organizations and institutions became increasingly interested in and engaged with the world. Foundations were particularly active in building international ties.[16] Among them were the Carnegie Endowment for International Peace, founded in 1910; the Rockefeller Foundation, established in 1913; and the Ford Foundation, created in 1936. Organizations such as the Carnegie Endowment were, as Rosenberg explains, "a private diplomatic presence" on the global stage during this period, as they would be during the Cold War, and their activities generally complemented official governmental policy and attitudes. Rosenberg observes that interwar internationalism tended to assume the "superiority and inevitable spread of American techniques and values," yet this cultural internationalism was complex.[17] While it undoubtedly focused on the spread of American values and capitalism throughout the world, it also opened communication with other countries and helped Americans develop a more global perspective.

This interest in cultural internationalism diminished during the Depression. In contrast to the 1920s, cultural relations during the 1930s were increasingly formulated in terms of national interest. Globally, culture became more politicized, notably in Nazi Germany and the Soviet Union.[18] The U.S. government's instrumentalist view of culture and knowledge would establish itself firmly after World War II. Yet even though the Democratic administration of

Franklin D. Roosevelt took some interest in how the United States might relate to the world through official programs, there was only minimal official cultural diplomacy activity during this decade. In 1938, the Roosevelt administration established the Division of Cultural Relations within the U.S. Department of State, with a primary focus on Latin America. The new division sought to involve—indeed, to rely on—the private sector for much of its work. But it also viewed cultural relations as a two-way exchange. That is, the division saw its role as communicating "the spiritual and intellectual values" of the United States to other nations, but it also wanted to help Americans understand other countries' cultures.[19]

Development efforts in the interwar period were, like cultural activities, largely confined to private-sector initiatives. However, David Ekbladh notes that the success of the Tennessee Valley Authority (TVA) provided an important model of how successful, large-scale modernization of regional areas might occur. As a New Deal project, the TVA was about more than just bringing electricity to a disadvantaged area of the United States. As Ekbladh argues, it was "a total project, vast in its scope, where social and cultural changes were integral." The intent was to fundamentally transform lives. At the same time, liberals were beginning to assert their model of modernization against totalitarian alternatives.[20]

What was the place of the book in the interwar period, and why did come to be seen as an important part of both cultural diplomacy and development efforts? The United States was a global pioneer in the provision of public libraries and in the professionalization of librarianship, and by the beginning of the twentieth century literacy and education had ensured the status of the book in American society and culture. Most library professionals believed that books would help produce an educated and informed citizenry who could participate effectively in public life. Through the end of the nineteenth century, libraries had served as key cultural institutions, providing moral and cultural guidance to the American people. Tied to the library was a faith in education and the belief that education could be a significant solution to social problems.[21] Thomas Augst writes that the modern library invested reading with a "public faith in secular ideals of individual and collective progress."[22] By the interwar period, however, books were competing with radio and cinema for public attention. Both the publishing industry and the library profession were thus concerned about promoting the relevance of the book and reading. Asserting the value of the book abroad could also be a way of asserting the value of the book at home.

Books played a small role in the various cultural internationalist projects that took place before World War I and during the interwar period. The Carnegie Endowment, for example, established a Division of Intercourse and Education that distributed American literature and books on American historical subjects to libraries in Europe, South America, and Asia.[23] The Carnegie Corporation of New York sponsored and funded Carnegie libraries throughout the English-speaking world, and these libraries were important resources in many areas in which access to libraries and books was otherwise limited. In South Africa, for example, where library access was generally restricted to Europeans, the Carnegie libraries were open to people of color.[24] However, on the eve of World War II, the place of the book in American activity abroad was still largely unarticulated and unacknowledged.

World War II: Propaganda, Cultural Diplomacy, and Books

During World War II, there was a definitive shift in the nature of cultural diplomacy and the role of U.S. state propaganda. Ideologies—fascism, communism, and democracy—were central to the imagining of the war, so propaganda and cultural and information activities were considered important enough to be undertaken by government. While the state recognized its responsibility, it undertook much of this activity with the cooperation of private organizations and industry, who made the most of this chance to ally themselves with the state. This allowed players such as the book industry to promote their product at home and abroad, and to lobby for increased trade opportunities. Other cultural industries, such as Hollywood, took similar advantage of the war.

Reflecting the book world's ongoing interest in cultural internationalism, U.S. book efforts began before the nation officially entered the war. For example, the American Library Association conducted a Books for China campaign in 1938 and 1939, with the goal of supplying books to Chinese collections devastated during the Japanese occupation (although most shipments arrived well after the end of the hostilities).[25] Government, too, began to establish promotional agencies before the United States entered the war. In 1940, Nelson Rockefeller was appointed to head the Office of the Coordinator for Inter-American Affairs (CIAA), an agency aimed at improving cultural, trade, and business relations between the United States and Latin America and introducing American corporations to this "vast underdeveloped market."[26] The CIAA's work included the translation and dissemination of American books.[27] Other areas of the globe eventually became the responsibility of the Division of Cultural Relations, which in 1944 moved into the State Department's new Office of Public Information.

Both the Office of War Information (OWI) and the Office of Strategic Services (OSS) were active in propaganda and cultural diplomacy during the war, and books and other printed material formed an essential part of their arsenal. By 1948, U.S. information libraries had been established in Europe, the Middle East, Asia, and Australia.[28] After the war they were the basis for an extensive global network of American information libraries. Wartime agencies also took an interest in the concept of psychological warfare. In 1942, General Dwight D. Eisenhower created a Psychological Warfare Branch within the U.S. Army that was to operate in North Africa. In 1944, a larger Psychological Warfare Division was created within the Supreme Headquarters Allied Expeditionary Force.[29]

The wartime approach tended toward the unidirectional; that is, government used various media forms as propaganda tools to promote American values and objectives.[30] However, the cause of cultural internationalism and exchange continued to be championed, notably by Archibald MacLeish, an American poet and the librarian of Congress, who was also the assistant director of the OWI. Clear tensions developed within government agencies between the idea of information activity, which largely moved in one direction, and cultural exchange, which implied a two-way relationship. Yet despite these tensions, the government's war efforts continued to harness private networks, industry, and organizations. As I have mentioned, the most important of these collaborations in the book and publishing field was the Council on Books in Wartime, a precedent and template for Franklin Publications.

The war was a boon for the American publishing industry.[31] Even before the nation's formal entry into the war, publishers had been interested in promoting the buying and reading of books, and one manifestation of that interest was the 1940 creation of the American Book Council.[32] During the war, publishing houses eyed the global market while professing patriotism and the promotion of democracy. For example, in November 1944, Simon and Schuster and Pocket Books joined forces "to expand and activate their postwar book publishing plans." Marshall Field III, who had purchased the two companies that year, declared in a press release: "I believe in better and better books for more and more people. I share their conviction that books will play an increasingly vital role in safeguarding and enriching the democratic way of life the world over."[33] Another notable wartime event in the book world was the formation of the American Textbook Publishers Institute in 1942, which aimed to "assist in helping to win the war and the peace that will follow by cooperating with our national government and its agencies."[34]

The formation of the Council on Books in Wartime showed that American publishers, librarians, and other book industry professionals wanted to support the war effort. It also signaled their desire to assert the importance of the book to American and global society. Much of the wartime discussion of books emphasized the contrast between the democracy of American reading and book culture and the Nazi book burnings.[35] The American Library Association enthusiastically embraced the ideological war against totalitarianism, exhorting librarians in December 1939, well before the attack on Pearl Harbor, to "mobilize all educational and cultural resources for the preservation and improvement of American democracy."[36] In 1942, after the United States had entered the war, the association formulated a statement on the profession's role in wartime that included a call for librarians to inform people about the war and the world they wanted afterward.[37] Librarians were also active in supporting the war cause and the aims and objectives of the OWI. Notably, libraries became sites for Victory Book campaigns, and the association emphasized the importance of the public library in a pluralistic democracy.[38]

The Council on Books in Wartime, in conjunction with the OWI, initiated and oversaw the publication of books in translation, known as Overseas Editions, intended to be circulated in European countries after their liberation. As John B. Hench notes, this allowed publishers "to establish a beach-head for their literary properties in Europe and elsewhere around the world." The council also published specially formatted books for American service personnel (known as Armed Services Editions) and engaged in home-front campaigns to promote the reading of certain books deemed valuable to understanding the war. During 1944 and 1945, seventy-two editions of forty-one titles were published as Overseas Editions, with more than 3.5 million copies shipped to Europe. The OWI selected titles for the Overseas Editions program based on their ability to meet propaganda goals, but the program also wanted to help reestablish and rehabilitate European publishing houses. The process of translating American books for this market served as a model for postwar translation activities. For example, for the program to work, American publishers had to be willing to provide translation rights at a reasonable price.[39] Furthermore, the books needed to be sold rather than given away because free books might have made some potential readers believe that they were worthless.[40]

As Europe was liberated, American publishers began to establish a presence on the continent and build up relationships with its publishers and booksellers. The American book trade was keen to continue pursuing these international interests after the war ended and sought government support to facilitate the circulation of American books abroad. Likewise, the State Department was eager to maintain the cooperation and assistance of private organizations and industry in its work. Thus, in 1945, the short-lived U.S. International Book Association was established. More than sixty American publishers became members, but the organization did not survive beyond the end of 1946. Subsequently, however, the American Book Publishers Council organized a foreign trade committee with the brief of promoting American books abroad. Hench concludes that wartime book programs contributed to the long-term expansion of American books abroad, even if they did not cause that expansion.[41]

After 1945: Finding Direction in Cultural Diplomacy

Wartime agencies such as the OWI were disbanded by the end of 1945, and the newly formed Office of International Information and Cultural Affairs took over the various programs and activities begun during the conflict. In the immediate postwar years, there was little direction in cultural and information efforts, but there were a number of structural reorganizations. The Office of International Information and Cultural Affairs gave way to the Office of International Information and Education Exchange in 1947, although funding for its activities was significantly reduced from wartime levels. However, by the early 1950s, growing Cold War anxieties were fueling a greater concern about information, and cultural diplomacy was back on the agenda.

The Smith-Mundt Bill of 1948 appropriated funds for a U.S. cultural diplomacy program and led to the creation of the Office of International Information and the Office of Educational Exchange. Two advisory committees oversaw these offices: the U.S. Advisory Commission on Information and the U.S. Advisory Commission on Educational Exchange. Both the education and the information programs struggled for support and funding from members of Congress who saw no reason to continue such activities after the war or were concerned about Communist infiltration of the State Department.[42] Still, a foundation was laid for the more substantial information work of the Eisenhower period.

The advisory commissions of both programs took an interest in the role of books and libraries in cultural diplomacy and information work. Committee members saw libraries as important purveyors of information about U.S. society and government policies to people abroad as well as essential distributors of scientific and technical materials.[43] In a 1949 report titled "Trading Ideas with the World," the Advisory Commission on Educational Exchange noted that U.S. libraries abroad were "among the chief outlets for American thought and culture." It championed traveling book exhibits as a way of promoting American books and thus American culture. The pamphlet also mentioned translation as "an obviously effective way of making United States ideas readily available to the peoples of other countries."[44]

During the Truman years, government funding was also used to create covert programs and to wage psychological warfare. National Security Council directives, such as NSC-10/2 permitted the setting up of covert international operations; and in 1950, NSC-68 began conceiving of the Cold War as a "total" struggle against the Soviet Union.[45] Importantly, NSC-68 made culture an integral part of American foreign policy activity, defining the concept as the means through which a particular, often idealized, vision of America could be projected internationally in a new ideological struggle. It would be facilitated in part by books and other media.[46] In April of that year, Truman launched the Campaign of Truth, a propaganda and cultural offensive with four principal Cold War objectives: generating confidence in America's leadership of the free world; countering the misrepresentation of America abroad, especially in Communist propaganda; asserting that the United States desired peace but was prepared for war; and undermining the confidence of the Soviet Union.[47] The Campaign of Truth was a markedly more aggressive propaganda and anti-Communist strategy, but it also relied heavily on the assistance of private organizations and institutions. Throughout this period, as official information activities and policy took shape, the State Department was honing the image of America that it wanted to project. As Frank Ninkovich notes, the department found it difficult to make a complete shift from the cultural liberal internationalism that had dominated in past years to a position of "reflexive, visceral anti-Communism."[48] Liberal discourse was therefore modified and harmonized with the demands of anti-communism, often by an articulation of the need to defend cultural and intellectual freedom.

Books and libraries were considered important elements of the new weaponry of information. U.S. Information Service (USIS) libraries, established during World War II, became central features of the government's overseas presence. Intended as clearinghouses for information about the United States, they often functioned as important centers for cultural activities that furthered the aims of U.S. information and cultural diplomacy work. In January 1952, the U.S. International Information Administration came into being as a semi-autonomous agency responsible for the government's information programs; and in June 1953, the United States Information Agency (USIA) was created. After much restructuring, the USIA became the home of information and cultural diplomacy efforts during the Eisenhower administration and remained so until the end of the Cold War, although some cultural activities, such as cultural exchange, remained within the State Department.

The bureaucratic reorganizing during this period highlights the government's struggle for a clear direction in cultural diplomacy and information work. Stakeholders could not easily decide exactly what government-directed cultural diplomacy should consist of or even if it should exist. The onset of the Cold War, however, meant that cultural diplomacy had become an ideological necessity, and policymakers were establishing an infrastructure for the future. They were also ensuring that culture and information would become important facets of American foreign policy. Increasingly, cultural internationalism was giving way to a nationalist, state-driven set of cultural and information policies within government-run programs, although it would not be completely extinguished.[49] The creators of these programs were preoccupied with integrating others into an American vision of the world, with American values (as imagined by government) as the perceived ideal. In other words, the postwar cultural offensive was becoming a one-way directive rather than a two-way relationship.

Truman's approach to the Cold War also included the development of the Point Four program, which aimed to provide technical assistance to countries for reasons that involved both national security and humanitarianism.[50] Technical assistance would be an explicit tool of U.S. foreign policy.[51] Gilbert Rist argues that the Point Four declaration inaugurated the "development age," helping to shift a global paradigm from colonizer-colonized to developed-underdeveloped and thus holding out the possibility that the underdeveloped might achieve development. It also presented development as *the* solution to the problems of humanity.[52] Later in this book, I will consider the importance of modernization, which was at least as crucial as official information and propaganda were in America's Cold War book activities. Here, however, I want to acknowledge the longer history of development ideas and the desire to modernize the world. Under the aegis of Point Four, new postwar government programs and structures initiated the process of technical involvement and transfer abroad.

In retrospect it is easy to see the imperial nature of such modernization efforts; but as Michael Latham explains, the Point Four program was originally framed as "an inherently anti-colonial venture." Development "promised a liberal, even altruistic means to meet and manage the ambitions of anti-colonial elites, . . . promoting economic growth, better living standards, and improvements in education and health care would satisfy nationalist aspirations and prevent radical alternatives."[53] Point Four and other U.S. technical assistance and aid programs were deeply bound up in the politics of the Cold War. To combat the appeal of the Soviet model of nation building and rapid development, the United States needed an American-style liberal capitalist model that would appeal to new and developing nations as well as the means to export it to the world.

The Technical Cooperation Administration, established in October 1950, was the first agency to oversee aid and development, although the PL-480 program, begun in 1949, was already shipping surplus food to thirty-six designated countries, and its money could also be allocated to book purchases. The 1950s Truman and Eisenhower administrations did not emphasize modernization in the ways that the 1960s Kennedy and Johnson administrations would, but they did begin to take American expertise to the world as a means of assisting nations to modernize along American lines. Books were not central to this vision, but some American publishers and bookmen were starting to conceive of their work as a potentially integral part of the modernization and development process.

Eisenhower and the Early Cultural Cold War

Shortly after coming into office, Eisenhower convened the President's Committee on International Information Activities, which became known as the Jackson Committee. It was headed by C. D. Jackson, who had pioneered ideas about psychological warfare while he was working in the OSS. Assigned to review America's current propaganda and information programs, the committee began its inquiry in January 1953 and issued a report in June of that year.[54] It called for a restructuring of America's propaganda apparatus, and in response the USIA was established as an agency separate from the State Department. Eisenhower believed in the power of psychological warfare, which he had seen in action during his service in World War II, and in

September 1953 he created the Operations Coordinating Board, whose mandate was to take the offensive in the global battle for hearts and minds.[55] Yet there was little evidence that psychological warfare really worked, and gradually the administration came to rely on cultural diplomacy and information efforts, primarily through the USIA.

According to Kenneth Osgood, the USIA "considered its principle charge to be the management of public opinion in the non-communist world."[56] Its primary concern was with unidirectional information flow across the globe, and the agency increasingly emphasized the need for quantifiable results related to information and propaganda work.[57] While Europe was an important target throughout the Cold War, the USIA was also increasingly attentive to developing and emerging nations. Its efforts were aimed at countries considered to be at risk from communism, but the agency also aimed to communicate information that would generally improve other nations' views of the United States, its policies, and its culture.

During the early Cold War, many American officials called for a more aggressive approach to promoting the United States and its values abroad. In his 1953 book *Truth Is Our Weapon,* Edward W. Barrett, who had served as assistant secretary of state for Public Affairs from 1950 to 1952, claimed that a "war of ideas" was "now going on." He argued that America must learn to "master the techniques of public persuasion" and concluded that it had "no intelligent choice but to keep its case continually before the world."[58] Oren Stephens, the USIA's deputy assistant director for Policy and Programs, in *Facts to a Candid World* (1955), noted the USIA's importance in communicating "that the objectives and policies of the United States are in harmony with and will advance [other nations'] legitimate aspirations for freedom, progress and peace."[59] One of the key themes that the USIA emphasized in its campaigns was the promotion of U.S. democracy, broadly defined as national self-determination and individual liberty. It was extolled in various USIA information campaigns, including books selected for distribution. The agency also promoted religious freedom and spiritual values in an attempt to counter both communism and any assumption that the United States was a materialist society. At the same time, the USIA campaigns of the 1950s emphasized the benefits of a modern consumer society for everyone, praising the United States as a nation of "affluence, progress and personal fulfillment."[60]

The first head of the USIA (until 1956) was Theodore Streibert, a former broadcasting executive and a former assistant dean at Harvard Business School. In his view, the agency's mission was to emphasize "the community of interest that exists among freedom loving peoples and [to] show how American objectives and policies advance the legitimate interests of such peoples."[61] An important element of the 1950s American approach to cultural diplomacy and information was its focus on cultivating local elites in countries where its offices operated. This sometimes contributed to anti-American sentiment but was nevertheless viewed as the most effective approach.[62]

Streibert saw libraries and books as valuable to American cultural diplomacy, although less important than the "fast media" of radio, film, and television.[63] An early example of book diplomacy in action was a 1952 shipment of crates of paperbacks to India. Each crate, containing 102 titles, was placed in a municipal library, a reading room, a student hostel, a labor union reading room, a school, or other suitable location. The shipments featured works such as Benjamin Spock's *Baby and Child Care,* *The Autobiography of Benjamin Franklin,* and other popular titles, including those that warned Indian readers of the dangers of communism, such as Richard Crossman's *The God That Failed* (1949) and Edmund Stevens's *This Is Russia, Uncensored* (1950). The crates also contained titles that promoted America's artistic activities.[64]

The USIS libraries were a more important method of book diplomacy. Located around the world, they were intended to "offer a comprehensive picture of the principles for which we stand."[65] USIA officials believed that the libraries made a "strong political statement about America" and were central to the assertion of the nation's presence around the world.[66] However, they quickly became controversial. In 1953, Senator Joseph McCarthy alleged that the libraries contained literature by writers, such as Howard Fast, who had links to communism, and he demanded that they be purged of any such material.[67] As I will discuss, the book industry condemned this action, but the controversy led the State Department to issue a clear statement on what books would be selected for government cultural and information programs abroad. In a press conference, Robert L. Johnson, the administrator of the International Information Administration, commented that books and libraries were helping "protect the good name of the American people, no less than their vital interests." The aim for selecting books for USIS libraries would be to present "an adequate cross section of American literature . . . for a better understanding of American life and culture but writings of Communists and Communist sympathizers should not be tolerated in any manner which would indicate their acceptance by the American people." The basic approach would be to make sure that the program "was not a soft spot for subversives," although government officials denied that they would be participating in any approach that could be seen as "book-burning."[68] Nonetheless, books were removed from USIS shelves, and a new directive declared that in future books would be chosen for their merits and their usefulness to government objectives.[69]

Books and libraries were also seen as having a more general role to play in the U.S. presence abroad. In 1952, Willard L. Thorp, the assistant secretary of state, published an article in *Publishers Weekly* commenting that information was essential in "presenting the free way of life to the peoples of the world." He noted that while government programs were important, books must also be exported in the conventional way: "Those responsible for the State Department's information programs realize that an American book read in a government library cannot have the same impact as the purchase of the same book by a foreign reader to be put on his own bookshelves." Thorp argued that American publishers had "a direct and important stake in a growing world economic system." Therefore, "the rapid extension of foreign trade in American books, both technical and cultural, is an important objective of United States foreign economic policy."[70]

As it sought to increase the number of American books in translation across the globe, the government began creating translation and publication programs abroad. In the early years of the 1950s, the book industry worked closely with the government to design such programs. In March 1952, *Publishers Weekly* recorded that Philip Hodge, the director of the translation program at the State Department's Division of Overseas Information Centers, had traveled around the world to study the possibilities for undertaking U.S. translation projects. According to the article, the State Department was "preparing the way for the publication in various languages of American books not generally available abroad because of lack of dollars." In the same year, the publisher Robert L. Crowell of Thomas Y. Crowell prepared a manual for guiding information officers in the translation, condensation, and serialization of American books. The effort was, according to *Publishers Weekly,* one example of the "close co-operation between the book publishing industry and the Department of State's foreign information program."[71]

Translation and publication programs posed a challenge because the government had to operate within commercial restraints even when book production was subsidized. Soviet publishing was openly state-directed and subsidized, but the U.S. government could not appear to be undermining its nation's commercial book trade. As Thorp told the publishing industry, "our final reliance must rest upon the export of American cultural and technical books through conventional trade channels."[72] Government support for the idea that eventually became Franklin was undoubtedly prompted by a need to collaborate with the publishing industry and to move publishers into new markets that were also of strategic importance in the Cold War. In an undated State Department memorandum, probably from 1952, an official suggested that the best way to combat Soviet propaganda was to support "a private non-profit corporation" to "translate, publish and distribute commercially" those American or other books which explain the true aims of the United States on the one hand, [and] expose and explode the communist aims and myths on the other."[73]

Throughout the 1950s, the publishing industry was focused on asserting the importance of books in American life as well as for the perceived betterment of global society and in service of American foreign policy interests. In 1952, the publisher and book industry activist Theodore Waller declared that books could serve "both as bullets in the cold war of ideas and as ambassadors of good will."[74] Franklin was a direct product of the government's Cold War cultural offensives, but it required the active participation and support of the publishing industry. Yet as the fight against communism and the censorship of USIS libraries were demonstrating, difficulties and complications lay ahead.

Books at Home and in the World

American book publishing experienced considerable growth after World War II. Thanks to the expansion of education, particularly higher education (boosted by the GI Bill and the influx of veterans into colleges), there was a huge demand for books. College-textbook publishers and university presses expanded; and with the postwar baby boom, children's publishing also increased considerably. There was also unprecedented growth in technical and scientific publishing.[75] At the same time, shifts in censorship laws and attitudes, the rise of mass culture (and concerns that television and other mass media would dumb down the population and reduce the appeal of books), the Cold War, and anticommunism challenged and stimulated the industry.

The book industry was also looking beyond U.S. borders. During the 1950s and 1960s, the American Book Publishers Council (ABPC), established in 1945 as the U.S. Book Publishers Association, worked to increase the export of American books, especially textbooks and scientific and medical literature.[76] One of its explicit aims was "to assist the industry by all appropriate means in increasing the demand for American books throughout the world."[77] At the same time, educational publishing was expanding, with bodies such as the American Textbook Publishers Institute (ATPI) specifically working to promote the value of textbooks and reference books, which many believed were important in the global spread of knowledge and innovation.[78] Publishers and librarians were keen to assert their role more emphatically and drew on a discourse that emphasized the importance of books and reading in the creation of a democratic, fulfilled citizenry.

During the early 1950s, book industry and library professionals strove to articulate their concerns and debate solutions to perceived problems. In 1951, many gathered at a meeting dedicated to the topic of reading development. Attendees included the librarian Lester Asheim; academics such as Harold Laswell, David Reisman, and Ralph Taylor; George Gallup, the director of the Institute of Public Opinion; and industry figures such as Datus Smith (still working at Princeton University Press), Harold Guinzburg (of Viking), John O'Connor (of Grosset and Dunlap), and Theodore Waller and Robert Frase of the ABPC's Committee on Reading Development. Participants discussed the public image of reading in the United States, arguing that the average "man in the streets" regarded book reading as a "high-brow" activity, a view they needed to change. They argued that books were essential to modern society—"as a means for learning more about the world, as a means of escaping from the world we know, as a symbol of prestige, as a piece of furniture, as any number of things beyond a mere instrument of communication." Unlike newspapers, magazines, radio, or films, books offered "solid value."[79]

This conference, and the views expressed at it, reflected the importance that academics, the government, and the book industry placed on books. Yet each faction had its own stake and invested its own concerns and values in promoting that importance. In 1952, for instance, participants at an American Booksellers Association meeting expressed concerns about declining book sales and debated solutions. Although speakers noted that modern life, television, and the uncertainty of the atomic age were creating pessimism in the book trade, most were optimistic that books were and would remain central to American life.[80] At the National Book Awards ceremony held the same year, the president of Yale University, A. Whitney Griswold, addressed fears that television and mass media had made people stop reading and argued for the ongoing value of books and reading in a democratic society.[81]

In 1953, Dan Lacy, a former government official, was named the president of the ABPC, thus linking the book industry with the government and public interest.[82] Then in 1954, the American Library Association and members of the industry established the National Book Committee with the aim "advanc[ing] the use of books and the freedom to read."[83] Cultivating a readership of children and students was considered particularly important: book publishers emphasized the importance of "devis[ing] ways and means of exposing students to a spontaneous and contagious enthusiasm for books and reading."[84] All of these debates and initiatives helped inform a broader postwar discourse about the value of the book within American society and culture, even as they promoted sales.

This same discourse took place on the global stage. Books were seen as a way of furthering the aims of Cold War cultural diplomacy, but they were also considered a vital means of education, citizenship, and modernization among those who envisioned a peaceful and productive global future. Expanding the American publishing industry into various parts of the world was a regular topic of discussion in the 1950s. A 1953 *Publishers Weekly* article noted that book exports were up by 15.1 percent; further expansion into foreign markets seemed, in those years, to be inevitable.[85] In September 1955, the National Book Committee held its Conference on American Books Abroad, sponsored in part by the Rockefeller Brothers Fund and convened at Princeton University. It enabled publishers, government officials, and representatives of public and private agencies to come together to discuss the expansion of the book trade and possibilities for cooperation; and representatives from Franklin, the Asia Foundation, the ABPC, and various university presses prepared working papers.[86] During the conference, American bookmen outlined their understanding of the industry in developing countries. For instance, Peter Jennison, who worked for *Publishers Weekly* and the ABPC, commented on an "absence of a productive and integrated book industry" in such nations. He also argued that American publishers were generally ignorant of the foreign-market possibilities for American books in translation, and he outlined current government projects for taking books to the world.[87]

Concerns about the global expansion of American books was motivated by anxiety over the flood of Soviet books into certain regions, but there were also commercial implications for American publishers who hoped to get into markets in areas such as Asia and the Middle East.[88] It was difficult to move into soft-currency countries (that is, developing nations where the currency value was subject to great fluctuation) because there was no financial incentive if no one could afford to buy American books. The U.S. government set up the Informational Media Guarantee program to try to deal with this problem. In this scheme the government would buy soft currencies with dollars and then use those dollars to pay for American books and magazines. But the program's impact was limited because it applied only to selected countries, and in many areas of the world commercial opportunities for American publishers were constrained by lack of money. In addition, some regions were traditionally considered to be the territory of British publishers (under what was referred to as *empire rights*), and many regions presented fundamental challenges of literacy, education, and book distribution.

Publishers' interests abroad were not limited to finding immediate markets for American books. Some advocated a longer-term approach that would help countries develop their own modern book industries and readerships. Dan Lacy, writing in 1954, argued in favor of technical assistance to libraries and the development of facilities for publishing and distributing translations and original works. In his opinion, books in vernacular languages were absolutely essential: "The appalling significance of this [lack] can hardly be stated for the half or more of the world's people imprisoned in tongues in which almost no part of the whole body of modern knowledge has appeared."[89] Theodore Waller had already noted in 1952 that the ABPC was talking "intermittently" with the Technical Cooperation Administration "in an effort to demonstrate that there are some parts of the world where collections of books on certain subjects would make a great contribution per budget dollar expended than could be made by a transient technician."[90] His comment foreshadowed Franklin's later emphasis on linking book programs abroad to technical aid, development, and modernization.

A variety of related concerns were often raised and discussed in the postwar period. They included censorship (domestic and foreign), improving book distribution, increasing the book market by encouraging better national reading habits (often referred to as reading development), and interesting the government in book activities.[91] Other issues included reform of domestic copyright legislation and promotion of international copyright to protect American works. Many of these concerns would later be raised during the Franklin years. For instance, copyright was one of Franklin's ongoing concerns, and the organization hoped to use its work and methods to raise awareness and promote good copyright practices in the developing world.

Many publishers during the 1950s expressed concern about the kinds of books that were being published.[92] Even as mass paperback publishing began to take off, many still preferred to focus on higher-quality content. In 1952, Harold Guinzburg of Simon and Schuster, who was an active member of the ABPC, was one of three industry professionals to give the Windsor lectures at the Library School of the University of Illinois. In his view, books were one of the most precious assets of humankind but could all too easily be reduced to cheap vulgarity. He called for "serious" book publishers to obtain greater support from American society and government.[93] Speaking in the same lecture series, Theodore Waller declared, "Increasing the use of good books is not alone and perhaps not even primarily a publisher's problem, it is a national necessity. It is necessary if we are to protect and extend the civic competence of our people. It is necessary to the vitality of free institutions."[94] Into the late 1950s, publishers continued to express concerns about what might happen to reading in a society that was too distracted by material prosperity and television.[95] Bringing high-quality books to the rest of the world became an important issue for Franklin bookmen, whose main translation sources were academic and scholarly books, which they believed both presented a positive and cultured image of America and would better serve the needs of the developing world.

Freedom of speech was another important issue for the book industry. Amid the heated atmosphere of the early Cold War and paranoia about Communist infiltration, the U.S. government became concerned about the influence of communism on culture, especially in books and films. As I have mentioned, at the height of the McCarthy era, books written by Communist or Communist-associated authors were removed from USIS libraries, and the American Library Association and the ABPC strongly challenged such censorship. In May 1953, they prepared a joint statement about the freedom to read. The opening paragraph clearly stated their position:

> The freedom to read is essential to our democracy. It is under attack. Private groups and public authorities in various parts of the country are working to remove books from sale, to censor textbooks, to label "controversial" books, to distribute lists of "objectionable" books or authors, and to purge libraries. . . . We, as citizens devoted to the use of books and as librarians and publishers responsible for disseminating them, wish to assert the public interest in the preservation of the freedom to read.[96]

Dan Lacy, speaking at a conference that preceded the release of the statement, argued for the importance of making available a "wide variety of intellectual experience." Conference participants rejected the idea that any author's works should be suppressed on the grounds of his or her political affiliations.[97] In another forum in 1953, Lacy stated that books were different from other media because they gave readers the power to discover ideas for themselves. Thus, "it would be fatal to the success of the libraries if their content were restricted to works eulogistic of the United States and its policies." Books were "one of the few competent vehicles for th[e] necessary commerce of ideas."[98] In a 1954 article titled "Freedom and Books," he stressed that all individuals should have access to ideas and knowledge, especially in an age "when the complex doom of the atom hangs over us."[99]

By standing up for the freedom to read, book industry professionals, many of whom were later active with Franklin, also asserted books' importance in informing and educating within a democracy, something that they believed would be far more effective in combating communism in the long run. While they recognized that there was better and worse material, they defended the "right of individuals to be selective in their own reading" and opposed efforts to limit freedom of choice.[100] This belief was also expressed by Franklin bookmen, even when it came into conflict, as it sometimes did, with government directives.

A discourse was developing during the decade, one that stressed the value of books and libraries in bringing people together and promoting world peace and international understanding. At the global level, this was most strongly advocated by the United Nations Educational, Scientific, and Cultural Organization (UNESCO). Established in 1945, the organization played an important role in promoting a postwar conversation about the worldwide importance of literacy, education, reading, and books.[101] In the years immediately after the war, its focus was on reconstructing war-devastated areas; but beginning in the late 1940s, a number of its programs focused on the developing world. They provided an important context for Franklin's work but also illustrated the ways in which books and reading were being linked to modernization, development, and world peace.

The U.S. government hoped to use UNESCO as a tool in Cold War foreign policy; thus, its relationship with the agency was tense.[102] Yet the ideas promoted by UNESCO influenced international thinking about books and libraries. One aspect of its work focused on securing the free flow of books across the globe, and the UNESCO Book Coupon program was established in 1948 to allow countries with soft currencies to purchase books and educational material.[103] The agency also promulgated the 1950 Florence Agreement, which stated that import duties should not be placed on books, publications, and educational, scientific and cultural materials. The agreement noted that the "free exchange of ideas and knowledge and, in general, the widest possible dissemination of the diverse forms of self-expression used by civilizations are vitally important both for intellectual progress and for international understanding, and consequently for the maintenance of world peace."[104]

UNESCO facilitated and supported library exchange and the dissemination of library education. It sponsored numerous library conferences and published a regular *UNESCO Bulletin for Libraries*. It also emphasized the importance of fundamental education, with a strong focus on eradicating illiteracy. These ideas, like those of the USIS librarians, were often tied to a discourse about literacy as an essential component of democracy.[105] UNESCO's new global rhetoric about books and their value would influence some of the American bookmen of Franklin Publications.

Datus Smith and the Men of Franklin

As an organization, Franklin embodied many of the tensions and complications of America's cultural Cold War. Datus Smith, who was president throughout much of its existence, was responsible for most of Franklin's expansion during its first decade, and his dedication and enthusiasm were central to the organization's early operations. Born in Jackson, Michigan, in 1907, he graduated from Princeton University and spent his early career as a writer and a journalist.[106] In 1930, he considered taking a job with Standard Oil in China or the Middle East but eventually decided against it. Soon thereafter he was hired as the assistant editor of Princeton's *Alumni Weekly*.[107] Beginning in 1940, he moved to Princeton University Press, first as an assistant editor, then full editor in 1941, and finally director in 1942. During this time he expanded his interests in the Middle East. The university itself had links to the region, having established the nation's first Department of Oriental Studies in 1927.[108] The press published many important books on the Middle East, and Smith credited his time there with giving him important skills for his later work in the Arabic world, such as learning how to transliterate Arabic script.[109] He also oversaw the publication of several best-selling nonfiction books, including *Atomic Energy for Military Purposes* (1945), also known as the Smyth Report, about the Manhattan Project.[110] In a 1952 tribute marking the tenth anniversary of Smith's tenure as press director, Julian P. Boyd, a professor of history at the university, wrote that he had won for himself "the right to be called the scholar's ideal of a university publisher."[111]

Initially, Smith took a leave of absence from his position at the press to begin the Franklin experiment. When the project looked as if it would succeed, he decided to resign from Princeton to continue his work.[112] He wrote little about his initial motivations for getting involved with Franklin, but he acknowledged that he was deeply interested in the Middle East—what in one letter he called his "notorious phil-arabism."[113] Because of his desire to remain "non-political," he rarely referred explicitly to the Cold War anti-Communist struggle, but he expressed passionate faith in the possibilities for global cooperation and exchange. Not long after the establishment of Franklin, he wrote that he believed that it was a matter of honor to persist in doing this work: "We have the prospect of an intercultural achievement absolutely unique in our history."[114] In a 1966 memoir, the publisher Victor Weybright wrote that Franklin "had been envisaged by some of the founders as an adjunct to American propaganda abroad." Smith, he observed, "soon established a policy that Franklin would never become a propaganda organization."[115]

Smith was a great advocate of university press and serious book publishing and saw Franklin as a good vehicle for promoting those presses and their scholarly books in both book diplomacy and domestic programs.[116] In June 1952, after being appointed president, he wrote to the new board of directors, sharing his thoughts about directions for the new organization. If its work were not handled correctly, he felt, they risked doing more harm than good.[117] It was essential to remember that commercial interests were "a means of serving the national interest" rather than the other way around. Smith knew that some of the board members were concerned that Franklin would be less about promoting American publishers' interests and more about preventing an invasion of Soviet publications.[118] So he stressed that any books provided through Franklin must serve the needs of the countries in which the program operated. He told the board, "The surest way of missing the Department's psychological objective would be to select titles on a basis of explicitness of American propaganda rather than on a basis of what books . . . the East will read." He acknowledged that "the graveness of the international crisis will motivate the thinking of many people with respect to this project. But it would be fatal if the work itself were approached as a crisis operation." It was essential, he believed, to take the long view.[119]

In this, Smith set out the first, and one of the most important and contentious, of Franklin's operating principles. The countries in which the program operated, not the United States, would select the books that Franklin would translate and produce. The principle of local selection was, for Smith, inviolable. It also reflected a basic commercial instinct—readers want to choose their own books—and this would help to secure a future customer base. The State Department was eager to publish books in English and proposed that it

Datus Smith outside his Franklin office door.

could obtain a special ruling from the Justice Department to protect Franklin from being sued under anti-trust statutes.[120] However, because it was essential to maintain good relations with American publishers, this option was not actively pursued, and Franklin chose to work only in translation.

Smith's letter to the board of directors set out how Franklin would approach its work abroad. It would begin by surveying countries to determine existing facilities and needs. After careful planning, it would then commence operations. While he acknowledged that Franklin would be doing work for the State Department (soon the newly established USIA provided the funds), he insisted that it must also seek outside support so that it would not merely be an "instrument of government."[121] In other words, while Franklin began its life as a private organization funded by the state, its founders were from the first wary of being seen as a government-directed entity. Smith also insisted that he, his staff, and their work partners must stay out of U.S. partisan politics and never comment publicly on American foreign policy at home or abroad.

Smith found much personal enjoyment and satisfaction in working abroad, as is evident in the many reports he sent home to New York when traveling on Franklin business. He was always fascinated by the countries and the people he visited, though he acknowledged that he primarily interacted with the elite, most of whom spoke good English. (He never learned more than a small amount of Arabic.)[122] Nevertheless, travel expanded his horizons.

In later years, some women would work for Franklin, but in the beginning nearly all of its publishing professionals were white men, a reflection of the industry at the time.[123] Networks of publishers, especially those with links to Washington, oiled the machinery for its operations. As the Franklin archives reveal, many of the program's projects were conceived of and developed during long luncheons and cocktail parties in New York and Washington and at ATPI and ABPC conferences. When Franklin bookmen traveled abroad, they took part in social events, tennis matches, dances, and other activities that allowed them to foster international networks.

Members of Franklin's board of directors were leaders in the publishing field and were often active in other professional roles, such as the ABPC. Some were notable figures in education, research, or the corporate world. A variety of motivations prompted their involvement in the project. For example, Arthur S. Adams of the American Council on Education told George P. Brett of Macmillan, "This new venture holds great promise of providing an effective means of reflecting clearly the essential features of democratic philosophy. The availability of our literature to the undeveloped countries of the world should be a potent force in combating the spread of Soviet ideology."[124] Douglas M. Black of Doubleday emphasized that the directors needed to know everything that went on with the organization (perhaps because of concerns about its links to government). Yet he was happy to be involved: "It should be a most interesting experience and it can do enormous good in the world."[125] Once established, Franklin also enjoyed the support of a number of other organizations. For instance, Joseph E. Johnson of the Carnegie Endowment for International Peace wrote to Smith in October 1952 to express his enthusiasm for the project.[126]

Many of Franklin's founders had gained government experience during World War II. Victor Weybright had worked closely with the OWI and spent time in England, where he became close friends with the publisher Allen Lane and helped bring Penguin's books into the U.S. market after the war. He subsequently established the New American Library and was also, at one point, an ABPC board member.[127] Theodore Waller was managing director of the ABPC from 1950 to 1953 and then became the editorial vice-president of the New American Library of World Literature. During the war, he had served with the United Nations Relief and Rehabilitation Agency, and he was the Washington representative of the United World Federalists, a group that aspired to develop a federal world government. Waller was active in many book promotion activities, including the 1951 formation of the Conference on Reading Development and the Rural Reading Conference.[128] He was also, after May 1953, the executive director of the ABPC's Committee on Reading Development.[129] Malcolm Johnson joined the publisher D. Van Nostrand as vice-president in 1945, after having worked as the managing editor of the *Atlantic Monthly* and an editor at Doubleday. During the war, he served on the Council Books in Wartime and was on the War Production Board's book publishing and manufacturing supervisory committee. His wife, Mildred Young, was a librarian who had headed the army's library program.[130] D. Van Nostrand was an important technical and scientific publisher and, as John Tebbel writes, "contributed much to the global distribution of technological innovation."[131] George P. Brett, the U.S. head of Macmillan, had served in World War I and after World War II chaired the book committee of Eisenhower's People to People program.[132] He stayed active in Franklin until nearly the end of its existence.

Franklin had close and cooperative relationships with many American university presses and their staff members, primarily because of its focus on scholarly book publishing and Smith's background and connections in the sector. Thomas J. Wilson, the director of Harvard University Press and the 1952 president of the American Association of University Presses, played a key role at Franklin, mainly as a member of its board of directors but also through his survey work abroad and his consistent advocacy of the project. Dana J. Pratt, who had worked with both the University of Illinois Press and Princeton University Press and who had served as executive director of the

American Association of University Presses, joined Franklin in 1955 as a field consultant.[133]

A number of people participated in survey activities, helped to raise funds, or worked in the New York head office. For example, Francis St. John, the Brooklyn Public Library's chief librarian and the 1953 president of the American Library Association, was active in Franklin's first years of existence, when he undertook survey work in the Middle East. St. John had been involved with the Council Books in Wartime as well as the 1941 Book Mobilization Conference that focused on how the book industry could advance the war effort.[134] Many Franklin bookmen were actively involved in the ABPC and participated in a variety of book-related campaigns and debates. Donald Cameron, who was executive secretary for the ABPC in the early 1950s, had joined the council's staff in 1946 but resigned in 1952 to work for Franklin. During the war years he had been involved in projects for the OWI.[135] Dan Lacy, who was the managing director of the ABPC from 1953 to 1966, had previously worked with the Information Center Service (ICS) at the State Department and had received a "high departmental award of merit" for the "work he ha[d] done to improve relations between book publishers and the Department."[136] Robert Frase was the head of ABPC's Washington office and since 1951 had served as the council's economic consultant. He had previously had a busy career in government.[137] Harold N. Munger had worked with Smith at Princeton University Press as its advertising director. He was subsequently the director of Rutgers University Press until 1953, when he left to work for Franklin.[138] From 1955 on, he served as Franklin's research director.

All of these bookmen, and many others (including, later, a number of women), contributed actively to the Franklin organization. Their experience in government and publishing persuaded them of the importance of actively developing the global book industry and promoting book culture around the world. Through Franklin, they took their domestic knowledge and experience abroad. Some were undoubtedly motivated by Cold War anti-Communist concerns, but many more were focused on advancing American values and professional practices and identifying commercial opportunities. A spectrum of patriotic, professional, and cultural internationalist views were evident in their work for Franklin.

Nevertheless, it is important to remember that Franklin was a government-funded organization. Although Smith immediately sought to declare its independence, the program relied on government funding for much of its life, especially in its early years, and its work was a form of American soft power. Franklin had been a government initiative, and its employees and board members never stopped grappling with the question of how much to say publicly about its government ties. In the 1960s, there were public accusations that the program was connected to the CIA. Early in Franklin's history, Malcolm Johnson tried to line up work for Franklin with G-2, a U.S. military intelligence program. While Smith was concerned about getting involved in such activities, Johnson argued, "We don't need to do everything on the surface, and any G-2 job will probably be fairly well concealed. . . . If G2 want to make . . . basic infantry tactics readily available to the Near East in Arabic I see no objection to helping out."[139]

There is no evidence that Franklin went on to engage in such covert government publishing work; in fact, Smith deliberately avoided it because of the damage it might do to Franklin's reputation. He felt that U.S. aims were better served by overt cultural activities, and he wrote in 1952 that Franklin's goals were "to strengthen the position of the U.S. and the free world, and to preserve world peace"; "to increase the foreign distribution of American books"; and "to help the peoples of the Middle East, and thus to further the welfare of mankind." He saw all of these goals as equally important. He knew that the people of the Middle East would be concerned about whether or not Franklin was "merely a front for the State Department." Thus, "our hearts must be pure. We shall be found out very quickly if we do not really mean it when we say that we take the long view of serving the United States through serving the Middle East."[140] Yet the reality was that Franklin was receiving ongoing USIA money, and some of that funding may have had CIA origins. The program was not a front for covert activities—although such activities certainly occurred—but it operated within tangled networks of government influence and funding.

In 1954, Don Cameron wrote to the publishing firm Alfred A. Knopf about Franklin's work overseas. He enclosed a form letter, also sent to other American publishers, to explain the program and its exciting work. Stressing that the organization was "private" and "independent," the letter emphasized that Franklin's activities would not detract from American publishers' commercial interests. Rather, the program would "combine the technical knowledge of American book publishers and the cultural resources of the United States with advice from educational and intellectual leaders in other countries, and . . . receive financial support from a variety of sources, both public and private" to "promote the freedom, dignity, and welfare of mankind."[141]

The letter thus appealed not only to publishers' patriotism but also to their humanity—and perhaps to their professional pride—in asking them to support the nascent work of Franklin. Publishers were not just businessmen and salesmen; they could also be cultural internationalists and book diplomats, and it was hard for them to resist such requests, especially in the intense Cold War atmosphere of the 1950s. Rather than promoting its work as anti-communism—which was creating censorship anxiety in the book world—the letter emphasized that Franklin's activities would benefit all mankind, furthering the progress of humanity and the cause of world peace and understanding. The fact that it might also offer commercial opportunities was important, yet the Cold War was the essential context for Franklin's creation of Franklin. How would this work play out in actuality? And how would the world respond to American books?

2

Book Diplomacy in the Middle East

During the 1950s, Franklin Publications set up a number of field offices across the globe while also surveying opportunities for new programs and maintaining its New York office. Its first field office was established in Cairo, with the goal of producing books in Arabic for a Middle Eastern Arabic readership. Yet Franklin's work in the Middle East was, as it would be elsewhere, deeply influenced by the politics of the Cold War, despite the various motivations of Franklin staff members and their affiliates and regardless of how the program's work was presented to people in the United States and the region.

In this decade, Franklin's work echoed the U.S. government's approach to information activities abroad, and the organization functioned largely as an adjunct to USIA cultural diplomacy programs. Franklin's bookmen, however, were beginning to embrace a more holistic approach to developing a book culture and industry abroad, especially as they responded to challenges on the ground. The story of their operations in Egypt reveals much about U.S. attitudes toward the Middle East and Americans' desire to bring their own national values into a region that was largely unfamiliar to them.

The United States in the Middle East

The Middle East remained largely peripheral to American interests and culture until World War II, when the area assumed greater strategic value, especially as the United States focused on access to Middle Eastern oil. During the Eisenhower administration, the United States became more deeply entangled in the region. Egypt was of particular strategic concern (as it also was for Great Britain, the historical power in the region). In 1949, the United States recognized the newly-established state of Israel, which led to considerable anxiety over possible Arab responses.[1] Arab-Israeli tensions would continue to mark the politics and history of the region.

In the postwar years, the Middle East was rife with sentiments of anticolonialism and nationalism. With the rise of the Soviet Union and its growing interest in the Middle East, American foreign policy increasingly focused on the area, and Egypt was regarded as a key power. In 1953, Egypt became a republic, with General Muhammad Naguib assuming the presidency. Over the next few tumultuous years, Gamal Abdel Nasser challenged Naguib's power, assuming first the prime ministership in 1954 and then the presidency in 1956. Nasser was anticolonial and a strong nationalist, and he was central to the 1954 Colombo and 1955 Bandung conferences—gatherings of new nations, most of which were former colonies. At these meetings, he pressed emerging nations to adopt a generally anticolonial stance and a nonaligned diplomatic position.

In 1955, Iran, Iraq, Turkey, and Pakistan signed the Baghdad Pact, which, by excluding the Arab states, meant that Egypt became more closely aligned with the Soviet Union. Nasser embraced modernization and development, introducing land reform and later requesting American aid money during the Kennedy administration.[2] His nationalization of the Suez Canal prompted the Suez crisis of 1956 and the withdrawal of British and French influence from the area. In the 1960s, he continued to assert Egyptian dominance in the region, often through military encounters with Israel. For the most part, however, Egypt's central ideology during this period was nationalism, not communism, despite U.S. fears.

Douglas Little, a preeminent scholar of U.S. policy in the Middle East, notes that, from the Suez Crisis to the 1978 Camp David Accords, American strategy in the Middle East remained fundamentally consistent: "Determined to protect Western access to Persian Gulf oil and promote the security of Israel, Washington sought to reduce Moscow's influence in the region and combat pan-Arab radicalism from Cairo to Damascus."[3] The United States remained generally wary of Arab nationalism and its radical potential.[4] The government's concern about volatility in the region, especially in Egypt, made cultural diplomacy vital, although American priorities were to establish and maintain political stability. Cultural diplomacy and information were regarded as weapons, a way to keep the Middle East sympathetic, or at least not overtly hostile, to the United States. But many in the region were deeply suspicious of U.S. motives, with the Soviet Union championing Arab nationalist aspirations. As in other parts of the world, the USIA approached this challenge by targeting local elites, which some nationalists saw as a form of colonialism.[5] Franklin's book diplomacy efforts were one element of this 1950s campaign to win hearts and minds.

Surveying the Middle East

As a preliminary step, Franklin needed to survey book needs and problems in the region, but interested bookmen found that it was not easy to obtain clearance to work abroad for the program. Everyone needed security certificates.[6] In August 1953, Don Cameron traveled to Washington to meet with Philip Hodge, the head of the State Department's Special Programs Branch within the Information Center Service, in an attempt to work out the details of operating abroad. The State Department was concerned that Congress would see such trips as junkets, so its officials requested that only one Franklin representative travel to the Middle East at any one time. As Cameron explained in his report to Datus Smith, "they [did] not want Franklin representatives to travel on diplomatic passports, but strongly urged the idea that Franklin representatives should appear to be American business men without governmental ties."[7]

In December of that year, Smith set off on his first trip to the Middle East as a representative of Franklin Publications. In preparing for the trip, he asked Dan Lacy for "the dope" on State Department and other American personnel stationed in the region as well as a list of local contacts.[8] He put out feelers for possible cooperation opportunities with a range of area organizations and people, including corporate industries. For instance, he tried to arrange a meeting with Harry R. Snyder of the Arabian American Oil Company (Aramco). Snyder, a former McGraw-Hill editor, was now responsible for training the Saudi Arabians who worked for Aramco. Smith wrote, "[Because you have an] interest in the development of a native technician class, I suspect that there might be special ways in which you might be able to advise us as to the Arab world in general, and just possibly with reference to specific projects in Saudi Arabia."[9] He did later meet with Aramco officials, although what advice they offered is unknown.[10] Aramco has been cited as an important example of "corporate diplomacy" in Saudi Arabia, and perhaps it offered Smith a model of how to interact with local populations abroad.[11] Indeed, the idea of an American corporate diplomacy can be applied in some ways to Franklin bookmen, who saw themselves as diplomats of the book industry.

Malcolm Johnson and Francis St. John accompanied Smith on this first trip, presumably representing their main employers (the publisher D. Van Nostrand and the Brooklyn Public Library, respectively), which took them, via London, to Beirut, Damascus, Cairo, Baghdad, and Amman.[12] *Publishers Weekly* reported that the trip would help determine Franklin's future publishing policy.[13] The three men met with various educators, teachers, intellectuals, and officials, and a key goal was "to find out what Arabia needs in the way of books."[14] Their experiences reinforced their belief that there was a great need for books in the region, a void that American publishing could fill.

Later Smith wrote that the men had been "received *everywhere* with courtesy and warm friendliness. Your travellers had a wonderful time." His report to Franklin's board of directors provides insight into a tumultuous period of change, especially in Egypt. Smith observed that "antagonism to U.S. government policy is universal, and its intensity has to be experienced to be believed." He also noted widespread ignorance about American society and culture: "Even the well educated people, of whom there are quite a lot, know French and British culture but not ours, except as it takes the form of movies and of such exports as Kuka Kula and Bebsi Kula." He concluded that "Palestine, not Russia, is the great world problem in the Arab mind, and the U.S. is to blame for creation of the Israeli state and its artificial support through capital gifts and other aid." But he did not think there was much evidence of communism "in a formal Marxist and Stalinist aspect."

> [I saw] some "Dogs of Wall Street, Go Home" scrawlings on walls in Lebanon but not many other direct evidences. But the Stalinists are able to use anti-American feeling, and the age-old resentment against Britain (still dominant in Iraq and Jordan) and the French (Tunisia, Morocco) for its purposes. The desperate economic plight of the Arab countries, and the feudalism which causes or aggravates much of it, are both identified with foreign domination. Most communist disturbances therefore have the public appearance of mere nationalism. "Down with the British, French, and Americans" is the surefire cry of demagoguery in the Middle East.[15]

Yet Smith believed there was "underlying goodwill" toward the United States in the region: "The Arabs I talked with seemed eager to believe that our Middle East policy [that is, American support of Israel] is explained by (1) Jewish ownership of all the newspapers in the U.S.; and (2) French and British blackmail taking the form of a threat to withdraw anti-Soviet support in Europe."

He saw Islam as "fundamentally antithetical to the Soviet [ideology]" but argued that Muslim conservatism was attracted to communism because the West persisted in seeing Islam as "bigotry and medievalism."[16]

While the book had a long history in Egypt, there were no features of a modern-style book industry in the 1950s. Printing presses had been introduced in the nineteenth century, and Egypt did have an active press, but existing book publishing was largely government directed.[17] Literacy rates were low, and there was little publishing infrastructure. In his report to Franklin, Smith said that he saw few books during his travels in the Middle East, and most were very expensive. The region had few translation programs, no copyright laws, and "practically no publicity or promotion." He argued that it was important for Franklin to produce American-style books for the Middle East: "There is such respect for the physical form of American books that all of our advisers urged us to make them just as 'American' as we can." Yet enthusiasm for the Franklin idea did not extend to the translation of "directly anti-communist or pro-America books." Smith told the board members that American commercial interests in the Franklin project would give it legitimacy and help dispel suspicions about U.S. intentions.[18] Later that year, he wrote that Franklin would be a "kind of intellectual Point Four" program for the region, and elsewhere he argued that "books will serve American interest, public or commercial, only if they serve the people of the Middle East."[19]

As Smith's observations about the Middle East demonstrate, there was clear hostility toward the United States and Americans during this time of political and cultural ferment. There was also animosity toward Israel and the former colonial powers of Britain and France. Moreover, the region's book industry was considerably different from American-style publishing. Thus, if Franklin were to succeed, it would need to learn to operate in an unfamiliar atmosphere and find a way to produce books in translation that would not raise significant popular opposition. The challenge was great, but the travelers were determined to rise to it.

Setting Up the Cairo Office

Initially, the State Department wanted to locate the first Franklin program office in Beirut because officials believed there was less anti-American sentiment there. Smith, however, recommended setting up a small Cairo office with an Arab manager, a secretary, and consultants. Office staff would select books from a list provided by the New York office and approved by the USIA, and the home office would then negotiate translation rights with American publishing firms. Most of the publication work would take place in Egypt, and local newspaper and magazine jobbers would handle distribution.[20]

First, however, Smith sought advice about potential problems. Before leaving to take up a professorship at Fuad University in Cairo, Lewis Awad, an Egyptian scholar based in the United States, wrote an advisory memorandum for Franklin reiterating that the program would certainly be met with suspicion:

> Many sections of the Egyptian public will be alarmed at the prospect of a foreign corporation, settling in, directly or by devious paths, not to invest, not to manufacture harmless goods, but to mould the minds of men. If that corporation comes from the powerful America, the America that has created the problem of Israel for the Arab world, the America that has allied herself with the enemies of Egypt, there is all the more reason to distrust its activities and even to resent this new form of penetration.

Awad thought the United States needed to change *its* attitude toward the Arab world before the Arab world could change its mind about America. He advised Franklin to work "from afar" through local publishers and to keep any relations with Jewish people to a minimum. He also wrote that the organization should emphasize that it was working "purely in the service of intellectual advancement."[21]

With these warnings, Franklin opened the doors of its Cairo office. By February 1953, the program had hired an Egyptian office manager, Hassan Galal al-Aroussy, and drawn up a list of initial book projects. Al-Aroussy had long had a close connection with U.S. interests. Described as "an active man of letters," he had previously worked for the Fuad University library and had a history of involvement with USIS activities.[22] He was also a former member of the Egyptian diplomatic service and a former professor of law at Fuad, and he was said to have operated as a "confidential adviser on Muslim affairs to the American public affairs office in Cairo." In addition, his wife was employed as the children's librarian in the city's USIS library.[23] Consultants for the Cairo office included Ahmad Zaki, a former minister of education and the former dean of the science faculty at Fuad, who would serve as a general science adviser and the supervisor of science translations; Hassan Mahmoud, a novelist and an editor who was also Fuad's former controller-general and a lecturer at the Higher Institute of Dramatic Art, who would advise Franklin on literature; and Habib Amin Kurani, the chairman of the School of Education at the American University of Beirut, who would advise on educational problems in Arab countries.[24] They would each be paid about US$50 per title published, a reasonable sum for the time.²⁵ Al-Aroussy would be assisted in the office by Hassan Mahmoud and Mrs. Sydney Adams, the wife of an American embassy attaché who had worked with Smith at Princeton University Press.²⁶

When offering al-Aroussy the position of manager, Smith told him that he was expected to pledge his full allegiance to the Franklin organization but that this would not conflict "with your loyalty as an Egyptian, an Arab, a Muslim and a Near Easterner because if you did not think this project was in the interest of the Arab world you would not be taking part in it."²⁷ Al-Aroussy responded that he was "accepting this job with complete conviction that I am doing the best I can for my country by doing the best I can for American Egyptian and Arab relations in a very vital field."²⁸ In a letter to Franklin's executive committee, Smith wrote that he thought al-Aroussy was working for Franklin "out of patriotism to Egypt." He added, "Religion is an important motive force in his work, and it is precisely as an Arab-Muslim-Egyptian, not a pseudo-American, that he is dedicating himself to the enterprise."²⁹

Yet Smith quickly realized that, with the Cairo office, Franklin was operating in a complicated, unfamiliar business environment. In addition to facing local suspicions, the program dealt with many mundane practical and logistical issues, such as how best to ship packages of books from the United States to Egypt and how to set up bank accounts.³⁰ Workers also found that they were competing with a range of other American book activities in Cairo. For instance, the American embassy and USIS were each commencing book translation activities.³¹ There was also a translation program underway at the Egyptian Ministry of Education, although Smith believed that it was "slow-moving and *very* long range and no problem at all."³²

In April 1953, Smith returned to the Middle East to visit the new Cairo office, located in a small one-room office in the main business district. Franklin paid a rent of US$36.75 a month and had a three-year lease on the space, which Smith described as "the smallest . . . in the best building" and thus striking "just the right balance between ostentation and humility."³³ (The program would move to a larger office in the same building a year later.)³⁴ He projected that the costs for running the office in 1953–54 would be about US$20,000, with production costs at about US$100,000. For the same fiscal year, he expected royalties of between US$20,000 and US$40,000.³⁵ Most of this money would go back to New York, although a small amount would remain in the Cairo office accounts.

Franklin planned to keep its Cairo operation small, and production would

Hassan al-Aroussy, Datus Smith, and Egypt's first president, General Muhammad Naguib, discussing Franklin books, November 9, 1953.

depend on contracts with existing Egyptian publishers and printers. The books produced would bear those publishers' imprints with the addendum "published in cooperation with Franklin Publications."[36] A number of local publishers and booksellers signed contracts with the Cairo office, including Dar al-Maaref, Dar al-Hilal, the Renaissance Bookshop, and the Anglo-Egyptian Bookshop. According to Smith, there were "two other houses (Dar al-Fikr al-Araby and Mustafa el-Baby el-Halaby) with which we would like to do business because of their excellent connections with the most conservative Islamic circles, and especially al-Ashar University." Unfortunately, he explained, "they are not very good publishers, and are noted for doing terrible looking books, but we shall probably make arrangements with them for one or two of our future books."[37] Some of these publishers were already accustomed to arrangements with overseas partners. For instance, Dar al-Maaref had been an agent of British publisher Macmillan for many years.[38] Established in 1890 by the Lebanese scholar Naguib Mitri and his brother Shafiq Mitri, the press had long worked, according to its own account, to promote Arabic books. After signing a contract with Franklin, it advertised in local newspapers to emphasize its ongoing commitment to that mission: "The Arabic reader will be able during all the states of his life to find the material which will help him keep pace with the modern developments in the various spheres of science, arts and culture."[39]

Franklin-Cairo generally received a royalty of 10 percent and also controlled the selling prices of the books.[40] It pushed for prices to reflect the market. As a pricing memorandum explained, books sold too cheaply might stimulate accusations of American "dumping, and lead to resentment of publishers and booksellers against foreign intrusions into their economies." Franklin had to work within "a natural commercial framework."[41] The policy reflected an ongoing commitment to American-style commercial operations and was a element of its approach to corporate modernization. By offering a commercial business model, Franklin not only remained true to free enterprise and capitalism but also provided a model for the local publishing industry to emulate. As time went on, the program began offering direct training to local publishers and booksellers in how to develop an American-style publishing industry, which in turn laid the groundwork for future commercial trade with Egypt.

Franklin was not the only American cultural and educational organization to operate in the Middle East during this period. The USIA ran other translation programs as well as USIS libraries, and the agency was also involved in book presentations to local elites. Franklin was initially an extension of USIA's work, but its management came to feel that the agency was undercutting Franklin's own activity and even directly competing with it. American colleges and universities also had a substantial presence, as did foundations such as the Ford Foundation.[42] In addition, British publishing activities in the region continued, and anti-American and Communist books also circulated.[43]

Producing Books in Arabic

Franklin quickly established an active publishing program. While its books were relatively inexpensive, staff members noted in September 1953 that they should never undersell "indigenous" titles "nor [should] they . . . be priced above what the average reader could afford to pay for personal and family reading matter."[44] In Smith's early plans for the Middle Eastern program, he had outlined the types of books Franklin should produce, ones that emphasized both Cold War and educational objectives. Books should, in his view, "give the people of the Arab states a realistic view of the world and their place in it," "help rescue the Arab heritage from its present plight as the exclusive property of bigots," or "further the development of free institutions with the objective of aiding political stability and economic health—or preventing a vacuum into which the Soviet can move."[45]

A list of titles dated January 11, 1953, included books that Franklin hoped to consider for translation and publication. The juvenile category included Louisa May Alcott's *Little Women;* Marguerite Henry's *King of the Wind;* books on Thomas Jefferson, Abraham Lincoln, and George Washington; science books such as Richard W. Bishop's *Stepping Stones to Light* and Hermann Schneider's *Everyday Machines and How They Work* and his *Rocks, Rivers, and Changing Earth;* and Sarah K. Bolton's *Lives of Poor Boys Who Became Famous.* The America category included Frederick Lewis Allen's *The Big Change* and Henry S. Commager's *The American Mind;* and the philosophy category included Hans Reichenbach's *The Rise of Scientific Philosophy* and F. S. C. Northrop's *The Taming of the Nations.*[46] Social studies, fine arts, agriculture, and reference works were some of the other categories under consideration.

Franklin's board members were not all convinced of the value of some of these titles. Shortly after Smith's report was circulated, George P. Brett wrote to express his concerns: "I am sure that we are not going to accomplish our purpose, which is primarily that of making American books popular in these countries, until we offer books that the common man can read, enjoy, and from which he can gain profit in translation, and the educated man our own best books in English which we might expect he would be interested." He continued, "I think that you are crediting your foreign customer in these Near East and Far East countries with far more intelligence than he has. I think that he won't like the books that you have suggested nearly as well as he would like different selections, principally culled from the supplementary reading books offered by the educational publishers in the United States." He also argued that Franklin should be distributing books in English "for the well-educated foreigner in these countries."[47]

Smith replied that he thought that the list was a start and that there had been an "informal resolution" not to publish books in English—a principle that quickly became fundamental to Franklin policy. His response went to the heart of not only his own preferred approach but also much U.S. government activity in the early Cold War. Franklin was producing books for "relatively literate" people "because they are the influential people who, according to one tenable theory of public opinion, represent the best target group for an operation of this sort." Smith believed that "we will be in serious trouble if we seek to publish for the masses *before* we have established our bona fides with the upper group."[48] Indeed, much of Franklin's eventual production was aimed at the literate elite in the countries in which they set up offices. Egypt's literacy rates remained low, reaching only about 30 percent by the early 1960s.[49] Yet as Brett's patronizing comments suggest, some within the organization were concerned with broader questions of literacy and the desirability of reaching out to or creating a broader group of readers. Johnson and St. John both told Smith that reaching out to the "barely literate man in the street" would give them a better chance to achieve "our long range objectives." Johnson said,

> Speaking in the broadest possible general terms, I think our publishing objective in the next two years is to produce a small group of books for the educated and ruling classes, a much larger group for the adult who can read but is otherwise not particularly educated, and a final group on the one hand for children and on the other in whatever equivalent of very simple English Arabic has to offer, for the border-liners who still, it would seem, hanker after the printed word.[50]

In the end, however, Smith's approach prevailed, and Franklin began its translation and publishing work with books that were "creditable and interesting and not carrying particular messages."[51] Smith championed titles such as *The Atlas of Islamic History in Arabic* because it furthered the program's objective of supporting "local values."[52] He argued in favor of Charles Lindbergh's *The Spirit of St. Louis* because it "stands as the personification of young Americanism and we believe this book will make a splendid ambassador for us." Lindbergh's history of anti-Semitism may also have made the book an acceptable choice in the anti-Zionist atmosphere of 1950s Egypt, and 10,000 copies in Arabic were slated for publication in 1954.[53]

To secure a book for translation, Franklin offered to pay American publishers a nominal sum to publish a selected text in specified languages. In return, it would share a small portion of the royalties and give the publisher three free copies of the book per each translated language. According to a form letter sent to Knopf, Franklin agreed to reproduce the copyright notice and the name of the original publisher as well as not make substantive changes. But "minor changes may be made throughout to aid comprehension by non-American readers or to avoid giving offense to readers in particular languages."[54] This particular form letter accompanied a permission request to translate two books by the popular contemporary writer John Hersey, *Into the Valley* and *A Bell for Adano,* for publication in the "local languages of the Near and Middle East." Those "local languages" included Arabic, Bengali, and Persian, but Franklin was primarily requesting Arabic rights. Don Cameron told William A. Koshland, Knopf's office manager (and later president), that the organization's practice of securing translation rights was in part motivated by a desire to model the practice in the countries in which it operated.[55] Knopf agreed to give Franklin permission to translate, and the Egyptian publisher Akhbar al-Yom released an Arabic version of *A Bell for Adano* in 1954.[56]

Franklin's publishing program was shaped by attitudes of the time, even as it sought to avoid being seen as explicitly pro-American and anti-Communist. By 1956, a number of its published books were selling well in the Middle East, including titles as diverse as Alcott's *Little Women,* Allen's *The Big Change,* and Carl Becker's *The Heavenly City of the Eighteenth Century Philosophers.*[57] In fact, *Little Women* proved to be one of the best-selling books in the Arabic program. Franklin was also releasing books that supported the transfer of technical knowledge, and they were often actively supported by local elites who worked as translators or wrote prefaces and thus helped to legitimize the text for a local readership. For example, Willy Ley's *The Engineer's Dream* was published in 1956, with a preface by Mohamed Ahmed Selim and Ahmed Aly Farag, who wrote that it was "really high time for every Arab to think seriously and resolutely of rendering the greatest service to his greater home 'The Arab World' by digging out and by exploiting the natural resources which have nothing to match them all over the world."[58] Franklin remained cautious about mentioning Israel or promoting cultural sensibilities that might not match Muslim ones. As St. John noted, the program worked to avoid including books on the "Zionist or Jewish question" and those that might be seen as conveying "extremely loose morals."[59]

A variety of motives determined translators' decisions to cooperate with Franklin. For example, Osman Khalil Osman, the dean of Ibrahim University Law School and the chairman of the subcommittee that was designing the new Egyptian constitution, chose to translate George H. Sabine's *A History of Political Theory* (first published in 1937) and write an introduction to the Arabic edition "on the grounds that public access to this book in Arabic is essential at this stage of Egypt's constitutional development."[60] Ahmed Zakey, the rector of the University of Cairo, translated the Arabic edition of James Conant's *Science and Common Sense.* The editor of a popular Egyptian fashion magazine translated the Arabic edition of *Little Women,* and her name was used in advertising to help sell the book to an Egyptian audience.[61] Nonetheless, Franklin's releases accounted for only a small number of the books that were circulating in Egypt and the Arabic world. At the end of the 1950s, Nasser embarked on his Thousand Books scheme to translate a range of books from other nations into Arabic. Many pirated translations of popular texts also circulated, including many Marxist-Leninist ones.[62] It is notable that all of these publishing programs—American, Soviet, and Egyptian—focused on the translation and circulation of foreign works at the expense of Arabic ones.

While Franklin books were undoubtedly read and perhaps even influenced some readers, they functioned within a much broader set of translations and thus could have only a limited effect on Egyptian readers. The program's real influence was on the book industry. In 1956, Franklin spokesmen boasted that it had created "a revolution" in the Middle East and elsewhere, particularly in book distribution techniques. The program had introduced a range of "modern" (that is, American) techniques such as direct mail and other advertising practices as well as bookstore displays and radio spots.[63] It had also influenced the appearance of Arabic books: "When Franklin books were first introduced, their design, and especially the method of cover-printing, were so distinctive that they were set apart from all other Arabic books; now most Arabic books look like Franklin's." In both Iran and Egypt, the spokesmen reported, methods of bookstore display and book promotion had been "notably Americanized, and the booktrade in both countries has looked to Franklin for leadership and instruction in both arts."[64]

I will detail Franklin's work in reshaping the industry and book culture later in the book. It suffices to say here that by the second half of the 1950s the program's work was already extending beyond a focus on the content of books as a conveyor of American cultural diplomacy objectives. Franklin bookmen desired to transform the Arabic book industry and to make it more American; ultimately, they envisioned reshaping book culture in the countries in which they operated. This vision extended well beyond the USIA's intentions when it agreed to supply Franklin with government funds, and the disconnect would cause tensions in the future. USIA book programs nearly always focused on the texts themselves and how they could further U.S. informational and foreign policy objectives, but Franklin saw its broader work in publishing and reading as vital to true and lasting success. Like the government, its work was about asserting American power and culture, but Franklin framed that vision differently.

Franklin under Attack

Like the USIA and other organizations identified with American power and cultural imperialism, Franklin Publications from its inception was attacked in the countries in which it operated. Although the program tried to downplay its links to the U.S. government, it was often reviled as a government agency. These criticisms, which frequently appeared in the Arabic press, said as much about debates over Egyptian nationalism as they did about American power and influence in the Middle East. They also suggest that Franklin was having some impact on the Egyptian cultural scene.

On January 13, 1954, Hassan al-Aroussy wrote to Datus Smith, telling him that "a kind of protest" had been made in Beirut against the "cheap books which Franklin publishes." The organization was accused of selling its books so inexpensively that it was killing Arab authors, and it was also charged with "cultural colonization." After consultation, al-Aroussy had decided to ignore these attacks: "It is best, I think, to let our books speak for us."[65] The source of the complaints was the publisher of the Beruit-based Egyptian newspaper *Rose al-Yousef*, who was subsequently imprisoned on charges of corruption. Smith was gratified to see "a come-uppance for a man who reminds me of our W. R. Hearst in his yellowest rabble-rousing days."[66] Of course, in a country that constitutionally protected freedom of speech, Hearst was never jailed for yellow journalism, but the irony of this difference appeared to be lost on Smith.

The next round of attacks came from Egypt. A May 1955 article in the magazine *Al-Adab* criticized Franklin for preventing Egyptian publishing houses from publishing literature "that meets the needs of the Egyptians or that may help to awaken in the reader a consciousness of his real position in life and society." The article criticized the members of the intelligentsia who were working with Franklin and also complained that the program's publications tended "to create a special intellectual and sentimental atmosphere in favour of American trends in politics and thought." The author recognized that it might be impossible to oust Franklin from the country, but he did advocate the creation of a "counteracting cultural body whose aim must be to defend Egyptian culture against parasitic inroads."[67]

In October 1955, Samy Dawood published "We Are No Enemies of Culture" in *Al-Gomhoureya*, a Cairo newspaper.[68] In his article, he argued that "the Arabic reader has, for some years, been subjected to a regular and methodical intellectual invasion." He worried about a future national culture in which Egyptian "minds and thoughts will be subservient to and following the lead of a foreign authority." Citing Franklin's publication lists, Dawood noted, "Franklin Publications, Inc., which is a foreign enterprise, issues every year about one-third of the whole amount of books published by all the national publishing houses put together." Its aim, he claimed, was "to Americanize Egyptian culture especially when these books are sold at cheap prices which cannot be beaten in competition by the native commercial houses. The inevitable result will be the ruin of not only Egyptian authors but also of any European or American book which is not arbitrarily selected for translation by that purely American corporation." Dawood regarded Franklin as a foreign corporation with a monopoly on book publishing and declared, "We are not enemies of culture . . . but we strongly resent and flatly refuse to accept the cultural drift which is being imposed on us. . . . National thought must be allowed to live and flourish."[69]

A subsequent article published in *Al-Gomhoureya* in October, "Danger to our culture," by Ameed al-Imam, was an even stronger attack on what was seen as the "infiltration of foreign influence into all the Arab countries." This writer condemned the dominance of foreign broadcasting, the imperialist monopoly over world news, and the fact that "our bookshops and libraries are stuffed with so many Arabic versions of foreign books sold at very cheap prices and often at less than the cost evidently [*sic*] for the same alleged purpose of enlarging our minds and increasing our knowledge and culture." He hoped for the eventual victory that would "crown our efforts and those of all freedom-loving nations until the day comes when imperialism shall be decisively beaten and annihilated."[70]

In a November article, Dawood continued his complaints against Franklin and called on the Egyptian government to do more to translate and publish books. He made it clear that he was not criticizing the local people who worked for the program, writing that "the majority of those who co-operate with Franklin are either my teachers or my colleagues for whose learning, loyalty, patriotism and dignity I have the highest esteem." But he opposed the "methodical and foreign cultural invasion which penetrated the country through different ways, namely by books and broadcasts and now through magazines and newspapers." He cited the example of Abbas al-Aqqad, a famous Egyptian journalist and poet, who had recently written a biography on Benjamin Franklin for a Franklin Publications series on geniuses. Dawood noted that al-Aqqad had written on many great figures from the Arabic-speaking world, including the prophet Mohammed and the first caliphs to interpret and apply Islamic legislation. So why was he writing about Benjamin Franklin? Dawood saw this tendency as "a predisposition, a self-prompting effect brought about by the various cultural relations I have explained before." He argued, "It is this inner influence that has induced Akkad to rank Benjamin Franklin with prophets and caliphs or at least drove him to start the series of modern geniuses with Benjamin Franklin."[71]

This time al-Aroussy responded, writing in *Al-Gomhoureya* that Dawood "simply aims at exploiting the present political situation for attacking Franklin and obstructing the enormous cultural and literary output which no seeker of truth can deny has greatly enriched the Arabic library and stimulated thinking and love of reading." Al-Aroussy felt that his work at Franklin was about the "policy of cementing pure Egyptian and Arab culture," and he looked forward to "see[ing] the Arabs again in possession of that glory which they had in the remote past when they used to give to the world as much culture and learning as they had taken."[72]

In the eyes of some Arab nationalists, Franklin was a clear example of American cultural imperialism and demonstrated that many Egyptians identified with their colonizers. They believed that the program promoted American culture at the expense of the much more important and necessary Arabic culture that would support and encourage Egyptian nationalism and cultural development at this crucial period in its history. Yet those who worked, wrote, and translated for Franklin regarded the program as a way to further Egyptian (and personal) cultural and political goals.

American Orientalism?

Race and the realities of Cold War foreign policy crosscut the U.S. presence in the Middle East. In the 1950s, American views on Islam and the Middle East tended to be both generalized and flawed, as a number of scholars have demonstrated. One component was a belief in the threat of Arab nationalism and the notion that the people of the region were, as Matthew F. Jacobs writes, undergoing a deep identity crisis that positioned them between tradition and modernity.[73] Americans also tended to regard Islam as monolithic, although more subtle and nuanced understandings began to emerge over the course of the decade.[74] These assumptions shaped Franklin's work and attitudes, as did the belief that the Middle East was in transition from tradition to modernity and that guiding the region through this transition could prevent its societies from being seduced by communism. Americans were quick to see and denounce the Communist presence in the Middle East; but as a Franklin report makes clear, "hyper-nationalism" was considered to be the primary obstacle to American books and publishing.[75]

The prejudices of the Franklin bookmen who traveled to the Middle East during this time structured their encounters with the local people. While their preconceptions were tempered by personal experience, they were never entirely dispelled. During his April 1953 visit to Cairo, Datus Smith reported back to the organization's executive committee, and his comments reveal something about the views that Americans took with them into cultural encounters. "I like Egypt, and I am charmed and interested in the overwhelming majority of the Egyptians I have met," he wrote. "Their *kind* of intellectual sophistication is not the same as ours, but it is not less engaging, or less challenging to the mind."[76] In a letter to Johnson about al-Aroussy, Smith noted that he admired the manager's "breadth of vision" but also recognized "his capacity for wishful, contrary-to-fact thinking" and a "free-wheeling quality of business administration that would drive either of us nuts in a New York office."[77] Smith's language is condescending and paternalist but also typical of the time, and it shaped Franklin's work as it related to both the Cold War and conceptions of Arabic society. Not only did such stereotypes affect the choice of titles, but they also structured basic assumptions about the capacity of local book people to take on the work of publishing. In other words, they were the basis of arguments about why Franklin's existence was necessary. Clearly the Middle Eastern book industry was in need of change, but it was American publishers who constructed the discourse that that industry was underdeveloped and proposed American-style solutions to the problem.

Arabic anti-Semitism and anti-Zionism also shaped the relationship between Americans and Middle Easterners and influenced Franklin's work. As Smith's earlier report made clear, the organization acknowledged that these sentiments were common in the region, and it sought to avoid challenging them. In 1954, for example, someone suggested that Franklin sell its Arabic books in Israel. Smith responded that this might be in the interests of Arab countries, although he didn't say why (presumably for commercial reasons or to improve relations). Yet he acknowledged that, because no Arab government would support the idea, to sell books in Israel might jeopardize the entire operation.[78] Franklin intended to primarily operate in countries with large Muslim populations and hoped that its plan to focus on Islam-friendly texts and authors (who would often be translated into a number of different languages) would establish a basic position of trust that could be drawn on when establishing new offices in the region. Thus, it had to make sure that its texts would neither offend Muslim sensibilities about Israel nor model culturally offensive morals and social behavior. Foreign policy concerns shaped Franklin's work even as its work played out those foreign policy concerns.

In April and May 1954, Smith was again in Cairo, and he wrote back to New York about Franklin's infant publishing program. More than twenty titles were scheduled for imminent release, "good going in any league," although the number was less than he had hoped for because of printers' strikes and "great civic turmoil." While sales had so far been low, they were, he argued, "impressive by local standards." Franklin was also having some success with exports to other Arabic-speaking areas.[79] Smith noted Egyptian enthusiasm about the publication of Sabine's *A History of Political Theory:* "It is in the hands of all the very best people in the country, so its influence, both in itself and as identification of America with that kind of broad objective thinking about major trends of thought in the history of the world, is far greater than the sales [of 1,500 copies] would indicate."[80] He believed that Franklin had met its goal of getting an influential political text into the hands of the Egyptian elite.

Franklin's office in Egypt remained the center of its activities in the Middle East and the distribution hub for its Arabic-language books. In 1955, at the Princeton Conference on American Books Abroad, Smith contributed a paper on American books in the Middle East, which was later published in the journal *Library Trends*. He discussed the progress and prospects for American publishers in the region and lamented the ongoing challenges of education and literacy as well as the still-limited nature of the local publishing industry. Nevertheless, programs such as Franklin and the USIA were helping to circulate American books in translation. The goal, Smith said, was not "to persuade the Middle East that Americans are fine fellows" but to help the region "attain the intellectual and moral and spiritual strength which gives the insight to expose Communist hypocrisy." He continued: "Mere client nations, without the inner strength, would be of small value to this country when the chips are down, no matter what fine views of America they may hold, and no matter how gratifying it may be to American representatives in the field or their principals at home to chalk up technical points scored against the enemy in the international popularity game."[81]

Smith's paper suggested a range of activities for promoting literacy and developing readers, libraries, and a more sophisticated book culture in the Middle East. He was convinced that implementing a general book culture was vital, but his vision of that culture was very American: it was unclear how the long heritage of Arabic books fit into it. Smith's conception of development work would become increasingly important to Franklin as it extended its activities globally. The organization's methods and rhetoric were not identical to the USIA's informationalist approach, yet they were extensions of U.S. power abroad and reflected a common belief that the Middle East and other regions should become more like the United States and hence more understandable and manageable.

3
A World of Books, an Empire of Books

The Franklin archives contain a world map dating from the early 1960s, showing the Americas at its center and highlighting the countries in which Franklin operated. Each is marked with the date when a Franklin office opened there and the language used for the office's publishing program. The map is a visual projection of Franklin's dream of an empire of books.[1]

As Franklin sought to globalize its book work, it reflected the globalized and universalist goals of American cultural diplomacy and modernization during the 1950s and into the 1960s, when all the world seemed to be a potential audience and market for American cultural products. The organization's experience in Egypt served as a template. Although Franklin worked with locals in each of its subsequent locations, it showed only a limited concern for how the context and history of each place might differ.

The 1950s marked the high point of the book abroad, especially the idea of the book as a propaganda weapon. While there was considerable political upheaval in the areas in which Franklin operated (notably the Suez crisis of 1956), the period was also a time of global optimism as new nations emerged from colonialism, asserted their independence and nationalism, and sought to industrialize and modernize. Books could foster national culture; and for some of these countries, assistance in developing a book and publishing industry had practical value.

Franklin's work in the 1950s followed a trail of American global interests: Egypt, Iran, Pakistan, Indonesia, and Southeast Asia. All were of vital strategic importance as the United States worked to keep them from succumbing to communism and to bring them into the American sphere, including U.S. markets. Franklin opened many new offices in Muslim countries, not only because of its apparent success in Egypt but also because it assumed that Muslim countries had certain useful commonalities. Importantly, many of these countries were seeking to establish themselves after years of colonial rule and the turmoil of World War II. State building, not religion, was their priority.

Datus Smith's attitude toward political crises in these areas was generally matter-of-fact. As he observed in 1956, the year of the Suez crisis,

> Crises are the order of the day nearly everywhere we work, and the Egyptian situation differs from the others chiefly in its anti-Western slant, and in the striking change from the situation of a year and a half ago. The Communists are extremely active in Indonesia, food riots and suspension of civil government have occurred in East Pakistan, and the vitality of the Pakistan Republic is openly questioned by a number of observers. Only in Iran, where a species of police state is in firm control at least for the moment, are things relatively quiet.

Nonetheless, he was optimistic about the surge toward modernity and believed that Franklin bookmen should keep working in these areas for as long as possible, regardless of political turmoil. In his view, the program had much to offer troubled new nations: "A time of political troubles, when other sorts of contact between the United States and the local population are difficult or impossible, seems to us precisely the time when Franklin can make its greatest contribution. We should make and hold every friend we can."[2] Smith declared that Franklin and its staff members would always stay out of politics, "whether national or international," and he later boasted that this approach had kept them alive in the places in which they operated.[3]

In 1957, Franklin assessed its impact, especially in the Middle East. While quantification was difficult, there was "a flood of evidence demonstrating that the Franklin Publications program is locally recognized as one of the most important cultural facts in the Middle East in the last five years." A report noted that various governments had shown support and appreciation and that some local governments had sought to emulate Franklin's work, proof of the model's efficacy. Communists in these countries had branded the program "an active danger, regarded as the more serious because the books are of solid educational value and hence tend to ingratiate themselves with students." Such criticism was a badge of pride and seemed to suggest that Franklin was having an impact. The report also cited evidence that its books were influencing educational activities. It had received orders that year from the ministries of education in Afghanistan, Pakistan, and Egypt. Its publications were being used as university textbooks; for example, Sabine's *The History of Political Theory* was now a text used at both the University of Cairo and the University of Baghdad. Bookstores in Cairo were selling Franklin books to students, and basic science books in Urdu would be used as texts in Pakistan's army personnel educational program.[4]

At the end of 1957, Smith reflected on the success of the Cairo office "during this year of unprecedented difficulty." He noted that Franklin's Arabic-language books were finding their way into shops in Casablanca, Rabat, Tunis, and other North African cities.[5] Bill Spaulding, a textbook publisher with Houghton Mifflin, had a similar reaction. Spaulding, who had headed up the editorial staff of the U.S. Armed Forces Institute during the war and later helped found the American Textbook Publishers Institute, had been named the chair of Franklin's board of directors. In 1957, he traveled to many Franklin offices around the globe and reported back on what he regarded as the organization's great success. He thought the office managers were "wholly dedicated to the Franklin idea" and noted that Franklin's books were on display in all the cities he had visited.[6] Such feedback gave the organization confidence in its ability to have a global impact.

During the 1950s and into the 1960s, Franklin operated in a number of countries that were of concern to American Cold War strategic interests. It did not work in isolation but was part of a mosaic of U.S. government and private initiatives that included publishers who were becoming aware of commercial opportunities in regions such as Asia and the Middle East. Yet while Franklin boasted of its positive impact, results on the ground were mixed. The program sought to create a world of American books, but its vision of American internationalism was difficult to realize. Moreover, Franklin was dealing with increasing tensions in its relationship with the USIA as the state-private network came under strain.

Expanding Franklin

After its relative success with the Cairo office and with the Arabic translation program that was bringing books into Sudan, Jordan, Morocco, Tunisia, Libya, and other Arabic-speaking countries, Franklin began to discuss expansion into new regions. Its bookmen had already surveyed potential locations, including India, Pakistan, and parts of Southeast Asia—Thailand, Vietnam, Malaya (known as Malaysia after 1963), and Indonesia.[7] Because the USIA's initial grant was for use only in the Middle East, the organization would require additional funding, which meant making a convincing case to the government about which countries would be best suited for Franklin offices. There was considerable pressure from the State Department to set up an office in Iran, something Smith initially opposed but later agreed to. In 1954 and 1955, offices were established in Tehran, Iran; Lahore, West Pakistan; Jakarta, Indonesia; and Dacca, East Pakistan (which became, after 1971, the independent state of Bangladesh). Smaller offices were established in Tabriz, Iran, and Beirut, Lebanon, in 1957; and Kuala Lumpur, Malaya, in 1960. There were active translation programs in Persian (Farsi), Urdu, and Bahasa Indonesia alongside the continuing Arabic one.

Franklin investigated a number of other potential locations, including Taiwan, which had considerable strategic importance for the United States. Staff members drafted a lengthy report on the possibility of producing books for the "Overseas Chinese." In the end, however, while acknowledging that there was a need for books to combat Communist influence in Taiwan, they recognized that Franklin could not replicate its Middle Eastern operations there but would need to develop a different sort of model.[8] In early 1955, Smith and Malcolm Johnson also looked into the possibility of working in Hong Kong, where they could publish books in English by Asian authors for distribution in the Middle East and Asia.

These surveys in China were prompted by U.S. government concerns about "a newly-emergent, dynamic and hostile Asian power which is attempting to mobilize other Asian nations against us." With Chinese communism becoming a source of anxiety, cultural diplomacy efforts in the region were ramped up, but no one knew what was likely to have the greatest impact. R. M. McCarthy, who worked with the USIS post in Hong Kong, wrote to Franklin to express his doubts about the current efficacy of USIA-promoted books, which he thought were "too American and anti-Soviet." He argued for books that identified more with "the interests of Free Asia" and related to current Asian issues and problems.[9] While Franklin never operated in Taiwan or Hong Kong, the proposals and discussions reflect the way in which the organization conceived of book diplomacy as global in nature. They also reveal concerns about focusing too much on pro-Americanism and anti-Sovietism without considering local concerns and desires.

In addition to establishing new field offices during the 1950s, Franklin undertook work on behalf of the U.S. government in several countries of strategic significance, mostly by helping them procure translation rights.

For example, in 1954, it helped the Turkish Ministry of Education obtain translation rights for a number of teacher-training books. Don Cameron noted in a letter to Johnson that Franklin was "not thinking of Turkey as a priority target, but in the chain of Middle East defense it is an important link, and the training given by the National Defense College there would be, I should think, paramount in our national interest."[10] Franklin also briefly worked with the Burma Translation Society in Rangoon.[11] At various times, its bookmen considered opening offices in Liberia, the Philippines, and India; but Smith and other Franklin employees thought the risks were too great—especially in India, where the USIA was eager to establish a presence.[12] India was far too large to effectively manage, Smith said, and it was clear that such a project would have to be funded wholly by the U.S. government and thus could severely compromise Franklin's independent status.[13]

Franklin was clearly revealing its global ambitions as it sought to establish a professional model for translation and publishing in countries around the globe. In 1959, Smith, then traveling in Africa, commented, "Everywhere I go there are theoretical Franklin possibilities, and if we were empire builders it would not be at all hard to justify our jumping in."[14]

Creating New Offices

IRAN, 1954

In 1953, Donald Wilber, an author and an academic, sent Franklin an advisory memorandum about the state of Iranian illiteracy (80 percent of the population) and recommended titles to publish and distribute in the country, including those in the areas of autobiography, biography, sociology, and anthropology as well as how-to books in technology and civic affairs and books about the United States.[15] Given the State Department's focus on Iran, Franklin felt pressured into establishing a presence there, and in 1954 opened an office in Tehran. Eventually, it opened a second office in Tabriz in the East Azerbaijan Province (a region that the Soviet Union had occupied during World War II). Beginning in 1957, the Tehran office also produced books for Afghanistan, and an office opened later in Kabul.

Despite Smith's initial reluctance, the Tehran office proved to be Franklin's most successful, and I will consider its story more fully later in the book. For now, it is important to note that Iran was central in U.S. strategic thinking after the war, not least because of its important geographical position. The United States did have some history with Iran, primarily in providing economic advice before and during World War II. However, its concerns intensified after the war, in part due to the Soviets' interest and presence in the nation. During the war, Iran's leftwing Tudeh party had grown in strength; and as the Cold War developed, the United States believed it was imperative to ensure a stable, U.S.-friendly regime in the country, regardless of whether or not it had a democratic government. In the late 1940s, American economic and technical consultancies in Iran increased, as did U.S. interest in Iranian oil (through the Anglo-Iranian Oil Company). Yet some elements in the Iranian population were disturbed by the growing U.S. presence. When Mohammed Mossadegh became premier in 1951, the United States and Britain became alarmed. They regarded him as a "dangerous fanatic," and believed he might turn Iran toward the Soviet Union.[16] In this environment, the United States helped engineer an August 1953 coup to bring down Mossadegh.

It was no coincidence that Donald Wilber was a major source of Franklin's information about Iran. A graduate of Princeton University, he was the author of books about the country. He was also a former OSS officer who lived in the Middle East, and had worked with the CIA to plan the coup, and thus had a major influence on the course of Iranian history. After the coup, the United States became the dominant foreign power in Iran, supporting an authoritarian government led by Shah Reza Pahlavi and making substantial investments in the economy. Just a few months after the change in power, Franklin established its Tehran office, an indication of American interest in constructing cultural ties. The office would be active until the 1970s.

The Tehran office opened in early 1954, with Homayoun Sanati appointed as manager. Sanati, who had a background in business and no prior publishing experience, was the son of a notable Iranian author and businessman, Abdolhossein Sanati Kermani.[17] He later recounted that he had been arranging an exhibition of Expressionist art in Tehran that year when an attaché from the U.S. embassy approached him and asked if he wanted to be involved in starting a publishing firm in the country. Sanati told the attaché that he knew nothing about books, but the attaché said that lack of experience was precisely what the Americans wanted. The belief was that he would be free of bad publishing habits and thus more easily trained in good (that is, American) ones.[18]

Like al-Aroussy's in Cairo, Sanati's work for Franklin was framed as an act of Iranian patriotism rather than U.S. collaboration. Sanati, Smith wrote, could be described as "first, last, and always a Persian, and he wears no man's collar. He has a sharp tongue, and is not backward about mentioning the things he dislikes in America and American policy, and in Persia and Persian policy. But he is one of the staunchest defenders of freedom and democracy and human dignity I have ever known." Although he had once been a member of the Tudeh party, "his Persian patriotism drove him from the Tudeh, and he is a devout and confirmed apostle of the kind of free society that you and I believe in."[19] He had never been a Communist, Smith averred, and indeed was denounced by Tudeh as an Iranian police and foreign agent.[20] Sanati did have some perceived shortcomings, such as "a freewheeling contempt for laziness and red tape which makes him sometimes barge ahead faster than is wise, [and] a little tendency toward intolerant generalization about other people's failings." But what Franklin needed, Smith believed, was a man with "ironclad Persian patriotism who believes that the advancement of American ideas through American books is of high service to his own country."[21]

Franklin received US$50,000 in USIA funds to establish the Tehran office.[22] Wilson Dizard, then the USIA's policy officer on Iran, recommended in 1955 that Franklin concentrate on producing books that would supplement USIA and Point Four activities in the "cultural and educational field." In particular, the program should produce a series of children's science books that could be introduced into schools; "such a project could strengthen the foothold that American influence has in the Iranian educational system."[23] In the same year, Franklin Burdette of the USIA traveled to Tehran and visited the USIS post there. He noted that the USIS cultural officer believed that Franklin's publications were being received positively in Tehran and that Sanati appeared to be a great success in the office. Burdette wrote that Sanati had brought together a group of advisers and translators that "represents the best minds and the most influential people in Tehran."[24] Another successful outpost of empire was in place.

WEST PAKISTAN, 1954, AND EAST PAKISTAN, 1955

Pakistan was also of strategic importance during the 1950s. In the early years of the decade, the United States cultivated the new Pakistani government, and a number of the nation's officials visited the United States. Although India and Egypt strongly advocated nonalignment with the Americans and the Soviets, Pakistan chose to ally itself to the United States. In 1958, after General Ayub Khan seized the government from Feroze Khan and established a military dictatorship, the United States, in the interests of stability, supported the new government. Important U.S. bases were located in Pakistan, and good relations were seen as essential to keeping the country oriented toward the

West.[25] Given such concerns, a variety of American book and cultural diplomacy activities were targeted at Pakistan, and the USIA's operations there increased by 80 percent between 1954 and 1956.[26] In 1954, Franklin opened an office in Lahore, West Pakistan, to support these operations. Under the management of M. K. Rehman, it would publish translations in Urdu. At the same time Franklin began working to set up a Bengali language translation and publication program in Dacca, East Pakistan.[27]

Books published in Urdu during the decade included Alcott's *Little Women*, William Saroyan's *The Human Comedy*, and Harold Lamb's *Tamurlane*.[28] Yet as it had elsewhere, the Franklin program in Pakistan faced challenges in convincing the population that the organization wasn't purely an American propaganda outfit.[29] In 1957, Smith observed that the office was underachieving. He thought this was due to a combination of factors, including the fact that many literate people in Pakistan were already able to read books in English. He also noted that the local publishing industry was not very productive and was limited by "a stolid bureaucracy" and the "solid weight of Pakistani inertia."[30]

The Dacca office in East Pakistan opened in 1955 under the management of A. T. M. Abdul Mateen, the former chair of the Department of Humanities at Ahsanulla Engineering College. Mateen had earned a degree from Cornell University, and the USIA regarded him highly. In that year's report on East Pakistan, surveyors Smith and Charles Griffith said there was an "almost overwhelming" need for books in the country, which was "eager" for them and "generally friendly to the United States and to Western ideas, but constantly threatened both from without and within." Griffith was the vice-president of the textbook company Silver Burdett, and he would go on to chair the book committee of President Eisenhower's People-to-People Program from 1957 to 1960. In their survey report, he and Smith recommended that Franklin should publish supplementary school materials, university texts, and other books that could help the country's educational expansion. They said that literacy rates were higher in East Pakistan than they were in West Pakistan and that books could be "an ideal means of reaching the true heart of East Pakistan public opinion." They noted that local publishers saw cooperation with Franklin as an opportunity for financial support. Among them was the Pakistan Book Cooperative, founded by N. M. Khan (who was also Chief Secretary of East Bengal), which was already receiving funds from the U.S.-based Asia Foundation, backed in part by the CIA with the aim of furthering cultural relations. Through correspondence and conversations with Smith and Griffith Khan had, they believed, expressed his "dedicated belief in the importance of books to his country."[31]

One of the first books Franklin published in Bengali was Jack London's *The Call of the Wild*.[32] General subjects recommended for publication were "nation-building stories showing social conscience"; "anti-communist books, preferably story treatment rather than heavy treatises"; "American river stories, such as Huckleberry Finn, which establish neighborly rapport"; "ideological books by local authors—for example, presentations of the principles and key concepts of democracy in terms of Pakistani experience"; and "self-help books on all subjects illustrating the dignity and personal benefits of physical labor and the never-ending constructive resourcefulness of a nation built of individuals, groups, and communities imbued with the spirit of self-help."[33] Their descriptions illustrate the way in which Franklin's bookmen promoted books that they believed could serve national purposes for a relatively new nation as well as further USIA and U.S. priorities.

By February 1960, the Bengali program was producing a number of books that appeared to have some local popularity. On a trip to Barisal, a port city on the Bay of Bengal, Smith observed many bookshops, and all of them were carrying Franklin books for sale. "All the booksellers we talked with," he wrote to the New York office, "said sales were sensational when they first got the books, but that as economic conditions worsened there has been a big fall-off." He added, "They love our books."[34]

As he did for every Franklin office, Datus Smith regularly traveled to the outposts of his book empire, and his observations provide a snapshot of an American abroad in the 1950s. In early 1954, he wrote about Dacca in a letter to Malcolm Johnson, telling him it was a place he "did well to miss. Intensely interesting, but living conditions fierce."[35] The year before, Smith had noted the many "outward manifestations of the British Raj [in Pakistan which] seem not to be changed at all." He felt, as an American, that it was embarrassing to have so many servants attending to him.[36] Yet he seemed to enjoy his role as a latter-day imperial adventurer.

During the decade, American publishers took an interest in the country's commercial potential. English was a popular language in Pakistan, and there was a large-enough English-literate population to form a potential market. In a 1955 article in *Publishers Weekly*, Robert Taplinger, who had traveled to Dacca for an international PEN (Poets, Essayists, and Novelists) conference, argued that there was tremendous demand for American books among educated Asians.[37] In the same year, he set up a nonprofit company to publish

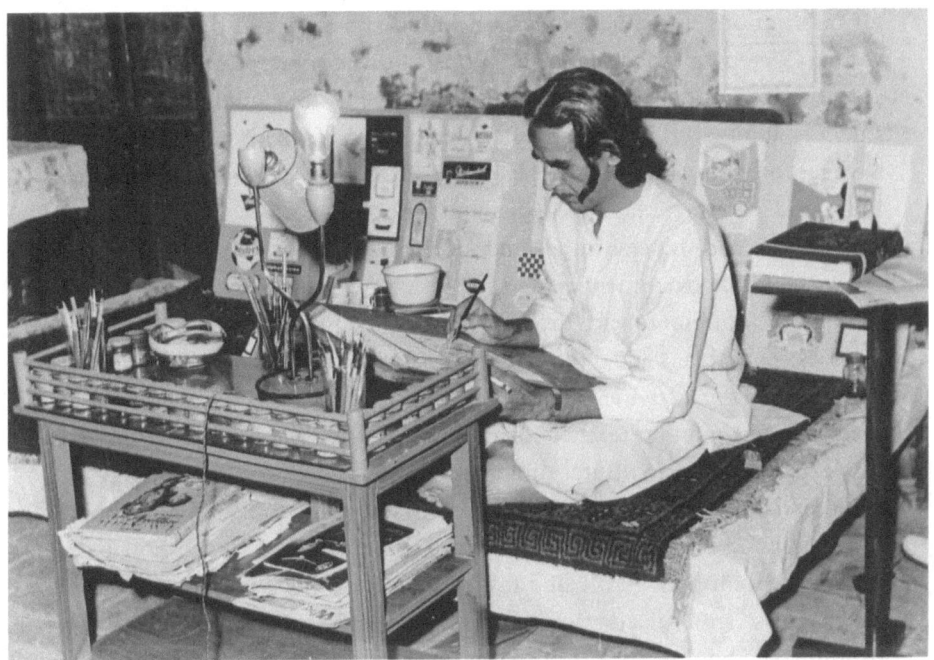

An image in Franklin's annual report for 1967, with the caption "A Pakistani artist preparing a jacket design in Lahore."

translations and adaptations of books by contemporary Asian writers.[38] Robert E. Banker of Doubleday Book Shops also went to Asia in 1955, on a trip sponsored by the USIA; he, too, wrote in *Publishers Weekly* that there was a potential commercial market on the continent, including in Pakistan.[39] As a result, the ABPC and the Asia Foundation cooperated to ship stock to a Pakistan-based exhibit of American books in December of that year.[40]

INDONESIA, 1955

In 1954, Franklin surveyed the possibility of expansion into Southeast Asia, a region already of commercial interest to American publishers. Smith traveled through the area early that year, along with his fellow surveyors Griffith and Francis St. John. They focused on Indonesia because it was predominantly Muslim, but American publishers had already flagged their interest in the country: two 1952 articles in *Publishers Weekly* had identified it as "a new market for American books." The three noted the country's many bookstores, its relative safety, and potential commercial and government connections.[41] For instance, the Indonesian Ministry of Information had "an urgent need for publications in the field of citizenship, democracy, and the technique of voting to prepare Indonesia for elections." Furthermore, it was "carrying on an intensive campaign against illiteracy as well as developing textbooks for students at all levels in the school system and adults, particularly those who have recently become literate."[42] Higher education was developing rapidly in Indonesia, and there was a great demand for textbooks.[43]

Indonesia had strategic importance during this period.[44] As with other such areas, the U.S. government undertook a campaign of cultural diplomacy to sway public opinion toward the West, which involved the expansion of USIS libraries, book translation (both Franklin's and the USIA's own programs), and cooperative activities with nonprofits such as the Ford Foundation that included training teachers of English.[45] While the publishing industry supported American cultural diplomacy work, it also saw the country as a commercial opportunity. One initiative was the American Book Shop, a demonstration bookstore in Jakarta with a display of 5,000 books donated by American publishers. According to its own press, the store was enormously popular as a "cultural show," with many Indonesians visiting the display and handling the books.[46] It was jointly funded by the ABPC, ATPI, the USIA, and the U.S. Department of Commerce.[47]

In their survey, St. John, Griffith, and Smith noted that the new Indonesian government was planning to develop school programs and adult "mass education" and that the new government had made Bahasa Indonesia the official national language.[48] The language was promoted as a nation-building tool and was part of an attempt to unify the country. The Indonesian cultural nationalists of this period envisioned a progressive, modernized nation; and as the government embraced that agenda, there was an increased demand for technical and scientific materials, especially in the form of textbooks.[49] An advantage was that Indonesia already had a strong book industry that American publishers could build on. Dutch colonial rule had left a printing, publishing, and bookselling infrastructure that was still in place after World War II and the nation's independence.[50] Balai Pustaka had been established in 1908 and continued to be the major government publishing house. It dominated the production of "official culture," and Indonesian nationalist leaders were strong believers in developing a nationalist literature to underpin the development of a new national culture.[51]

In the mid-1950s, a number of American publishers, including McGraw-Hill and Macmillan, sent representatives to Indonesia and other parts of Asia to take stock of the potential market. Even as Griffith was working with Smith in surveying the region for Franklin, he was also representing his firm, Silver Burdett, in considering a move into the Indonesian market.[52] McGraw-Hill launched an Asian textbook program in 1956, publishing textbooks in Japan for distribution to Indonesia, Burma, the Philippines, Pakistan, Thailand, Ceylon, and elsewhere.[53] In his 1955 report, Banker of Doubleday Book Shops argued that Indonesia was the greatest regional opportunity for American books in English, largely because British books did not have the same foothold as they did in other Asian markets.[54]

Indonesia was, like Egypt, an area that "absolutely fascinated" Datus Smith.[55] He believed the possibilities for Franklin there were "enormous."[56] His affection eventually led him to write *The Land and People of Indonesia* (1961), in which he described the nation as "one of the most important countries of the modern world." In September 1954, however, Franklin was still planning its Indonesian program, and had just received US$50,000 from the USIA for establishing its office there. In the proposal he sent to the agency along with a request for that funding, Smith emphasized, as he had in other locations, that Franklin would work with a diverse list of books and argued for the principle of local selection. He said that "books of direct 'doctrinal' value" would ruin "local belief in any support of the project in general; and it would be an error for Franklin to force concentration on such titles." He recommended some emphasis on Islamic-focused books, given the "recent appearance of a hardening of Muslim groups in their attitude toward Communism." American books such as Edward R. Murrow's *This I Believe* could, he argued, be of "high doctrinal usefulness."[57] But subject matter on the recommended list varied enormously. For example, it included Richard Boleslavsky's *Acting: The First Six Lessons* because the president of the local Akademi Theater wanted to revive acting and modern plays in Indonesia. Such books were clearly of interest to Indonesian readers but did not advance the U.S. cultural diplomacy agenda. Even the publisher who assigned Don Cameron the rights for the translation suggested that Franklin should consider it a potential money earner rather than "a weapon or argument" in the Cold War.[58]

Hassan Shadily, the Jakarta office's new manager, had worked at Cornell University on an Indonesian-English dictionary. He had no experience in printing or publishing, but Smith argued that he, like Mateen in Dacca, had been "chosen because of our estimate of their integrity, responsibility, and general intelligence." One of Shadily's greatest assets, he said, was the fact that he had "friends and supporters well scattered through all the non-Communist parties."[59]

Despite its existing infrastructure, Indonesia posed challenges for book and publishing work. Purchasing power was low, and local publishing was hampered by the high cost of production and a lack of good material to publish, especially educational texts.[60] There were also practical problems. For example, in 1958, there was an imminent major paper shortage, and Franklin had to ask the U.S. government for PL480 funding to acquire paper.[61]

Ongoing political unrest and the strong nationalist sentiment also posed unforeseen challenges. In July 1955, Smith wrote home to his wife that "life is peaceful and orderly in Djakarta, and if it were not for the newspapers you wouldn't know anything unusual was happening."[62] He was probably referring to the run-up to Indonesia's elections. In a report that year, Smith and Johnson wrote that the country's "geopolitical and cultural relation to other Afro-Asian countries is unique and critically important; it is playing with tremendous stakes in the game of being wooed by East and West."[63] In 1957, Smith noted that Franklin's start in Indonesia had been slowed by political upheaval.[64] But the program persevered, despite an often hostile climate. It initially produced only a small number of books, but Franklin believed that "the importance and influence of the people reading Franklin books is great, and as literates are naturally most numerous among the young we believe the effect on the rising generation is in itself a justification of the Franklin program."[65]

Indonesia was not particularly enamored of American cultural efforts, unlike countries such as Iran, which was eager to cultivate a close relationship with the United States. Its government actively promoted a strong nationalist culture, especially after 1957, when President Sukarno introduced "Guided Democracy." After 1958, Sukarno's regime was based on martial law, and he rejected what he regarded as foreign solutions to Indonesian problems.[66] Many Indonesians believed that Americans failed to understand the Asian "psyche" and did not know how to deal effectively with Asian people.[67] The U.S. government had a difficult relationship with Sukarno throughout his years of power (1945–67), and this affected Franklin's operations.

LEBANON, 1957, IRAQ, 1957, AND MALAYA 1960

The Franklin empire continued to expand over the course of the decade, but the other offices it established in the 1950s had comparatively little impact or success. In 1956, it opened small new offices in Beirut and Baghdad and planned to use Lebanese and Iraqi citizens as Arabic translators.[68] The Beirut office, which was intended to supplement the Cairo one, was headed by a part-time manager, Mohammed Najm, a professor of Arabic literature.[69] Although both the Lebanese and Iraqi offices were intended to be, as Franklin's annual report noted, "a small hedge against the worst eventualities in Egypt," the Beirut program later became more important as the center of the organization's English-Arabic dictionary project.[70]

The Baghdad office came under the supervision of Dr. Mohammed el-Amin, a German-educated archaeologist and academic who had formerly worked at the University of Pennsylvania. According to a 1958 Franklin memorandum, "no country without a book industry needs one more clearly than Iraq."[71] Yet even though the organization saw a Baghdad office as essential, it ultimately accomplished very little. Staff member Dana Pratt recognized that Franklin faced a tough job there, given the strong anti-American sentiment that began spreading after a coup that year overthrew the Hashemite monarchy in favour of a republic. On a visit to Baghdad, he noted that Franklin books (which had been temporarily banned) had been "replaced by a welter of books with the smiling faces of Khrushchev and Mao Tse Tung adorning the covers."[72] The book industry in Iraq was small, as was the literate population, and it remained difficult to establish any kind of presence there. Over the course of its existence, the Baghdad office produced only a tiny number of books in translation. In 1967, the Iraqi Ministry of Culture seized the office, and Franklin decided to shut it down.[73]

In 1960, Franklin opened a small office in Kuala Lumpur, Malaya, under the management of Ghazali Yunus, a former magazine editor and journalist. The aim was to distribute books produced in the Jakarta office and to improve regional methods of bookselling and distribution.[74] The office did receive support for a few small projects to develop the Malayan book industry. In 1962, for example, the Asia Foundation gave it US$43,000 in local currency for a program of supplementary schoolbooks.[75] But like the Baghdad office, the Kuala Lumpur office produced only a small number of books in translation.[76]

All three of these offices had only a minimal impact on the U.S. cultural Cold War and did little to contribute to Franklin's mission of cultural internationalism and industry building. Their activities were marginal at best, but their existence does attest to the thinking that underpinned Franklin. American book diplomats and publishers recognized that the globe was up for grabs, and almost every place was worthy of consideration as an outpost in the Franklin book empire.

Global Visions, American Imperial Culture, and the Politics of Translation

As Franklin established a global network of offices and American books, its bookmen imagined a world brought together by common reading, common values, and a nation-building book industry and culture. This vision was an element of American postwar imperialism. As the United States became involved in countries around the world, it sought to find frameworks for understanding that world, and cultural diplomacy served as one such frame. Franklin, USIA, and book-industry surveys contributed to a network of global knowledge, but they also labeled and thus approached nations as "traditional" or "underdeveloped." While these labels sometimes reflected reality (for example, a lack of infrastructure), they, along with Cold War imperatives, also constructed and reinforced particular understandings of the world. For example, Franklin reports about Iran focused on the sinister influence of clandestine Communist publications to justify the organization's operations.

Franklin sought to project American culture and values globally because its stakeholders assumed that these qualities had universal applicability. For example, it chose to circulate Alcott's *Little Women* in a number of countries because it believed the book would be meaningful to people in many places and cultures while also transmitting American social notions about, for instance, gender roles. As cultural internationalists, U.S. publishers imagined that people were more alike than different, so they tended to regard the so-called undeveloped readers of other countries as being basically just like Americans: all they needed was better literacy, more education, and greater inculcation into American culture. As these attitudes framed the dimensions of American imperial culture, they crowded out the particularities of local cultures.

Franklin's understanding of Islam also projected an American vision of the global. As I have made clear, Franklin's operational focus, especially through the 1950s, was on Muslim nations. A 1956 report noted that its work had met with "general Islamic acceptance" and that a number of Muslim religious figures in Egypt, Iran, and Pakistan supported the program. The report also mentioned that the Islamic Congress, "an organization for relations among Muslim countries which was formed during the pilgrimage to Mecca, has brought more than 1,000 Franklin books to send to Islamic institutions all over the world."[77] Franklin thus aided U.S. government efforts to support Islam—to an extent—as a bulwark against atheistic communism. As I will discuss, the translation and publication of Murrow's *This I Believe* in a variety of countries was explicitly seen as a means of countering Communist influence by promoting religious and spiritual values.

Translation had particular significance in the Western vision of postwar global relations. UNESCO, for example, saw it as a way of creating common understanding among disparate nations and peoples.[78] A 1957 *Publishers Weekly* article about the second Conference on American Books Abroad commented that translation was important for "cultural and political reasons" and should therefore be increased.[79] Many embraced the idea of translation as a form of cultural relations, but many also saw it as an essential part of propaganda and development.

Franklin's publishing work engaged in a politics of translation and language. This was evident in its choice of languages and the relationships it forged with local translators. Moreover, as I have noted, American books were translated into other languages, but few books from other cultures were translated into English. This has been a long historical pattern: as recently as 2015, only 3 percent of books published in the United States were titles in translation.[80] Thus, Franklin's decision to focus on circulating translated works rather than discovering or nurturing indigenous writing also meant that it created conditions that made it harder for such writing to be produced and published.

In 1954, when Franklin was considering its options for future work and expansion, Smith advised against working in certain languages, including Armenian and Kurdish, which he categorized as "divisive." He also spoke against languages such as Pashto, which he saw as both a "divisive" language in northwestern Pakistan and an "unsuccessful national" one in Afghanistan, as well as Tagalog in the Philippines, which, he argued, "offer[ed] no promise." English, he said, would be a better language for American publishing in the Philippines, and Persian was better for Afghanistan.[81] Debates over language choices continued into the 1960s. For instance, in 1965, Dariush Homayoun, who worked with the Tehran and Kabul offices, promoted Persian as "the mother tongue of a majority of Afghans and the lingua franca of the country, whether some officials admit it or not. . . . Persian is bound to become the cultural language of Afghanistan."[82] Homayoun advocated that all books for Afghanistan should be planned around Persian translations, despite the fact that the country contained multiple languages and ethnic groups. In other words, he was reflecting his own desire to assert Persian cultural nationalism. In Iran, Franklin and the national government worked to shift the preponderance of translated texts from French, which had dominated before the war,

Cairo exhibit of Franklin's publications, 1958.

to English. A number of Franklin-translated books won regime-endorsed cultural prizes—the first American-derived translated texts to do so. In Indonesia, Franklin supported national government efforts to establish Bahasa Indonesia as the national language.

Reviewers (that is, the people who selected books for translation) and translators were a major point of collaboration between Franklin and the people in countries where they worked. Reviewers for the Arabic program were required to complete a questionnaire for each book they examined. Questions included "Is the book biased in favor of a certain point of view?" and "How useful will the book be to readers in . . . Arabic countries?" The questionnaire also asked them to consider the political and religious consequences of the book and to note if it would need modification, editing, or revision before publication in Arabic. Translators and revisers were told, "It is agreed upon that the translation should be strictly consistent with the original in letter and spirit. Nevertheless, changes in some parts of the book may be permissible, . . . and in this case, it is necessary that the matter be referred to Franklin Office for its views."[83]

Franklin often recruited prominent figures to translate books or write prefaces to translated editions. As I discussed in chapter 2, a number of notable Egyptians translated Franklin publications; this model was followed elsewhere. In 1957, S. A. Rehman, the chief justice of West Pakistan, wrote the preface for the Urdu translation of D. C. Coyle's *The United States Political System and How It Works*. In it, Rehman praised the great progress the United States had made as a relatively young nation and called it "the standard bearer of democracy." Because he believed that it was important to understand the U.S. political system, he recommended Coyle's book, which "should be of immense use and importance to every serious-minded person to make a study of the various aspects of this most important modern Power."[84] In Iran, key members of the shah's regime and family were involved in Franklin's translation and publication programs. Princess Ashraf, his twin sister, translated Spock's *Baby and Child Care* as well as a book on nursing.[85] Three prime ministers contributed chapters to an edition of Noah Fabricant's *Why We Become Doctors*, and another translated Arthur Nussbaum's *A Concise History of the Law of Nations*.[86] Prominent politicians in Egypt, Lebanon, Pakistan, and Iraq all contributed to Franklin's publications as translators and writers.[87]

Adaptations and edited editions were produced specifically for markets abroad. In Iran, the Golden Books for young readers included illustrations that editors thought would be more suitable for Iranian children. For example, "the bears' cottage" in that edition of *Goldilocks and the Three Bears* "looked typically Caspian and Goldilocks' hair . . . [was] more auburn than yellow."[88] For publication in Pakistan, Franklin adapted a children's book that originally included a scene in which parents worried that their children might be in an automobile accident. In the Pakistan version, they were depicted as worrying about a tonga, or carriage, accident instead.[89] A Persian version of *The Columbia-Viking Desk Encyclopedia* involved a range of editorial interventions, including the elimination of entries relevant only to American readers and the insertion of items related to Persian history, Asia, and Islam.[90]

To offer further insight into the way in which Franklin created wholly new cultural products for its intended audiences, I want to turn to the history of three books: Sarah K. Bolton's *Lives of Poor Boys Who Became Famous* (1885) and *Lives of Girls Who Became Famous* (1886) and Murrow's *This I Believe* (compilations published from 1953). In all three cases, Franklin's versions of these books were not straight translations. Each became a new text invested with new significance for the organization's book diplomacy and cultural internationalism. *Lives of Poor Boys Who Became Famous* was a late nineteenth-century classic that profiled a series of famous self-made American men. Since its original release, it had undergone a number of revisions to include more recent famous figures. Thus, it seemed perfect as a vehicle for adaptation. For the Arabic edition, Franklin planned to include a selection of Americans along with famous men from the Middle East and the surrounding regions. An early list of possibilities retained the chapters on Benjamin Franklin, Charles Dickens, Abraham Lincoln, and Thomas Edison from the American edition and added ones on Kemal Ataturk, Omar Makram (an early Egyptian nationalist leader who had resisted the French), and Ali Mubarak (a late nineteenth-century Egyptian education minister). Deleted figures included John D. Rockefeller, Calvin Coolidge, Will Rogers, and Pope Pius XII.[91] The Urdu edition published in Pakistan included an introduction by Abdul Majid Salik, a newspaper editor and writer, who emphasized that the Muslim figures would serve as models for the nation's young people.[92] The Iranian edition added a chapter about the shah's father, supposedly written by the shah.[93] Franklin was focused on using this edition to impress the shah. Thus, when staff members learned that it might not be ready in time for a national holiday because nearly all of the workers would be away and the binding machinery was not working, the Tehran office manager, Homayoun Sanati, had to help assemble copies by hand at the printing plant, assisted by the head printer and people called in off the street to help.[94] The story perhaps attests as much to fear of displeasing the shah as it does to Sanati's dedication to Franklin's mission.

The Cairo office prepared Bolton's *Lives of Girls Who Became Famous* for publication in 1953. A number of figures were omitted from the Arabic edition, including Sister Elizabeth Kenny and Eleanor Roosevelt, but Amelia Earhart, Helen Keller, Marie Curie, and Harriet Beecher Stowe were retained. Under the heading "Famous Women of the East," new chapters featured Houda Sharawy, a pioneering feminist; Nazik al-Abid, who had played a role in the Syrian independence struggle after World War I; Fadwa Toukan, a Palestinian poet; and Marie Agamy, a professor of Arabic literature.[95] The Urdu edition, published in 1958, included profiles of Queen Noor of Jordan; Hazrat Aisha Siddiqa, a wife of Mohammad; and Hazrat Mahal, an early Indian freedom fighter.[96]

This I Believe was a series of popular anthologies based on Murrow's 1951–55 radio show and composed of short pieces by notable Americans on the subject of faith. Some were directly religious, while others discussed spiritual and philosophical issues. Smith was initially cautious about producing a translation, worrying that "conservative Muslims might be unwilling to join with Christians in a book with the idea of 'belief' in it."[97] Eventually, however, his enthusiasm for the project grew. *Lessons Life Taught Me* was the early working title for the Arabic edition. Smith was keen to use a local Egyptian publisher, Dar al-Hilal, "because they have been the most successful to date in large distribution of cheapest books, especially using newsboys and kiosks," although he believed the publisher was not appropriate for most Franklin books.[98] In a November 1953 letter to his wife, he said that the book might be his "tiny contribution . . . to both Islam and Christianity through helping our Muslim friends to see and feel their brotherhood with us as children of God . . . [for] they do believe this very deeply, but perhaps they do not realize that this is a feeling that good Christians share with them."[99] The Arabic-language version included twenty-five of the original American pieces and a number of new ones written by Arab leaders, including President Nasser of Egypt.[100]

When the Murrow book appeared in Egypt, it sold well, in part because "the personal philosophies of westerners and easterners appear[ed] in the same book thereby showing a spiritual and intellectual identity between two people probably not heretofore recognized by 'the men in the street.'" Franklin believed that adding the Nasser piece was an element in the book's success, as was "the fact that the religious overtones in the statements by both Americans and Arabs could all be embraced by Islam."[101] As of April 1954, *This I Believe* had sold 30,000 copies and Bolton's *Lives of Poor Boys Who Became Famous* 18,000.[102] Murrow's book was eventually translated into Persian, and that edition included a number of notable Iranian figures. The print run was 25,000 copies, which, according to Franklin, was probably the largest in Iranian book publishing history to date.[103]

Many books went through a process of selective editing and adaptation. That process was driven by a variety of factors, and these were not always political or religious. For example, in 1955, Franklin agreed to work with Iran's new School of Public Administration, which was being established by the local government in conjunction with the University of Southern California. Franklin's task would be to translate and publish certain texts related to public administration, including sections from two textbooks: Albert Lepawsky's *Administration: The Art and Science of Organization and Management* and Herbert Simon, Donald Smithburg, and Victor Thompson's *Public Administration*. "Because of the intensive nature of [the] program," any passages relevant only to American students would be omitted.[104]

Franklin continued to adapt and translate a variety of texts into the 1960s. In 1961, its Arabic program released George Antonius's *The Arab Awakening*, D. R. Bates's *Space Research and Exploration*, Crane Brinton's *A History of Civilization*, John Dewey's *School and Society*, John Kenneth Galbraith's *The Affluent Society*, Arthur Nussbaum's *A Concise History of Law*, Stewart Schackne's *Oil for the World*, and Noel Streatfield's *The First Book of Ballet*.[105] A 1965 *New York Times* article noted that Franklin had, by this time, assisted in the translation and publication of 43 million copies of 2,500 books, with many adapted for local readership.[106]

Certain books were translated in order to create a particular impact in particular countries. For instance, in July 1965, Najaf Darybandari wrote to Smith about the Persian translation of William L. Shirer's bestselling *The Rise and Fall of the Third Reich*:

> We have provided the Persian intelligentsia with a much needed analysis of the Nazi movement which had, before and during the war, its sympathizers in this country too. What pleases me most about the success of the Shirer book is that I think it washes away the residue of the Nazi legend which I am sure has been lurking somewhere in the minds of those who once sympathized with Hitler. This is no small service on the part of Franklin.[107]

Other books selected for translation demonstrated the importance of technical aid and development. For example, Franklin obtained the rights to a number of *Scientific American* books for its Arabic and Persian programs because "one aspect of the Franklin program which we find eminently appropriate is to be able to offer to the Middle East the fruits of American scientific research."[108]

It is difficult to find responses to many of these books, other than commentary from translators and preface writers. Nonetheless, I think it is fair to say that their welcome or rejection usually depended on the recipients' own criteria and needs. In an address at the launch of Franklin's school library project in the early 1960s, Hamid Ali Khan noted: "Translations of good books into national languages can play a valuable role in the development and progress of a country's literature, provided they are accepted as a supplementary to and stimulant for genuine literary creation and not its substitute."[109] His comment is a salutary reminder of the real problem underpinning Franklin's work. While the bookmen believed that their work would benefit the target audiences as much as it benefited the United States—perhaps even more so— they often overlooked what was necessary to make local audiences embrace books: an indigenous literary and scholarly culture promoted through the circulation of locally written texts.

Franklin's Relationship with Authors and Publishers

Franklin's relationship with American authors and publishers was generally positive during the early Cold War years. The book industry supported its surveying work and its identification of possible future markets. Publishers were eager to expand abroad, not only for national and commercial reasons but also because of a "humane interest in broadening [the] scope of men's lives throughout the world." Various conferences and initiatives were trying to overcome the barriers to distribution overseas, whether they were tariffs or simply a lack of awareness about American books.[110] Some publishers, such as Charles Griffith, were moved by a feeling of "deep responsibility to our country in its 'time of troubles.'"[111] In his memoir, Victor Weybright wrote that he wanted to help Franklin secure translation rights because he believed that the books his firm published were well suited for the task. His authors, he said, "were more delighted with a collection of their works in an impressive variety of foreign languages than if they had received a vast sum of money."[112] But publishing was ultimately a commercial endeavor, and it was important for Franklin to avoid hampering the activities, present or future, of American publishers.

Many Franklin authors were happy to have their books translated for an overseas audience, even if that meant that they would receive no royalties. This was not surprising: most of the books that Franklin produced were scholarly and thus had never been released in the expectation of generating large profits for their authors or publishers. But occasionally Franklin had to deal with authors or literary estates that were not willing to grant unfettered translation rights. For example, readers in numerous countries were interested in translations of Margaret Mitchell's *Gone with the Wind,* but Stephens Mitchell, who handled his mother's literary estate, was notoriously difficult about granting rights and permissions. He would agree to the possibility of Franklin's translating and publishing it only if the estate were to receive full royalties: "I wish to do the patriotic thing and help the cause of American literature and Western culture in the Middle East. However, I do not believe that our prestige is heightened by gifts of American art and letters to nationals of other countries, to enable them to profit from the work and property of nationals of this country." He wrote to Cameron to express his "doubts about giving things to people." "When you give to charity," he said, "you often lose respect for the recipient. The recipient often lacks regard for what is free."[113]

Datus Smith doubted the suitability of *Gone with the Wind* for Franklin's program as it was, in his view, "neither a major contribution to knowledge nor a work of high literature."[114] However, Hassan al-Aroussy, the manager of the Cairo office, disagreed, arguing that the book "is about the best known American fiction through the cinema and through reading in both English and Arabic." He anticipated that the book would be a success.[115] Ultimately, Arabic and Urdu translations were produced, with the royalties going to charity—in the case of the Arabic translation, to the Palestine Aid Fund set up through the American University of Beirut.[116] The book was clearly popular in the countries in which it was distributed. But a pirated Arabic condensation appeared just before Franklin's full translation was released (the estate did not permit abridgment), undercutting the edition's potential sales.

Franklin worked effectively with American publishers throughout the 1950s. For instance, Knopf, which also worked directly with the USIA, frequently granted the organization cheap translation rights. Franklin's Knopf books included Carleton S. Coon's *The Story of Man* (1957), Robert R. Palmer's *A History of the Modern World* (1950), and Hans J. Morgenthau's *Politics among Nations: The Struggle for Power and Peace* (1948).[117] The USIA and Franklin occasionally requested rights for translation into the same languages, suggesting that they had little coordination in this area and were perhaps even competitors.[118] In early 1954, for example, the USIA requested translation rights from Knopf for Willa Cather's short story "Neighbor Rosicky."[119] In mid-1955, Franklin, hoping to translate the story into Urdu, requested the same rights but was referred to the USIA.[120] The agency had, as it turned out, already given Urdu rights to a local publisher but did offer to consider giving Franklin other language rights as long as that arrangement did not conflict with local missions.[121]

As the decade wore on, publishers' attitudes toward government bureaucracy became less enthusiastic. In 1957, Alfred Knopf wrote to Arthur Larson, then the director of the USIA: "Book people could be helpful, [so] why don't you use them effectively?"[122] This was a recurrent refrain that the government failed to effectively address, and publishers' support for government book activities, such as overseas exhibits, declined by the end of the 1950s. In 1959, for example, *Publishers Weekly* reported that ABPC members were not eager to support such exhibits without "legitimate sales potential." Publishers were also concerned about the low amount of money they were being pressed to accept for translation rights.[123] Nonetheless, they continued to advocate for certain other government-supported programs, especially the International Media Guarantee program that allowed them to take their English-language books to a number of countries that otherwise could not afford them. In 1959, Knopf sent a letter in support of the program to various members of Congress: "[It] has enabled publishers to sell certain books, the reading of which would be calculated to improve the understanding of the American way of life on the part of foreign peoples, for local currency in many countries which would otherwise have been unable to buy American books because of shortages of exchange." In his view, cuts meant that "some countries whose friendship and understanding we are seeking are unable to obtain good American books in sufficient numbers."[124]

Publishers' open dissatisfaction with government bureaucracy did not mean that they were necessarily opposed to Cold War principles. In 1957, Curtis Benjamin, then the president of the ABPC, released a statement on the industry's behalf. Pointing to the vast amounts of print material being exported by the Soviet Union, he argued that the United States was falling behind. There were two obstacles to increasing the export of American books, he wrote. One was the high cost of book production, the other the shortage of dollar exchange. He also criticized the funding cuts in the International Media Guarantee program. Emphasizing that the Cold War was primarily a battle for people's minds, he asked why more money was being spent on the American defense budget. Benjamin believed that the "international exchange of books leads directly to a better world understanding, and thus to peace."[125] Yet his appeals to Congress to restore the program were in vain.

Franklin's Relations with Washington

In 1958, William J. Lederer and Eugene Burdick released their novel *The Ugly American,* which, they acknowledged, was "based on fact. The things we write about have, in essence, happened." The novel tells the story of American embassy officials in Asia, focusing on their crass behavior and their refusal to engage with local culture and populations. The book's subject matter mirrored growing public concerns about American behavior abroad. While Lederer and Burdick wrote their tale to assert the need to keep fighting communism, they also believed that the United States was failing at the task because it was using the wrong people for the wrong jobs. Their novel worked to show why.[126]

Franklin was keen to set itself apart from the Ugly American image. Indeed, Smith wrote to Storer Lunt of W. W. Norton, which had published the book, to express his outrage when Lunt suggested that it must have given him "some discomfort." Smith agreed the book's argument was correct, but "for crying out loud, Storer, can you really think that I could have traveled in Asia as long as I have and then make common cause with the Bad Guys instead of the Good Guys?"[127]

Smith was doubly frustrated by Lunt's assumption because of Franklin's own ongoing travails with the government. As I have discussed, Franklin was government-supported but had a complicated relationship with Washington throughout its existence. Smith wanted its operations to remain open and transparent and sought to distance the organization from any obvious alliance with the government. At the same time, he shied away from publicly revealing its funding arrangements for fear of damaging its reputation. He actively sought to avoid any mention of Franklin during congressional hearings and was outraged when the program was named in the 1954 House Appropriations hearings: "Once the decision is made to handle the thing partly off the record, it surely must be done with greater finesse and sophistication than is evidenced here."[128] Smith hoped that more care would be taken in Senate hearings because, he believed, Franklin's "usefulness could be terribly destroyed by any more of the on-and-off the record technique that was used in the House hearings." He added, "The combination of 'cloak and dagger' suggestion on the one hand with inescapable identification of Franklin on the other (even including complete reproduction of our unique title list!) could be fatal."[129]

Even though it could not hide its participation and complicity in American foreign policy, Franklin resisted the USIA's attempts to control and accelerate its operations. Correspondence between Johnson and Smith suggests that the pressure to make rapid decisions was evident from Franklin's inception and that they had agreed, in 1952, that "nothing could be more fatal to our purposes."[130] As time went on, they also became concerned about the way in which the government viewed Franklin. In 1956, Smith confided to Johnson that he thought they had more to fear from their "bureaucratic and congressional friends . . . than [from their] enemies." He explained,

> The friends instinctively try to show that this is a slick trick we have been putting over on our Asian friends. We flatly deny that it is, and we know that if it were a trick, or not in Asian interest, it would have been exposed and halted long since. But the argument of caginess is so easy to make, and is so appealing to congressmen, that I feel certain Franklin is going to be presented in the wrong light by people trying to help us.[131]

Title selection was an ongoing source of tension between Franklin and the USIA. In 1953, both entities had agreed that the State Department would indicate which titles it objected to on Franklin's lists but that Franklin would have the freedom to make its own decisions about the remaining titles.[132] In September 1954, Smith wrote to Franklin Burdette of the USIA's Information Center Service. He was concerned about their telephone conversation the day before, when Burdette had told him that the USIA felt that, all along, Franklin should have been publishing "hard-hitting anti-communist books." Smith said, "I am only one of several Franklin Directors who declined to enter the [Franklin publications] project until assured that [the Information Center Service] took the same long-range view of the book as a propaganda instrument that we do, and that direct propaganda was not in our assignment." He argued that any attempt to make Franklin "hard-hitting" or "political" would be "immediately self-defeating." He would rather terminate the contract between Franklin and the USIA.

> There is no quarrel with the fact that the content of Franklin's program should be "politically" determined. It would be naive to think you could support the project otherwise. But our initial tentative thinking on this subject has been made a ringing conviction by our field experience; and we are now sure that, even in the most hard-boiled propaganda terms, our method of publishing books which reflect American culture and thought and which can be wholeheartedly and publicly endorsed by the cream of the intellectual and civic leadership of the foreign country is the only method by which we can help reach ultimately valuable political objectives.
>
> There is a theory that apolitical general-interest books are all right as bait or camouflage—as a method of sneaking up on the locals, so to speak—but that the real work of a book program is done by the propaganda items for which the general books provide protection. This will not work with us. Without local endorsement and sponsorship our program would fail; and local people of eminence—some of whom are understandably timorous and all of whom are proud—will not lend their name and influence to a program including "hard-hitting" books even in high dilution.

If the government wanted anti-Communist and "hurray for America" books, it should publish them itself, he argued.[133] Smith's strong response won him few friends in Washington and jeopardized Franklin's ongoing funding. At a December 1954 board of directors meeting, Johnson mentioned the USIA's displeasure but reiterated the importance of sticking to the principle of local selection. In his view, maintaining this approach was integral to Franklin's success.[134]

Despite these tensions, USIA continued to fund Franklin's work, and the agency's director, Theodore Streibert, wrote to Johnson at the end of 1954 to confirm that the USIA had earmarked funding for Franklin for the next fiscal year and assure him of its "deep and continuing interest" in the program.[135] But in 1955, tempers flared again when Smith expressed concern about time-wasting bureaucratic procedures associated with a particular anthology marked for translation. At first, the USIA had stipulated its right to approve the inclusion of every contributing author, but then it changed the clearance rules while Franklin was still working on the book.[136] Smith's memorandum about the incident defined, from his perspective, Franklin's preferred relationship with the USIA and asserted the necessity of "independent action." USIA and Franklin titles should not follow the same rules and procedures, for "the value of Franklin's program could not be reckoned in terms of the effect of any single title or type of title, but rather in terms of the broad interest in and understanding of Western ideas which the publication of a great variety of books alone can foster."[137]

Burdette's response assured Smith that the USIA had no desire to interfere with Franklin's regular program and suggested that editors and reviewers attach a brief statement to each title stating its contribution to USIA objectives. "In cases where the purpose of the project is related to something other than the content of the book, Franklin could submit, in place of the foregoing statement, a designation of what Franklin believes the project could accomplish and a copy of the book, since we would probably have no staff appraisal of the book if its content were marginal to the mission of the Agency." The USIA would try to decide quickly about titles, and an independent review would be required only when "sensitive" subject matter was involved. "I should emphasize that we are fully aware of the advantages to be gained from occasionally including a book which has a usefulness not directly related to its content. However, our approval of such a book must be recognized mutually as an exception."[138]

Dissatisfied, Smith asked for an example of a title that "match[ed] the stated criteria" and for clarification of the accompanying bureaucratic process. In a letter to Claude Hawley of the USIA, he agreed that freedom might be a valid objective but asked, what about titles that upheld freedom but were not strongly American?[139] In a separate memorandum to Hawley, Smith stated that title selection was not a uniform procedure and that Franklin had many special advisers helping it settle on title lists. He emphasized that the principle of local selection meant that Franklin had to trust the "local leaders of distinction" with whom the program worked: "Our entire effort would be destroyed if there were any tendency to veto books which are neither harmful nor of unacceptable quality." He reminded Hawley that Franklin had the competence to be responsible for its own operation and that it was far better to have a functional program "rather than imperil the whole enterprise by trying to impose an American-selected list."[140] A few months later, the USIA vetoed Franklin's inclusion of Paul H. Landis's *Helping Children Adjust Socially* without any clear explanation as to why it was unacceptable other than that it had been written for middle-class American children. Smith wrote a long letter of objection, noting that the books had been approved at the local level and that should be good enough.[141]

The USIA believed that Franklin had value because it dealt with "certain types of books which would not normally be used in the USIA program."[142] But criteria for title inclusion created tensions through the 1950s and beyond as the government tried to assert its own priorities in the work that Franklin did. Meanwhile, Franklin had difficulty making the USIA understand not only its principles but also its budgeting, particularly when it needed to retain funds to carry over projects from one year to the next rather than use up all of its funds by the end of a given fiscal year.[143] The lack of funding for long-term projects was a constant problem, and Franklin frequently complained about it.

There were also problems generated by shifts in USIA policy and direction, as the leadership shifted from Streibert, to Arthur Larson, to George V. Allen, to Edward R. Murrow by the early 1960s. In December 1956, Johnson expressed his unhappiness about "dangling at the whim of various individuals." He believed there needed to be a commitment to continuity, which he saw as a "sound publishing practice."[144] While the USIA remained committed to books as a Cold War weapon, it wanted complete control over titles that were translated and published abroad. The agency regularly had to justify its expenditure to Congress, and appropriations depended on its ability to demonstrate that its work was directly contributing to the fight against communism. It was hard for the USIA to fund Franklin's projects "if there are not a substantial number of titles that have some demonstrable relationship to the Agency objectives."[145] For its part, Franklin was increasingly concerned about waning government interest in its projects. The USIA's own low-priced books program was not established as competition, but it invariably became so.[146]

Franklin's industry professionals continually queried the government's publishing competence, and studies of the USIA have generally agreed that its staff members lacked the skills needed for a variety of activities. According to

Richard Arndt, limited training and a less educated cohort of recruits meant that the agency increasingly struggled to handle cultural work. By 1961, he notes, doctoral degrees were no longer "usual" in the USIA, and a culture of non-intellectualism prevailed. Moreover, by this time, the instrumentalist view of information had risen to dominance; in the 1960s, the USIA was no longer concerned with two-way exchange but with a one-way flow.[147] Its primary preoccupation was countering Communist information; indeed, it was unlikely that Congress would have given it the funds for anything else. Minutes from a meeting of the Advisory Committee on Cultural Information are filled with anxious commentary about Communist influence in Africa, India, and the Middle East.[148] Such worries lay behind the USIA's decision to narrow its book focus to projects with explicitly anti-Communist values or functions.

By the end of 1958, Franklin staff members were talking about sending a declaration of independence to the USIA. Smith spoke of "the cumulative effect of lots of things, especially . . . the USIA tendency to blurt things out at one moment and at another to follow procedures appropriate only to a cloak-and-dagger outfit." He cited one ridiculous example: the USIA sent a non-classified bibliography, available to anyone coming to the New York office, by registered mail, wrapped in a double envelope and with a transmittal letter marked "confidential."[149] Smith was eager to distance Franklin from the USIA and to reassert that the program was not a government agency.[150] He wanted to make this separation clear to other Franklin funders as well. In 1961, for instance, he told a Ford Foundation employee about a misunderstanding between Franklin and USIS-Cairo: "We felt that we were being asked to serve merely as an instrument of USIS Cairo, rather than having our traditional freedom to act as a responsible professional organization."[151]

During the second half of the 1950s, the USIA became more directly involved in producing books for the overseas market. Although it still saw Franklin as an important player, the agency had decided to produce its own low-priced editions of American books for distribution in a number of countries. Many of those books were released as *ladder editions,* written in what the USIA termed as "simplified English." Others were translated into local languages.[152] The agency believed its low-priced books in translation program would show the world the value of American literature, help explain the American system of government, and prove that the nation had a "cultural and spiritual foundation."[153] Production of these cheap books was "essentially the Agency's answer to the vastly increased Communist book program." In 1956, the USIA allocated US$1.5 million to the program, distributing the money to American contractors abroad, who in turn subcontracted to local publishers.[154] In late 1956, the agency began planning an abridged books program as a response to the flow of Soviet books in Asia and the Middle East. Each selected book was shortened to 120 pages and its vocabulary level reduced to about 2000 words. American publishers gave the USIA rights for these works.[155]

In the late 1950s, the agency's low-priced books in translation program published a variety of texts. Those in Arabic included Chester Bowles's *New Dimensions for Peace,* Massimo Salvadori's *Liberal Democracy,* John Foster Dulles's *War or Peace,* R. Ernest Dupuy's *The Compact History of the United States,* George Soule's *Introduction to Economic Science,* and the locally written *Abu Shadi in his Adopted Land.*[156] It also produced books in Gujarati, Hindi, and Persian. Those in Persian included Alfred Zauberman's *Economic Imperialism* and Phillips Russell's *Jefferson: Champion of the Free Mind.* Its largest print run in Persian was for Allan Nevins and Henry Steele Commager's *A Pocket History of the United States.*[157]

Advisory committees composed of members of the book industry helped the government make decisions about selecting and using books; addressing publishing and library-related problems; and creating links with American individual, groups, and private institutions.[158] Yet members of the ABPC expressed their concern that the agency's book program was being carried out by USIS officers who had no experience in publishing (a familiar situation that had been part of the original justification for Franklin's creation), and Knopf for one frequently complained that the government ignored publishers' useful recommendations.[159] As I have mentioned, Franklin staff members saw the government approach as generally counterproductive. In 1962, Smith argued that the organization would be better off folding than compromising its principles.[160] Yet Franklin stayed alive and continued to run its programs as best it could, despite a steady reduction in USIA funding. After 1959, more than 56 percent of its support came from sources outside the U.S. government, and the program began to shift its focus from book diplomacy to book modernization.[161]

In 1958, Malcolm Johnson, who had been active in smoothing the relationship between New York and Washington, died of a heart attack at age fifty-five. He was a Cold Warrior who took American books abroad as a patriotic duty. But he was also a publisher who loved books, and he worked hard to promote both the industry and book culture globally. According to Smith, Johnson "did more than any one other person to open the eyes of American publishing to its world responsibilities."

> He would have rejected indignantly any suggestion that he was a do-gooder [and] . . . he refused to talk sentimentally about world brotherhood, yet he established warm friendships and an attitude of reciprocal respect with hundreds of Asian book people of every race, religion, and skin color. . . . Every action he took as a publisher was weighed in terms of moral responsibility. Both America and the countries of Asia and the Middle East are permanently in his debt.[162]

Not long before his death, Johnson suggested to the National Book Committee that it should support a program to translate foreign books into English for an American audience—in his words, a "reverse Franklin" program. He argued that those who had worked with Franklin were "aware how slight has been the traffic the other way."[163] The publishers who worked with Franklin believed that Americans had much to learn from the literature and culture of the world, and such a program would also boost the credibility of America's global cultural work. Commenting on the proposal after Johnson's death, Bill Spaulding said it would be "a sincere demonstration of America's interest in the literature of 'Franklin' countries, [and] its effect could be invaluable."[164] Yet the program was never established, and cultural traffic continued to run primarily from the United States into other countries, reflecting the era's power relationships. Translation had become an instrument of American cultural imperialism.

By the late 1950s, Franklin had established offices around the globe, going some way to fulfilling Johnson's vision of an empire of American books. By November 1956, the organization had produced more than a million books in Persian, Arabic, Urdu, Bengali, and Bahasa Indonesian.[165] Among its projects, the two most successful were, and would remain, the Arabic program that operated from the Cairo office and the Persian program that operated from the Tehran office. The shah's regime strongly supported the Franklin-Tehran office, which was a crucial factor in its success. Yet the tensions between Franklin and the USIA over the types of books suitable for book diplomacy was forcing the organization to rethink its mission. By the end of the decade, it was looking to expand into other activities, most of which focused on assisting countries to set up and develop their own book industries. Increasingly, Franklin's work intersected with efforts at modernization and education.

4
Book Work as Modernization

In 1960, Datus Smith reported on a Franklin-sponsored program in West Pakistan known as Books for Village Aid. In his view, it reflected President Ayub Khan's commitment to "democracy at the local level." He explained, "In other words, it is *not* double-talk using the word democracy such as we have encountered in some other countries."[1] In fact, however, Khan was a military dictator, and the country was under martial law at the time of Smith's report. The contradiction inherent in his statement attests to the complicated politics of book modernization projects.

Book diplomacy, as we have seen, was riddled with Cold War demands and cultural internationalist aspirations. Book modernization work also raised difficult political and moral issues, including the need to work with and support undemocratic regimes. Franklin did not abandon book diplomacy in the 1960s, but it did strategically turn to modernization and development frameworks to sustain and expand its work. It became involved in a range of programs that sought to change communities and even societies. Franklin believed that countries should embrace American-style publishing and commercial models and assumed that American values should be an aspirational ideal for all societies. At the same time, it promoted the benefits of development for the countries in which it worked. In a 1962 plan for expansion, Franklin's stakeholders envisioned coordinating all of its future programs with educational and development projects.[2] They emphasized the importance of allowing private enterprise to develop "naturally," thus reinforcing their underlying commitment to publishing as a capitalist enterprise (although the results were more mixed in practice).[3] In Smith's words, publishing was, for every society, a "basic mechanism of development," not "a frill."[4]

Nonetheless, financial problems during the decade limited Franklin's effectiveness. In 1962, Smith commented that the organization was "in desperate need of dollars" and that government funding was in short supply.[5] Although the Kennedy administration paid lip service to the importance of books, libraries. and development aid programs, it was concerned abroad primarily with what it called the "book gap"—the gap between the amount of American and Soviet publications in the global sphere—and continued to use books in an instrumentalist way to address communism.[6] The USIA linked funding to the way in which programs were meeting government policy objectives, so Franklin was given "performance credit" only for titles that the agency saw as furthering its own agenda.[7] The organization steadily explored various other options for funding, including philanthropic foundations, new government entities such as the U.S. Agency for International Development, and (after 1964) private donors. It also received funds from the countries in which it operated.[8]

During the 1960s, U.S. foreign policy shifted under the Democratic administrations of Kennedy and Johnson. There was a greater emphasis on using development aid to encourage countries to modernize and move toward democracy (and hence reduce the attractions of communism).[9] Yet a focus on containing communism and keeping countries allied to the West continued to dominate foreign policy, and the government largely saw cultural programs as mechanisms for winning them over. It increasingly accepted the need for "military modernization," a model in which authoritarian regimes took control of countries and directed the path of development, often at the expense of individual rights and democracy.[10]

International organizations became increasingly concerned with development and modernization, and those goals shaped a variety of cultural and educational programs. UNESCO, for example, pursued universal literacy, with a strong focus on establishing education and literacy programs in developing countries, although literacy was often conceived of as part of economic productivity rather than an element of individual or community empowerment.[11] During the first half of the decade, many activists had faith in the power of science, industry, and technology to effect global change and development. Among those who were eager to spread the gospel of American-style publishing to the world, the future seemed bright—though that optimism would be challenged by the end of the 1960s.

Technical Aid and Modernization

By the early 1960s, many believed that developing countries were undergoing an inevitable process of modernization. According to Robert Jervis, both the United States and the Soviet Union imagined models of development that would spread and shape the world, yet neither country saw the world as it actually was.[12] Nonetheless, an elaborate ideological discourse underpinned U.S. programs as the government sought to guide the nature and process of modernization in ways that favored its worldview. American global development programs, first established during the Truman and Eisenhower administrations, increased dramatically.[13]

Modernization theorists of the 1950s and 1960s argued that social, economic, and political changes were fundamentally integrated. They believed that all countries developed along similar lines as they moved from a so-called traditional state to a modern one, and they declared that modernization (in American versions of this theory) would eventually guide all countries toward democracy. Michael Latham writes that modernization as an ideology framed 1960s understandings of foreign policy and aid, providing a "powerful and appealing narrative" that promised "sweeping changes" and rapid transformation.[14] According to Nils Gilman, American modernization theorists saw the ideal terminus of development as "an abstract version of what postwar American liberals wished their country to be."[15]

Modernization theory's key advocates included Gabriel Almond, Edward Shils, Walt Rostow, and Lucien Pye, and important works in its canon included Daniel Lerner's *The Passing of Traditional Society* (1958) and Rostow's *The Stages of Economic Growth* (1962). The theory is complex, and there were various manifestations of it in the postwar period. Yet most Western theorists agreed that modernization was an inevitable path for all societies, that the U.S. model was desirable and necessary, and that economic development was a necessary first step before political development could proceed. Thus, it was vital for the United States to contain and shape countries' paths to modernity.

Modernization in both theory and practice was deeply political. Indeed, as Michael Adas writes, it came to supplant "the beleaguered civilizing mission as the preeminent ideology of Western dominance."[16] Latham likewise emphasizes the political uses to which modernization was put, arguing that it even revived a sense of Manifest Destiny. The concept was articulated in terms of an idealized American self-image, and it had a complicated relationship to colonialism.[17] Those involved in modernization projects, such as Franklin's bookmen, believed their work was the antithesis of colonialism because it focused on "self-respect and development of self-reliance." The employees in its overseas offices, they declared, were not thought of as "locals" in a way that captured "the patronizing overtones of the 19th century colonialist expression 'natives.'"[18] Rather, Franklin was helping these countries "achieve that mood of cultural and spiritual independence that will permit them to remain loyally on *their own* side [rather than come over to the American side]." Franklin's bookmen believed that the organization's operating method, not the books it produced, was its greatest contribution to the anti-Communist struggle: "This turning away from the sahib-native relationship of the past has been as surprising as gratifying to local people. No Soviet enterprise and virtually no other business or educational project sponsored by the West has given the emphasis to self-respect and human dignity that Franklin has tried to maintain in all its work."[19] Yet development itself positioned its recipients as subjects, thereby extending a new form of colonialism. As Nick Cullather suggests, the colonial subject became the "developmental subject" who was still being imagined and manipulated by foreign "experts."[20]

Modernization shaped various foreign policy initiatives in the Kennedy era, providing programs such as the Peace Corps and the Alliance for Progress with, in Latham's words, a "conceptual framework."[21] It was also influential among Franklin's bookmen, who were already internationalist and developmental in outlook and who already believed in the value of education, literacy, and good books for the benefit of society. Modernization offered an image of Americans abroad helping other countries become more like their own: more democratic, more economically successful, more educated, more developed, and so on. In Franklin's eyes, such global involvement was not aggressive, nor was it aimed solely at furthering American interests. For some adherents, modernization was even akin to missionary work. They could be, as the sociologist David Riesman once declared, "apostles of modernity."[22]

In practice, however, modernization rarely followed the theorists' ideal path. Those on the receiving end usually contested and negotiated it in a variety of ways, and American implementation was not always benign or altruistic.[23] Modernization was enmeshed in American foreign policy self-interest. Some theorists accepted that the military could function as an important tool for modernization; and stability, even if authoritarian, became a key word in foreign policy approaches to developing countries.[24]

Franklin saw modernization as an appealing framework for its work and recognized that it would also allow the organization to pitch its work to a broader range of funding sources. While there was undoubtedly some cynicism involved in Franklin's adoption of this approach, its stakeholders were deeply committed to development and aid as a means of ensuring social progress. They believed that the United States could "serve as a great catalyst for change in 'stagnant' societies."[25] Not only would book modernization activities help keep these countries from becoming Communist, but they would also nurture commercial industries that could eventually become part of American trade networks. Now Franklin needed to find ways to act as "a great catalyst" in the development of the necessary infrastructure.

Books, Publishing, and Modernization

During the 1960s, there was an increased domestic focus on education and the role of books, not least because of demographics, now that the baby boomer generation was entering high school and college. Anxiety about being outstripped by the Soviet Union in scientific and technological development also led to increased government support for education. Before the Vietnam War began to suck up government money, the Johnson administration was notably concerned with education policy, and the publishing industry benefited financially from the public education acts passed during his tenure. Concerns with education were also global in dimension and were tied to modernization and development. Influential theorists such as Daniel Lerner advocated literacy as the best "index and agent" of modernization.[26] According to this argument, because books were a foundation of education, they must also be important in facilitating development.

Industry leaders were aware of the potential in global literacy programs, education, and publishing, even though they still largely pitched such work within a framework of anti-communism. A 1961 article in the *National Book Committee Quarterly* considered the future of "American books abroad" and declared that "more than half the world is in a race to catch up with the Twentieth Century. It is a race that India, Indonesia, Ghana, and the other underdeveloped countries believe they must win. . . . Nothing less than the future of the free world is at stake." The article noted that these nations' leaders knew that a technological elite was not enough. They also needed "an enlightened citizenry who are aware of the forces of change that are loose in the world, and who can help put them to good account rather than be demolished by them. In short, the removal of ignorance is a paramount goal of every underdeveloped country." The article emphasized that American books were particularly important in this regard and urged the book industry to work harder to facilitate their flow into developing countries. Yet it did not advocate a singular focus on "the triumph of American ideology over Russian." Rather, "by making widely available through books our intellectual, scientific, and cultural resources that they find useful, we will strengthen the community of purpose that can help these nations to withstand Communist pressures and take their rightful places in the society of free nations."[27]

In May 1962, Thomas J. Wilson, Bill Spaulding, and Datus Smith put together a paper titled "Books in Industrial Development" that advocated similar views. They argued that education and literacy were fundamental to growth and that books and a local publishing industry were "an essential element of industrial development." Indigenous book industries were far more effective than anything "laid on from abroad" and needed to be "closely aligned with educational initiatives." A book industry was, they asserted, "the handmaiden of progress."[28] During the 1960s, Franklin frequently presented its work in such terms, although, as Smith cautioned at an annual meeting of ATPI, publishers needed to take the "long view" in getting involved with the developing world.[29] In the same vein, W. Bradford Wiley urged publishers at an ABPC meeting to continue to connect profit motives with a "sense of social responsibility" because books were "vital to the development of a major part of the world."[30]

As the American book industry began to conceptualize its role in programs of modernization and foreign aid, Franklin turned to AID for financial support. Established by the Kennedy administration, the agency reflected the president's goal of making the 1960s the "Development Decade."[31] It was the successor to the International Cooperation Administration (ICA) and its predecessor, the Technical Cooperation Administration, which had overseen aid and technical assistance programs abroad. Early on, Franklin had worked with and received small amounts of funding from the ICA—for example, support for the organization's work in producing public administration, agriculture, and trade books in cooperation with the Indonesian government. However, Smith had been less than impressed with some of the ICA field staff. After meeting two of them at an Iranian Ministry of Education dinner in 1957, he commented, "In addition to general crudity, ignorance, and dullness, I was struck by the complete anesthesia under which they must keep themselves."[32] He hoped for better from AID.

AID signaled that it saw books as "significant tools in economic and social development" and, beginning in 1962, founded its Central Book Activities unit to stimulate book-related work in developing countries.[33] Seeing an opportunity to distance itself from its strained relationship with the USIA, Franklin set out to construct a potentially more fruitful relationship with AID. Its staff members explained that books were "one of the major factors in building the human resources required for political, economic, and social development of a nation."

> [They are] a tool for stimulating leadership and the general public in thinking about political, economic, and social issues. They offer information which is vital for a balanced understanding of social, political, and economic processes with which an emerging nation has to deal, and they are a record of action taken in dealing with social and economic problems. They serve as a medium for the transfer of knowledge and know-how in the education and training process.

The "challenge," they argued, "is not merely to counter-act Communist literature but to give the people in the underdeveloped countries access to the intellectual resources and the technical skills of the Western World."[34] Franklin thus conceptualized books as "handmaidens of educational and economic development of every kind" and proposed that its interests and AID's were basically similar: to find "ways and means for a nation to modernize its educational and technical possibilities."[35]

At the same time, Franklin briefly entered into discussions with the newly established Peace Corps, proposing that Peace Corps workers would work with local groups to prepare books and that Franklin staff members would help them with editing and publishing.[36] The Peace Corps was typical of U.S. government efforts during the early 1960s, many of which centered around the optimistic expectation that a combination of idealistic volunteers and state aid would help underdeveloped areas and counter the image of the Ugly American.[37] Although little came of Franklin's proposal, it does illustrate the organization's desire to find new avenues for developing book and publishing work as well as the increasing prominence of the rhetoric of development and modernization in the discourse of internationalism.

Franklin did receive some financial support from AID. For instance, in 1963, the agency funded the Books for Paper deal, in which it purchased Franklin books with dollars then used by Franklin to buy paper from the United States, Pakistan, India, the Philippines, and Finland.[38] A 1964 contract funded training for would-be publishers to travel to the United States for Franklin-run training seminars managed by Byron Buck, a former textbook editor for Macmillan.[39] In 1965, a Franklin newsletter noted that a major goal had become "the training of people to construct and operate local book industries" and that the organization had received funding from AID's participant training program to run U.S.-based workshops to train overseas book illustrators, designers, booksellers, distributors, and others. By the middle of the decade, Franklin had trained nearly a hundred people through this program.[40]

Training and the transfer of technical skills and knowledge were central to Franklin's vision in the 1960s. If book diplomacy was about giving people books to read, book modernization was about giving them the skills and infrastructure to create books for themselves. Franklin's overseas employees were viewed as the "nuclei of modern technical knowledge in their own countries and a source of ideas and stimulus to the entire book trade with which they are in contact."[41] In summarizing the organization's activities in Pakistan in 1965, a Franklin report noted that "technical assistance to aid development of Pakistani publishing is regarded as a vital objective in its own right, not merely in connection with Franklin-sponsored books."[42] The organization's increased focus on technical assistance demonstrates how it mirrored not only America's involvement in the modernization of emerging nations but also employed a rhetoric that emphasized empowering locals in their own progress.

Nonetheless, Franklin was not able to secure much ongoing funding from AID. For example, the agency was unenthusiastic about the organization's idea for a Nigerian reading materials program that would provide texts to new literates and young readers and so help indigenous publishers develop a market. As Rowan Wakefield, an AID employee, told Spaulding, "it is not the type of project . . . that can be readily put into the AID programming process."[43] Spaulding despaired of getting any real AID assistance, despite the agency's unanimous "verbal support" of Franklin's programs: "I think there isn't much hope of getting anyone in AID to develop any fire in his belly over the most critical area in the whole field of education."[44] Franklin's main problem was fitting its book projects into AID's bureaucratic processes and conventional project agreements.[45] In 1966, Smith echoed his earlier comments about USIA staff when he observed that few of AID's employees understood books.[46] That same year, the agency withdrew its funding for Franklin's training program.[47]

Given the general U.S. focus on technical aid and education, Franklin began to consider the importance of promoting library development. In 1963, Smith commented in the *American Library Association Bulletin* that many countries lacked library facilities, yet "both libraries and the library spirit are essential for wide and deep book development in any country." Hence, it was important for Franklin to continue its work in this field and to include librarians as assistants in its programs.[48] Jay E. Daily, a librarian and the author of training manuals on library cataloging, worked as a consultant for Franklin in the 1960s and promoted awareness of Franklin's work within his own profession. In a November 1964 article in the *Library Journal*, he highlighted the value of books in the "industrialization process" and outlined various Franklin projects for developing the book industry abroad, from providing paper, to encouraging banks to loan money to publishers, to teaching book distribution methods. For his librarian readership, he emphasized that a book industry underpinned education and that education underpinned economic growth. Franklin's work would be done "when the habit of reading and the institutions which support it are self-sustaining and an integral part of a country's social and economic life."[49]

Franklin helped establish school and village libraries; more generally, it promoted the library profession through its books.[50] But library development was a large and difficult area to tackle. In 1966, Lester Asheim, the head of the American Library Association's International Relations Board, published the results of his survey of librarianship in developing countries. During his travels, he had found that there were great challenges to the development of libraries and librarianship. He wondered if these countries really wanted American help and if American methods were in fact the most appropriate for such different contexts. He concluded that it was better to "adapt, rather than adopt" American methods and procedures, but adaptation was not easy to achieve, given most nations' limited financial resources.[51]

In Iran, Franklin's arguments in favor of library development did result in change: by the late 1960s, many town and provincial libraries were being established around the country.[52] Franklin also supported the establishment of school libraries in Afghanistan, East Pakistan, and West Pakistan during the decade.[53] It was involved in a project, launched in 1963, to provide free copies of 140,000 American books in Urdu to 815 high schools and more than 100 training colleges and normal schools in West Pakistan.[54] Yet as Smith noted, some local publishers objected to the program because they believed schools were being forced to take the books whether they wanted them or not.[55]

Franklin engaged in a variety of other technical aid projects aimed at educational and publishing industry development, and internal reports and grant applications frequently refer to the organization's "catalytic function" in helping to develop the book industries of other countries. Projects included training printers and conducting seminars on book distribution and sales.[56] Franklin also worked to help local publishers and printers obtain sufficient paper stocks, negotiate for paper imports, and understand the economics of paper supply, thus serving as a catalyst for "possible paper-industry developments."[57]

Franklin's work in Afghanistan illustrates how it imagined its modernization function. Afghanistan became increasingly important in the Cold War of the 1960s and 1970s, largely because of the Soviet presence there but also because it was regarded as so "backward" that it was in dire need of development aid, including book assistance.[58] The country posed problems for Franklin because it had limited book infrastructure, no publishers, and few bookstores. The Franklin office in Kabul was funded primarily by a grant from the Asia Foundation, and its work included remodeling the Ministry of Education's printing plant (supported by a US$100,000 Asia Foundation loan), training personnel, and producing American textbooks in Persian and Pashto.[59]

Franklin's American staff saw their work in Afghanistan as potentially revolutionary, although they viewed the country's nationalism with caution.[60] During a 1964 visit, Don Cameron observed that there was a "teen-age" quality to its nationalism and that national maturity was still some way off.[61] Yet on his own visit to Afghanistan that year, Smith reported, "There is a terrific show going on here—in the country I mean, not just in Franklin— and I think all of us are going to be proud in future years to have had some small part in building the new Afghanistan that is growing up right before our eyes."[62] He later commented, "I am most terribly happy we are here."[63] Smith's enthusiasm suggests that Franklin's involvement in modernization personally appealed to him, perhaps more than book diplomacy did. It certainly convinced him that the organization was involved in momentous work and could help bring about historic change.

Franklin's work in Afghanistan was influenced by political concerns, most of them linked to Iran, which wanted some control over the nation's development and politics. At first, the Afghan textbook project operated out of the Tehran office; and after the establishment of the Kabul office, Iranian staff expressed general dissatisfaction with the rate of progress, perhaps because they now had less control over what was being done. In 1965, Dariush Homayoun, who managed the Tehran office, noted that the personality of "their man in Kabul" (the manager Atiqullah Pazhwak) was slowing progress because he was not enough of an entrepreneur. The Tehran office, he said, was eager to "wash its hands from Kabul affairs."[64]

Franklin's work in Afghanistan was not aimed solely at national development; its bookmen continued to consider the possibilities for a commercial market in the future. In August 1964, for instance, Smith alerted American book publishers to the existence of the Afghan textbook project and pointed to opportunities for "getting in on the ground floor as the first book-publisher in a fairly important country which, after decades of holding back, is now moving into the modern age."[65]

It is important to acknowledge that the governments of many of the countries in which Franklin operated openly embraced modernization and development, sometimes even more enthusiastically than the Americans did. Modernization appeared to offer a rapid route away from colonialism and disadvantage. Both the United States and the Soviet Union provided models, but more importantly they provided practical assistance. The elite of many of these countries advocated for a variety of forms of local modernization, without necessarily agreeing that the ultimate goal should be American-style liberal democratic capitalism. At a basic level, they saw books as a means to education and self-improvement.

Franklin's most-requested titles in 1961 were related to popular science and self-improvement.[66] Such books spread or encouraged particular ideas and understandings in the countries in which it operated. In 1964, the organization drafted an article emphasizing the importance of education to development and the role of translated books in promoting education, insisting that these books were "indispensable to broadening horizons [and] injecting new ideas." The article also highlighted the ongoing importance of book work to American foreign policy aims. Franklin was helping "emerging nations of the world to become self-supporting economically, free and independent politically, and socially progressive."[67]

Franklin's focus on health and child-raising issues illustrates the way in which individual books could be matched to modernization goals. For instance, there was much emphasis in Iran on the translation and production of Spock's *Baby and Child Care*. Scholars have noted that the book, first published in 1946, conveyed a vision of a cooperative and consensus-oriented society that countered the violence and disorder of the war years.[68] Spock's vision of permissive parenting was intimately tied to his own society and culture, and the attempt to export these views is an interesting example of American cultural imperialism at work. Franklin's edition was a bestseller in Iran at least in part because, as I have mentioned, it was translated and promoted by the shah's twin sister. Yet it also suggests that certain aspects of

American culture appealed to the people (or the leaders) of other countries. It was not the only such book on the Franklin lists. The organization also released numerous books on child and educational psychology, sex education, child mental health, and parenting.[69]

Books on government and administrative topics were also seen as valuable tools for helping countries become more modern. The USIA and Franklin were both pleased with the impact of the Arabic edition of *The Federalist Papers*, for example, because they believed that the university students who would read it would "shape future policies in the governments of their countries."[70] *Industrialism and Industrial Man*, by Clark Kerr, John T. Dunlop, Frederick H. Harbison, and Charles A. Myers, was translated into both Bahasa Indonesia and Persian and promoted as a "clear and informative analysis of the problems of labor management in the industrial societies of the world, and in the societies that seek to industrialize themselves."[71]

In 1966, Smith published *A Guide to Book Publishing*, which neatly sums up Franklin's 1960s worldview. Addressed primarily to "those in developing countries," it sought to summarize the major operating principles for successful commercial book publishing. The book itself was a form of technical transfer and conveyed Smith's fervent belief that book publishing was "the key to educational and social and economic development and hence to true nationhood." Readers were tutored in the economics of commercial book publishing while also learning that book publishers had "an obligation to society." Many of the topics—editorial processes, book design, promotion—would have been familiar to any aspiring American publisher, but Smith also discussed the importance of reading development and libraries.[72] His book encapsulated the holistic view of the industry that Franklin advocated even as it reflected American power in the model offered for emulation.

Franklin and Philanthropic Foundations

A Ford Foundation grant supported the release of Smith's *A Guide to Book Publishing*, a reminder of the importance of philanthropic foundations as sources of Franklin's funding in the 1960s and early 1970s. Not only were the organization's government funds insufficient to cover its expenses, but Franklin also saw private funding as an essential part of its image as a semi-private organization with broad support. Both the Ford and Rockefeller foundations played important roles in American overseas work after the war. Generally internationalist and liberal in outlook, they sponsored various projects connected to development, education, science, and medicine and were an essential source of funding for programs in developing countries.

During the Cold War, these foundations usually supported and supplemented the work and interests of the U.S. government. As Gary Hess has shown, their enormous postwar expansion was due in part to a commitment to promote orderly social and economic development as a way of stopping communism.[73] There are allegations that some foundation funding came from the CIA. Yet even though foundations and other international organizations undoubtedly took part in the Cold War, they sometimes also played subversive roles—for example, by promoting the idea that the world was interdependent and in taking an internationalist perspective.[74] The Rockefeller Foundation noted in 1951, partly as a response to the anti-Communist hysteria of the House Un-American Activities Committee, that its mission was to focus on "the life of the mind, [and] the outreaching of the human spirit," which it saw as "fundamental to the well-being of mankind."[75]

Books and libraries had never been a significant aspect of American foundation work. Nonetheless, during and after World War II, the Rockefeller Foundation supported the American Library Association's work in developing libraries and collections overseas and encouraging international library exchange.[76] For the most part, however, foundations were more concerned about education, especially in the developing world. Projects such as the support of newly established universities in countries such as Nigeria and Uganda became a significant part of their work.

Franklin relied heavily on the ongoing support of the Ford Foundation, which gave it millions of dollars in grants over the course of its existence. Established in 1913, the foundation had become the world's largest philanthropic institution by the end of the 1940s.[77] In the 1950s, it supported some book and education work, including the Southern Languages Book Trust, an agency in India that produced books in translation and published locally written books in the primary languages of southern India.[78] By the end of the decade, the foundation had developed a focus on Africa. According to a 1966 estimate, it had invested more than US$56 million in African development since 1958, with nearly US$34 million of that money going toward education.[79] The foundation was also an active supporter of scholarship and university press funding during the 1950s. *Publishers Weekly* noted in 1956 that it was providing a US$1.7 million grant to help subsidize university press publishing.[80]

Franklin regularly applied to the Ford Foundation for funding. In 1960, for example, it received foundation support to produce a Persian dictionary and train Iranian editors.[81] Another large grant helped Franklin staff fund their New York office through the early 1960s and supported important survey work in Africa.[82] (As I will discuss in chapter 5, much of Franklin's work in Africa was subsidized by Ford.) The modernization framework had given Franklin access to a language that was meaningful to the foundation and underpinned the long relationship between the two entities. In a 1962 application, for instance, Franklin argued that its work would act as "catalytic agent" and was "essential to nation-building."[83] Foundations embraced the agendas and programs of modernization and development, although, as Ron Robin makes clear, they rarely supported organizations or research whose work or approach involved criticism of the United States and its official policies.[84] Like the USIA, Franklin occasionally found that philanthropic support was hindered by private donors who wanted some authority over title selection rather than agreeing to Franklin's basic principle of local choice.[85] Nevertheless, foundations were an essential source of income and an important facet of the Cold War state-private network.

Franklin also pursued corporate support for its work, sometimes in conjunction with foundation funding, and its quest for corporate donors ramped up from the late 1960s into the 1970s. One example of its combined-funding strategy involved the Cairo office's English-Arabic dictionary project. The Rockefeller Foundation supported the project, which, Franklin staff members believed, would enlarge the number of Arabic-speaking people who could read English and thus would purchase English-language books and magazines.[86] Franklin staff also argued that "identification with this great cultural monument should bring public relations advantages as well as practical benefits for many years to come."[87] The dictionary was promoted as also being useful for companies that ran training programs. Hence, Franklin asked for and received additional financial support from Aramco, which offered US$30,000 over the three years between 1964 and 1966.[88]

The Tehran Office and the Politics of Modernization

As I discussed in chapter 3, Iran was strategically important to the United States. After the shah came to power in 1953, the country was seen as an "island of stability" in a volatile region, and the U.S. government worked to support the regime at many different levels, even though the shah had little affection for democracy and ruled his nation via a form of "popular authoritarianism."[89] While both the U.S. and Iranian governments focused largely on the economy and technical aid, they also had considerable interest in cultural programs. Franklin's highly successful Tehran office was one such program, and it was central to bringing American books and book culture to Iran.

Franklin's history in Iran demonstrates that modernization was a political tool not just for the United States but also for regimes that were seeking to advance their countries' development. The shah was a keen modernizer, and his support for Franklin was one way in which he cultivated American strategic, financial, and military support.[90] His White Revolution (1963–78) was essentially a series of reforms through which he attempted to emphasize and increase the pace of modernization and shape Iran's political and economic scene. At the same time, he suppressed dissent, often violently. According to Ali Ansari, the White Revolution was the shah's way of finding a "legitimating myth" for his regime: that is, of identifying his government with progress and the development of a "model" country. Its effects had a mixed impact on the Iranian population, who suffered from the resulting economic changes and land reforms.[91] Nevertheless, it did include education and literacy programs, although these often had inconsistent results. The repressive regime was eager to cooperate with Franklin, and Franklin was eager to cooperate with the repressive regime, each for its own purposes. This pattern was replicated elsewhere (for instance, in West Pakistan), but the Iranian relationship was probably the most effective and productive because of the clear benefits it brought to both parties.

In 1957, after a meeting with the shah, Datus Smith reported to New York that he "showed a most enlightened and far-seeing view of the importance of our work."[92] At the time of their meeting, Iran had long possessed a strong book culture. Printing houses had been in place since the nineteenth century, and a number of private publishing firms were founded during the twentieth century. Their focus was on Persian-language texts, including many books about ancient Persia.[93] While the state had controlled much of this publishing work since the beginning of the reign of Reza Shah (1925–41), the leftist Tudeh party, a major force in Iranian politics before the shah came to power, had continued to operate a large publishing and bookselling concern until the party was outlawed in 1949, although it continued to operate underground. According to Smith, the Tudeh party's clandestine publishing work was continuing to have "psychological importance out of all proportion to its volume because of its saucy impudence in . . . pop[ping] up again each time it is announced to have been 'completely and permanently suppressed.'"[94] Smith's comments, while dismissive, suggest that a variety of texts, including leftist political texts, were in circulation despite official censorship.

Official censorship increased drastically after the 1953 coup, and books that touched in any way on socialism, the Soviet Union, or China were banned.[95] As Farid Moradi writes, the shah's crackdown on the left significantly hampered intellectual growth and damaged the quality of the nation's book industry. During the 1960s, the shah's cultural grip relaxed, but new cultural growth and nascent intellectual freedom were suppressed again in the 1970s when they began to threaten his regime.[96] Franklin thus operated in an environment of ongoing censorship, a situation that the bookmen never comment on in their reports—an ironic silence, given the American publishing industry's complaints about U.S. intellectual censorship. Franklin's desire to remain, in its own view, nonpolitical blinded its employees to their collusion with a questionable regime.

Franklin's books quickly gained recognition in Iran. In March 1956, its edition of George Sarton's *The Life of Science*, translated by Ahmad Birashk, won an annual prize, and its editions of Charles W. Leonard's *Why Children Misbehave*, translated by I. Ahmad Saidi, and B. Pazargad's *Contributions to Political Theory*, an original volume of Iranian commentaries on American political philosophers, won Imperial Court prizes. Smith told the Franklin board of directors that "these developments are especially gratifying because the prizes, which attract as much attention as Pulitzer Prizes do with us, have heretofore reflected the French bias of Persian culture. Only very rarely have they gone to translations from English, and never before to a book of American origin."[97] In 1960, Smith himself received two awards from the Iranian court—the Order of Homayoun and the Medal of Honor of the Imperial Organization for Social Service.[98] The Tehran office benefited from court and government support, including financial backing. For instance, the Persian version of *The Columbia-Viking Desk Encyclopedia* was funded by both the Ford Foundation and Princess Ashraf; and as we have seen, the princess's translation of *Baby and Child Care* was a best seller.[99]

Children's books were important elements of Franklin's Iranian program. Nonfiction publications, including introductory science texts and translations of Dorothy A. Bennett's *The Golden Encyclopedia* and Else Jane Werner's *The Golden Geography*, were popular. Younger readers enjoyed translations of Golden Books. Amina el Said, an Iranian journalist and Franklin's translator for *Little Women,* supported the organization's emphasis on children's books, which she saw as key to the establishment of a new publishing industry in Iran. Franklin eventually produced all of the nation's early-grade textbooks, which were then distributed free to schools through a subsidy scheme run by the Imperial Social Services Organization. Several Franklin publications appeared on the Iranian Children's Book Council's lists of recommended books—not a surprise, give that Franklin had helped to establish the council. They included editions of E. B. White's *Charlotte's Web,* Scott O'Dell's *Island of the Blue Dolphins,* and Ian Fleming's *Chitty Chitty Bang Bang.* Mark Twain's *The Adventures of Tom Sawyer* was assigned as school reading.[100]

Franklin's Tehran office produced more than a million textbooks for Iranian schools, with "a definite stated objective to improve and modernize the existing texts" through "use of adapted translations of American texts and ... substitution of texts and illustrations created by the Persian-American educational teams." It worked with local publishers and printers as a way of facilitating their direct relationship with American textbook publishers.[101] For the new textbooks, Franklin worked with an American base text and drew on American educational principles, but the Iranian Ministry of Education retained editorial control.[102] For example, even though *The Golden Geography* was the basis for the geography textbooks, Iranian geographers had a significant influence on the final product.[103]

The Tehran office also supported the Iranian government's literacy programs, helping prepare roughly 320,000 literacy-teaching books as well as materials for newly literate readers.[104] In 1963, the regime launched an initiative, the Army of Knowledge, whose literacy corps program sent urban dwellers into rural and underdeveloped areas to teach reading. The shah saw illiteracy as a major obstacle to development and was also concerned about a lack of nationalist fervor (and loyalty to him) in parts of the country. In his view, by teaching literacy with texts that promoted the Persian language and conveyed nationalist values and patriotism, the corps could solve multiple problems.[105] Franklin also published a magazine, *Peyk* (Persian for "messenger"), for newly literate readers and anticipated that the periodical would eventually have a circulation of 600,000.[106] The magazine was modeled on *American Scholastic* and included both content and suitably modernizing advertisements—for example, for fertilizers that could assist in agricultural development.[107] John Spaulding, the vice-president of Scholastic's magazine arm, conducted the preliminary work for *Peyk*. The intent was to help "consolidate Persian in areas where this language is not the mother tongue."[108]

Various editions were produced for different age groups, and most of its production staff worked in Franklin's Tehran office.

As Byron Buck noted in his report on textbook production in Iran, a major issue for the nation's publishing industry was the lack of qualified professional editors who could manage the work of a production team. In American publishing, the editor was a highly significant force in the production of a book, but in Iran there was no traditionally equivalent role. Hence, Franklin's training programs took on great importance. In 1960, staff members ran a workshop that brought Iranian personnel—educators, book production specialists, and artists—overseas to study Western-style textbook publishing. During a session in Paris sponsored by the French Ministry of Cultural Affairs, the trainees spent two weeks visiting publishing houses and meeting textbook editors and educators. Under the auspices of the British Council, they spent a similar month in England. In the United States, they spent three months attending seminars on all aspects of textbook production and visiting schools to "observe the role of the textbook in American education." Buck was careful to report that the visitors were "representative of *all* segments of Iran's intellectual and educational life, rather than merely an already Western (or anti-Western) oriented elite."[109]

Because existing Iranian printing plants could not support all of the proposed textbook production, Franklin developed a plan for a new offset printing plant in Tehran that could also be used "to satisfy the ever-increasing public appetite for trade books, including the books which the USIA hopes to see published in Persian for distribution both through trade channels and for secondary and university consumption." The shah, other members of government, and ten leading Persian publishing houses all invested in the project, whose estimated cost was between US$250,000 and US$350,000. Smith originally anticipated arranging a loan for part of this amount using money from a special USIA fund; but when that fund's availability came into question, he decided instead to use the earnings from textbook sales. The printing cooperative would repay the loan over a ten-year period. Despite the complicated financial arrangements and lengthy period of repayment, he convinced Franklin's board of directors to make the loan. Assuring them that the plant would have a qualified director, he explained that "other Persians would be trained in printing administration and cost-accounting in Germany with the help of the manufacturers there, and lesser employees would be trained in Iran."[110]

In 1957, Sherkat Sahami Offset opened, and soon it was doing more than half of Tehran's offset printing work. The plant offered work and training to 180 employees, many of them recruited from an orphanage in a village near Kerman, home of the father of Franklin's office manager Homayoun Sanati—an example of the networks of patronage in operation.[111] Don Cameron noted that, because of its connection with the shah, Franklin was assured "of proper treatment at every level of the government, and whatever the degree of Franklin's participation financially, that amount would be safeguarded by every possible legal precaution available under Iranian law."[112]

Franklin also helped Iranian printers acquire paper, including imports purchased from Finland with PL480 money. Many years later, Smith recalled that while the Suez Canal was closed, the Tehran office decided to bring paper in through the Soviet Union in sealed cars.[113] In 1962, recognizing the ongoing difficulty of securing adequate paper supplies, Franklin helped establish Pars Paper, the first paper production plant in Iran, which is still in existence today.[114]

Another Franklin project, begun in 1960, was the introduction of titles in pocket-book format in conjunction with a new bookselling infrastructure known as Ketabhaye Jibi or the "wire rack project." The Tehran office produced 10,000 copies of every title, which were then sold at between 20 and 30 rials each (equivalent to between US26 to US39 cents). One title was published per week, and the books were widely distributed on wire display racks in bazaars, newsstands, and shops. Shop owners received seventy-two books on consignment, and each week Franklin representatives would refill the rack and take a percentage of the sales.[115] Franklin staff explicitly modeled the plan on "Western methods of paperback distribution" and also saw it as a way to facilitate Iranian national unification.[116]

At first, Franklin reports on the project were positive: "For a short time it seemed that a revolution had taken place in the publishing industry." But ultimately the costs of book distribution were too high compared to the returns, and sellers were forced to raise prices. Although the project was not a financial success, Franklin staff members saw it as proof that the Iranian book market was larger than they had previously thought. As a result, they believed, the local industry had "become far more ambitious and aggressive." Yet they also admitted that it was impossible to "import" the necessary relationships between publishers and booksellers. These could only develop organically.[117]

Despite the political compromises Franklin made in order to work in Iran, its activities had a long-term impact on Iranian publishing. Even today, local publishers acknowledge the importance of the Tehran office's work, praising

Sanati in particular for his contributions to the development of the industry. According to Beytolah Biniaz, the "know-how of professional publishing organizations being transferred to Iran from the West" was extremely important, despite the censorship and repression of the shah's regime.[118] Likewise, Farid Moradi notes a number of valuable innovations that Franklin brought to modern Iranian publishing: introducing proper editing processes; improving book design; fostering the editing, designing, and writing of textbooks; and founding Sherkat Sahami Offset.[119]

Continuing Book Diplomacy

Alongside its modernization activities, Franklin still participated in book diplomacy, primarily through its translation projects. During the 1960s, the USIA expanded its translation programs, putting American books into circulation around the globe and coordinating with publishers and private organizations to support this work. During the Kennedy presidency, the agency sought new ways to justify its book diplomacy work, and it reiterated, especially to publishers, that such activities were a means of fighting communism. At the 1961 meeting of the American Book Publishers Council, Robert Beers of the USIA warned publishers that they could not continue with a "business-as-usual" approach, given "the gravity of the cold war in which the nation is engaged and of the strategic role which government expects books to play."[120]

Throughout the decade, the Soviet Union was producing large numbers of books in various languages. By 1961, it had published more than 40 million books in English, French, German, several Indian languages, Arabic, and Persian. In 1962, it had added Hausa, Sanskrit, and Swahili to its publishing programs. Soviet scientific textbooks, manuals for learning Russian, and a variety of political texts formed the bulk of this output.[121] Hence, American publishers were pressed to continue to support U.S. government book programs to battle this flood of Communist texts.

The low-priced books in translation program remained the USIA's largest venture, one intended "to acquaint teachers, students, and general readers with the rich variety of paperback books available from the United States at extremely low prices."[122] In 1962–63, the agency produced 5,577,805 copies of 974 volumes in translation and 485,900 copies of 106 volumes in English, many aimed at Middle Eastern nations such as Lebanon, Syria, and the United Arab Republic.[123] In 1964–65, the USIA reported publishing Arabic translations of Theodore Berland's *The Scientific Life*, Allan H. Cullen's *Rivers in Harness: The Story of Dams*, William B. Given's *Reaching Out in Management*, Frederick R. Kappel's *Vitality in a Business Enterprise*, Wheeler McMillen's *Land of Plenty: The American Farm Story*, Robert Leckie's *Conflict: The History of the Korean War*, Reginald Parker's *A Guide to Labor Law*, and F. Shilwi's locally written *Science and Prosperity*. Books in Urdu included Booth Mooney's *The Lyndon Johnson Story*, Howard R. Penniman's *The American Political Process*, Roger Burlingame's *Men and Machines*, Hugh Seton-Watson's *The New Imperialism*, and Owen Wister's *The Virginian*.[124]

Ladder editions were also produced throughout the 1960s. They were primarily aimed at teachers and suggest that some USIA objectives were intersecting with broader educational objectives. These editions sold for ten cents each or the local currency equivalent.[125] Titles included William Saroyan's *The Human Comedy*, Charles Shore's *Heaven Knows, Mr. Allison*, Nathaniel Hawthorne's *The Scarlet Letter*, Isaac Asimov's *Inside the Atom*, and Wister's *The Virginian* as well as various nonfiction books about China and Russia, life in America, and science and technology. Cooperating publishers included Bantam, Avon, Dell, and Pocket Books. A 1969 USIA study of ladder editions concluded that, while little research had been done on their effectiveness, fiction dominated sales, biographies and science books did well, and anti-Communist books sold poorly.[126]

The USIA continued to administer USIS libraries and gift programs. Richard T. Arndt, who joined the agency as an assistant cultural attaché in 1961 and was initially sent to Beirut, noted that these libraries were seen as a "carrot" to lure people into American spaces, where they would then be hit over the head with the "stick" of propaganda—an approach that may have ultimately limited the libraries' popularity.[127] USIA book gift programs, made possible with the cooperation of publishers, often involved presentations to "figures of influence." For example, an April 1963 report from the USIS post in Ibadan, Nigeria, noted that the office had sent copies of James D. Calderwood and Harold J. Bienvenu's *Patterns of Economic Growth: The American Experience* to economics teachers at the universities of Ibadan and Ife as well as to government economists, selected business leaders, and members of the Ibadan Rotary Club.[128] An October 1962 shipment of books to the USIS post in Dar es Salaam, Tanganyika (now known as Tanzania), for distribution to school, libraries, and reading rooms, was accompanied by a note: "The books included in this shipment have been donated by the publishers as a gift in furtherance of international understanding."[129] The gift program brought positive publicity to the publishing industry; in 1962, Edward R. Murrow issued a press release praising it for donating books to people abroad.[130] USIA files contain a number of thank-you letters from places in countries such as India and Kenya, many from school principals.[131]

Despite this cooperative activity, relations between the government and the book industry were strained, primarily because of the continuing subordination of books to government control. In 1962, the U.S. secretary of state convened the Government Advisory Committee on International Book Programs so that leading figures in the book industry could help the government "determine the most effective means for increasing the number of readers abroad of American books." Curtis Benjamin was appointed chairman, and other members included Bill Spaulding, W. Bradford Wiley, and Thomas J. Wilson, all of whom had worked with Franklin and other government book programs. Government representatives included Lucius Battle, the assistant secretary for educational and cultural affairs; Donald M. Wilson, the USIA's deputy director; and Frank Coffin, AID's deputy administrator for operations.[132] Yet creation of the committee did little to maintain good relations between the government and the industry or to advance book diplomacy initiatives. In 1964, Alfred Knopf wrote to Dan Lacy about a meeting in New York between ABPC members and government representatives. Knopf, who had found the meeting "increasingly embarrassing," felt that the agencies were doing little to communicate effectively with the industry. "In summary, I don't honestly know which group should be more offended: the ones from Washington, who certainly got darned little out of the meeting up to the time I left, at any rate, or those who attended the meeting and in my opinion got darned little out of it. It seems to me that each group made a sad impression on the other."[133]

Franklin managed to retain reasonably good relations with American publishers during the 1960s, perhaps because of its niche position as the translator and publisher of serious (and hence less financially valuable) books but certainly because of industry goodwill toward colleagues who were active in contributing to book promotion and research. Yet it did have to adjust its policies to placate book industry demands. For example, in 1963 it reconfigured its rights and royalties template. Franklin would still receive "token amounts" for translation rights "into those languages from which American publishers customarily receive no income," but it agreed "to recognize that royalty payments are justified in the case of books that run into substantial editions"—that is, more than 5,000 copies.[134]

Franklin continued to invest a great deal of value in the book as cultural object and a source of industry pride. It claimed to have transformed the production and design of books in its targeted countries and took credit for "the revolution that has occurred in the last five years in the design and manufacture of modern Arabic books, many of which may now—as in the Golden Age of hand-produced manuscripts—be regarded as works of art instead of the ugly examples of utility printing which most of them were before Franklin started work."[135] In cooperation with the Institute of Applied Design in Cairo, it began sponsoring book cover design competitions for its Arabic-language texts. It also continued to promote serious books that presented a vision of America as intellectually engaged and progressive. It promoted the view that books were not cheap entertainment but could facilitate relationships between the United States and other countries. In a 1967 manifesto, it described them as "a priceless bridge between cultures. And in a world whose tradition has been disturbed by the pursuit of development, building bridges between cultures would seem to have a very high priority."[136]

Franklin continued to have strong views on what type of American book should be published globally. In 1969, when Karim Emami of the Tehran office expressed a desire to publish Grace Metalious's bestseller *Peyton Place* (1956), Harold Munger of the New York office replied that he believed in "freedom of choice" and was prepared to try to get the rights to it. However, he told Emami that, among most Americans, "*Peyton Place* is a synonym for the cheap and vulgar level of much contemporary American fiction" and said that he was "unhappy at the thought of *Peyton Place* appearing on a list of Franklin-sponsored books." Munger worried that its presence would give Franklin's detractors ammunition and asked Emami to reconsider: "If the book were a good one, whatever its reputation, I would not be concerned, but I hate to see Franklin put in that vulnerable position over a book that is not first-rate."[137]

In 1967, the Johnson administration released a policy statement officially noting that books had a "special role in foreign relations" and envisioning a coordinated effort between government and private industry to make book and library resources more available to developing countries.[138] But Johnson soon left office, and the Republican administration of Richard Nixon showed little interest in book diplomacy, book modernization, or the contributions of the publishing industry in such work. Even the U.S.-Soviet book gap was no longer an issue—not because it had been solved but because it was no longer a priority. Book modernization remained an area of interest for Franklin into the 1970s, but the organization found much less support for a vision of "books for the world" now that certainties about the United States as a model progressive nation had begun to vanish. In 1968, Franklin's annual report noted that the "transfer of knowledge is unquestionably the greatest task confronting this generation." Countries' survival would depend on adequately meeting their need for books.[139] The challenges were great, but Franklin was committed to continuing to work to address them.

5
Book Modernization in Africa and Latin America

In 1961, Franklin Publications noted that its number of programs had quintupled during the past four years.[1] In 1962, staff members drafted a "Plan for Worldwide Development" in which they envisioned expansion into Africa and Latin America. Their global goal was twenty-six offices, thirty-eight sub-offices, and representation in thirty-one countries.[2] To reflect this expanded vision, which would include both modernization and diplomacy work, they decided in 1964 to change the organization's name to Franklin Book Programs. That year's annual report noted that the new name placed the "emphasis on books, where it belongs, and avoids suggesting an organization that is itself a publisher." In addition, the report pointed out the inclusion of "programs" in the name, which staff members saw as a way to better indicate their great variety of projects.[3]

Franklin's programs in sub-Saharan Africa and Latin America were reactions to the concerns and preoccupations of the 1960s. Yet in contrast to the organization's experience in Iran, it achieved mixed results in both of these regions. Franklin's work in Africa was shaped by a number of issues and challenges, including the preexisting entrenchment of British publishers as well as the many languages spoken within single countries—for instance, in Nigeria. Its activities in Latin America were part of a long history of U.S. involvement in the region, but the region's book needs were very different from those in the Middle East. This meant that Franklin's work there remained small-scale and limited. Neither Africa nor Latin America was suitable for Franklin's one-size-fits-all approach, and by the end of the decade stakeholders realized that the organization had overstretched itself. Nevertheless, despite its failures, Franklin's work in these regions helps us comprehend the global ambitions of American book diplomacy and book modernization during the Cold War while revealing the obstacles the organization faced in executing its programs.

Franklin in Africa

In 1959, Datus Smith spent African Freedom Day, April 15, in Monrovia, Liberia's capital, fishing for barracuda during the day and dancing quadrilles with his hosts in the evening.[4] His trip to Liberia and other parts of West and East Africa—the first he had made to Africa south of the Sahara—was part of a survey mission. He was investigating the possibility of launching Franklin operations on a continent in which many new countries were emerging from European colonialism. In the ferment of decolonization and nationalism, Franklin identified an opportunity.

As African countries moved rapidly toward independence in the late 1950s and early 1960s, Americans engaged in a variety of educational, philanthropic, and commercial ventures across the continent. As Frederick Cooper writes, Africa became "the world's project for uplift."[5] Among U.S. policymakers, it served as an experiment for fashionable ideas of development and modernization. Academics began establishing African studies programs at their universities and seeking support for research related to Africa.[6] Philanthropic foundations actively backed development and education programs in various African countries. Yet here as elsewhere, American foreign policy was primarily driven by anti-Communist concerns, especially given that some of these newly independent countries had quickly established relationships with the Soviet Union. Thus, the U.S. government supported (or at least not did not condemn) white supremacist regimes in South Africa and Rhodesia and lingering colonial powers such as France in Algeria. It also supported undemocratic authoritarian governments, even intervening to install a friendly regime in the Congo.

At home, racial attitudes and politics were shifting in response to the civil rights and Black Power movements, but foreign policy was slow to reflect these social and political changes.[7] American dealings in Africa were rarely free of racism or colonialism. Larry Grubbs suggests that it is possible to see a continuity between Cold War development discourse and the colonialist discourses of civilization and race. Indeed, many of the development activities in Africa were paternalist, operating on assumptions about a stereotyped "transitional African" who was on a path to modernity.[8] Smith's experiences in Africa challenged him to reflect on his personal prejudices, yet his descriptions of his activities suggest an imperial high life. In a letter to his wife, he claimed that his 1959 trip had "washed away any last tiny vestige of immature prejudice about black people which may have been lurking unconsciously."[9] Nonetheless, Franklin's programs and other American interventions were shaped by deep-seated beliefs in the cultural and technological superiority of the United States.

The Kennedy administration emphasized educational and economic development as keys to African progress and to keeping nations allied to the West, and it founded both the Peace Corps and AID to assist in that work. In addition, it saw Africa as a source of potential economic benefit and encouraged private business investment in the continent. While such investments would be good for the United States, the administration believed they would also boost local economic development and transfer important business and technical skills.[10] Franklin seemed to be a perfect fit for this approach to American involvement abroad.

In the early 1960s, a number of African countries were seeking rapid development, especially in education and industry. The Africanization of colonial infrastructure, including the publishing industry, was emphasized in this nation building. To some observers, a program such as Franklin's seemed to offer a means for developing a local book industry largely run by Africans, and certainly the organization tried to convince African countries that its work would have long-term benefits. In 1961, after a preliminary survey visit, Byron Buck commented that Franklin's work in Africa could be "an important step toward tomorrow."[11] The continent was, in these years, a limited market for American book publishers, but Buck argued that they should "give more thought to Africa today in anticipation of the Africa of tomorrow."[12] In 1961 and 1962, Franklin sent Smith and Bill Spaulding to further investigate the African book scene and Curtis Benjamin, Dan Lacy, and Francisco Aguilera to survey Latin America.[13] Their reports helped both Franklin and the American book industry as a whole identify and assess future commercial opportunities.

In their subsequent report on Ghana and Nigeria, Smith and Spaulding noted that African countries wanted freedom from foreign propaganda and the eventual Africanization of the largely British-dominated publishing industry.[14] Speaking before ATPI, Spaulding emphasized how important it was for both countries to develop their own industries. Franklin, he said, could help them with translations, training, and publishing in vernacular languages. Because books in English would also be important, the organization could encourage the importation of American paperbacks.[15] Alden Clark, the vice-president in charge of Franklin's African affairs, sent a memo to ATPI in which he declared that the organization's aim in Nigeria was "to encourage a healthy, responsible, indigenous book industry."[16]

Franklin eventually opened several offices in sub-Saharan Africa, with a primary focus on Nigeria, which had achieved independence from British rule in 1960 and was a key U.S. target for economic and technical development. The educational market became the focus of Franklin's programs in West Africa, and in July 1963, Alden Clark began his tenure with Franklin.[17] Clark had been an editor at Holt, Rinehart, and Winston and was a former president of ATPI, and he brought his experience with educational and textbook publishing to his work in Africa.[18]

Franklin was not the only organization interested in developing book programs and libraries in Nigeria. UNESCO, for instance, had located its African demonstration library in the eastern town of Enugu.[19] The new Nigerian government saw education as a priority; in a country composed of numerous ethnic groups, education and culture could help "create Nigerians."[20] Higher education institutions, such as the University of Ibadan, became important intellectual centers. It is not clear if Nigerians saw efforts such as Franklin's as an aid to their government's nationalizing agenda, but they did cooperate in the programs, at least initially.

Publishing infrastructure in these years was limited, although the Nigerian government was enthusiastic about developing an indigenous industry. The few existing publishers produced predominantly English texts, but most books were imported from overseas. In addition, there were a few local printers, among them the Publishers and Stationers Supply Company. In 1963, *Drum,* a South African magazine that was an important venue for African journalism and literature, investigated the possibility of publishing and distributing mass-market books, which offered some hope for the growth of a local publishing scene.[21] In his reports, Buck noted the importance of missionary presses in Nigeria and pointed out the contributions of the East African Literature Bureau, which published sixty to eighty titles a year and was eager to work as a development organization.[22] Yet all of these operations were limited in scope and audience.

In Nigeria, Franklin shifted its emphasis from translating and distributing American-authored books to setting up publishing infrastructure.

It established an office in Lagos under the management of 'Femi Oyewole and a second in Enugu under the direction of John Iroaganachi. Oyewole was a British-educated teacher, headmaster, and textbook author; Iroaganachi was an American-educated teacher who had previously managed the audiovisual division of Eastern Nigeria's Ministry of Education.[23] Both saw their work with Franklin as an opportunity to develop a Nigerian publishing industry, and they were strong advocates for the program, which was funded by the Ford Foundation and AID.[24] One aim was to develop new material for schools as well as to publish existing school materials in various local languages. Developing new material was a challenge because Franklin staff members first had to identify original material and manuscripts, something it had rarely done before. They planned to work in the country's dominant languages, including Yoruba, Igbo, and Hausa, as well as in English.[25] In 1964, AID (which had signed a more general aid agreement with Nigeria) gave Franklin money to help bring Nigerian publishers to the United States for training, and the Nigerian offices ran local workshops in writing, publishing, and graphic arts.[26]

At first, American publishers supported book efforts in Africa. In a 1962 circular letter to all American publishing firms, Franklin invited them to contribute to a special Africa fund for developing industry infrastructure and promoting American publishing on the continent.[27] By 1963, a number of firms had donated, including Bowker; Doubleday; Little, Brown; McGraw-Hill; the New American Library; Random House; Knopf; Time, Inc.; and Wiley.[28] At a 1964 ATPI meeting, Clark spoke enthusiastically about Franklin's work in Nigeria. Despite a strong British presence in the country, he said, American textbook and educational publishers could and should take advantage of the nation's rapid expansion of education. One way forward, he suggested, was to invest in Nigerian-run publishing firms.[29] Some publishers had already undertaken their own commercial explorations. In 1963, for example, sales executives from Wiley surveyed the market for American scientific and technical books and a delegation from the American Association of University Presses visited several African countries to study sales prospects for scholarly books.[30]

Some Nigerians showed their support for Franklin's operations. A. Babs Fafunwa, the head of the Harden College of Education at the University of Nigeria, wrote to Smith in 1963 to congratulate him on establishing an office in Nigeria and to say that he hoped it would "mark a new era in the history of mass communication in West Africa for the teeming millions who are starving for reading materials of all types."[31] At a Franklin-run training workshop in Nsukka in May 1966, Fafunwa declared that education was the "greatest hope of a nation."[32] In 1964, the Nigerian printer E. A. Etudo wrote to Shirley Smith, a Franklin employee, to thank her for the publishing seminar he had attended: "There is no doubt that whatever I publish from now on would show evidence that I have not attended the seminar in vain."[33] However, not all Nigerians welcomed Franklin's work. For instance, in 1965, at the inaugural meeting of the organization's Midwestern Nigeria Advisory Board, a board member accused the Americans of promoting "American literary imperialism."[34]

Franklin also considered opening offices in East Africa and sent Clark to survey the possibilities. In his August 1964 report, he noted the predominance of British books in the region.[35] Although he recommended setting up offices in Kenya, Uganda, and Tanzania, a number of publishers disagreed, advising Franklin that "chances for book publishing in East Africa are slim."[36] Nonetheless, in 1966, Franklin opened an office in Nairobi and hired as manager Hilary Ng'weno, a young Harvard-educated journalist.[37] The office intended to publish in Swahili and other East African languages but ultimately accomplished little. Its main contribution to the local book and literary scene was to fund Kenya's National Book Week.

Franklin contended with several issues as it considered expansion into Africa. One was language. As I have mentioned, Franklin's choice of operating language was, consciously or not, often political. This became extremely complicated in Africa, where a single country might encompass many different languages and dialects and where governments often did not favor one over the other. In addition to creating political difficulties, the multiplicity of languages was a barrier in the development of literacy and literary programs.[38] The U.S. government pressured Franklin to work in what it described as "world languages"—that is, French, English, or Portuguese—and Franklin recognized that most African vernacular languages did not have market viability.[39] Yet its founding principle was always to work in local languages. Moreover, its legal counsel had advised the organization to refrain from working in English in Africa, "lest a disgruntled publisher not on our Board of Directors, but viewing the distinguished heads of houses sitting on our Board—bring action against us as a combination in unfair competition."[40] The best option was to focus on training and technical expertise rather than engage in major translation programs.[41]

Another issue was the presence of British publishers and books. As I have noted, the survey teams were aware from the beginning of a well-established British publishing presence in Africa.[42] Oxford University Press and Longman were both important players in the market, especially in educational publishing.[43] The survey teams recognized that it would be difficult to introduce American books into such an environment but argued that the "African reader should not be denied the opportunity to buy the American books he would like and can afford."[44]

After independence, British publishers began Africanizing their operations. In 1964, for example, Heinemann planned an office in Lagos that would employ an all-Nigerian staff.[45] In 1963, W. P. Kerr, who worked for Longman, wrote to Smith about Franklin's surveys of West Africa and told him that Longman intended to Africanize its operations there immediately.[46] At the time of independence, the firm was already rapidly expanding on the continent.[47] Other British publishers were pursuing a similar strategy. Like American publishers, they saw enormous opportunity in the African market, and they were motivated by both idealism and commercial gain.[48] Their programs to develop African writing and publishing—for instance, Heinemann's African Writers Series—worked to bring regional writing to a global market while producing books by and for Africans. Such efforts had mixed results. On the one hand, they allowed African writers to find a global audience; on the other, they made little contribution to developing a long-term local publishing industry.[49]

Clearly, the views of British and American publishers had significant overlap, but their commercial competition blocked any cooperation. British publishers strongly opposed the entrance of Franklin and other American publishing interests into African markets. In December 1962, the writer and journalist John Ardagh, who had little sympathy for the British firms, observed that they were very concerned about the American offensive and accused them of operating "in wasteful competition and without adequate backing."[50] Nevertheless, the British maintained their grip on the African market and did their best to resist American incursions.

The situation was detrimental to Franklin's work. In March 1963, Smith wrote to J. E. Morpurgo of Penguin Books arguing that publishers from both nations could work together in Africa to develop indigenous book industries.[51] In the same year, Clark visited several English publishers, including Oxford University Press, to discuss Franklin's programs.[52] A year later, after Ronald Barker of the U.K.-based Publishers Association wrote to Bill Spaulding to object to what he saw as an attempt to "displace" British books in West

Africa, Clark replied that Franklin's goal was to "create a viable, free enterprise book industry," not simply to publish books in Nigeria.[53] By the end of 1964, he was lamenting that Franklin's progress in Africa had to depend on what he called "British types."[54]

The situation was worrisome. Clark wrote to Spaulding to ask, "How can we engineer books that are even as good as those the British are purveying?" He fretted about the lack of publishing expertise in Nigeria, which affected the entire book production process.[55] He was also concerned about the dominance of British usage and spelling in the education system. American publishers had hoped to establish "American English as the language of instruction in Africa," but the goal seemed impossible to achieve.[56]

In the end, Franklin was never able to make inroads into the African publishing scene, in large measure because of British publishers' entrenchment and their suspicion that Franklin was trying to capture their market. In September 1965, Clark, lamented that Harold Macmillan, who, after serving as Britain's prime minister, had returned to chair the family publishing company, was "turning into a real active, devious one, all over the landscape. Right on the heels of discovering his invasion and capture of Northern Nigeria, I find him over here in the midst of a huge ploy." Clark was referring to the firm's attempt to set up a joint-enterprise publishing company in Kenya, Uganda, and Tanzania, with the host government taking 51 percent of the profits and Macmillan 49 percent. Macmillan's aim was to monopolize the schoolbook business in East Africa.[57]

Macmillan got its publishing deal, and in 1967 it signed agreements with nine African governments to manage their state publishing.[58] Other publishers, including British competitors such as Longman, were taken aback, questioning the deal's legitimacy and its implications of a monopoly. One journalist reported that Macmillan's action was, "in effect, helping Africans to nationalise publishing," a move that ensured that American programs would remain relatively marginal.[59] Franklin had already noted that many of the new African governments felt that states "should be the most important or the exclusive publisher[s] and printers, and perhaps even booksellers."[60] Nonetheless, the organization's complaints about Macmillan's monopoly were ironic, given its own ongoing collusion with the Iranian government. Franklin's programs seemed to function best when the local government was an active supporter and funder of its work. While it aspired to participate in a fully commercial publishing scene, such an outcome was rarely viable in the countries in which it operated.

Franklin did receive some AID support for its work in Africa.[61] Yet while the two organizations shared common interests, the agency's relative newness made it wary of committing significant funds to any single program.[62] Conflicts with individual AID officials were also a problem. In a 1964 letter, Clark called the agency's director "the most impossible jerk."[63] In the same year, Spaulding lamented the insufficiency of current AID funds and the agency's failure to "develop any fire in [its] belly."[64] In 1966, Clark wrote bluntly, "AID is awful."[65]

Originally, Franklin had sought government support for the Nigerian operation, but in September 1963 it decided that its Nigeria office should be a privately funded operation with neither Nigerian nor U.S. government involvement.[66] Its decision was shaped by broader issues. Like other developing countries with a limited state infrastructure, Nigeria was rife with corruption, which large amounts of foreign aid money encouraged. Pat Belcher, who worked at USIS-Lagos from 1957 to 1962, later reflected, "The money we threw at them was not very good for the Nigerians."[67]

By the 1960s, Franklin was employing more women, and a number of them traveled to Africa during the decade—among them, Shirley Smith, Clark's assistant director. In early 1965, she met with publishers in Lagos and visited various Nigerian cities, including Kaduna in the northwest and Onitsha in the south, as well as locations in Ethiopia, Kenya, and Uganda.[68] In her reports, Smith noted Ethiopia's need for books but was uncertain about how Franklin could help. She also commented on the British publishing presence in Ethiopia (Oxford University Press was currently engaged in a four-year project there) and wrote that she did not see an opportunity for Franklin to enter the field. In Kenya, she attended the opening of the East Africa Publishing House and promoted Franklin's ongoing work in Nigeria.[69]

Smith saw her the trip as a positive experience and described her job as "[one] in a million." She reported that "the good will and support" that Franklin staff members had "established is apparent at every encounter. I'm so lucky to be working with you and think you should know it."[70] Her letters to the New York office reveal both the perils and excitement of working in Africa. At one point, she was stranded beside Lake Victoria when London flight engineers went on strike.[71] In Nairobi, she had dinner with the British high commissioner, met the British writer and broadcaster Alistair Cooke and the aviator Charles Lindbergh, and was driven back to her hotel in a Rolls-Royce. By the end of her trip, she was convinced of "the rightness of Africa and Franklin in tandem."[72]

Smith resigned from Franklin in 1966 after she got married, and Esther J. Walls replaced her as the assistant director for Africa. As a librarian and an African-American woman, she differed from many other Franklin staff members, and her experiences are worth considering in some detail. Walls had joined Franklin in 1965, though she had already undertaken some project work for the organization before coming on full time.[73] Previously, she had been the supervising librarian at the New York Public Library's Countee Cullen Branch and was one of the highest-ranking African American librarians in the system. She brought to her job at Franklin her deep experience with both library work and New York City's African American communities. While working at Countee Cullen, she had overseen the North Manhattan Library Project, designed to engage neighborhood readers.[74] In a speech, she noted that working in Harlem had driven her desire to "help people reach for some idea of change, of betterment through the rich cultural programs which we offered [at the library] and through books, to awaken in them a sense of their own self worth." Emphasizing the Christian motives that guided her life, she argued for the importance of the "global community" to which all people belonged.[75]

In Africa, Walls was Franklin's primary advisor on library, writer, and publisher projects and also helped acquire translation rights for the organization's field offices. However, her tenure at Franklin was brief, perhaps because its commercial imperatives ran counter to her public service ethic. In 1974, when Michael Harris, then the organization's president, wrote a reference for Walls, he mentioned that "unhappily she was not interested in the commercial side of publishing, and we were unable to recruit her."[76] After leaving Franklin in 1971, Walls remained dedicated to library work and cultural internationalism, involving herself in UNESCO and UNICEF library activities and in promoting International Book Year. She became the director of the U.S. Secretariat for International Book Year 1972, which had the theme "Books for All."[77]

Esther Walls's engagement with Africa was different from the engagement of bookmen such as Datus Smith because of both her ongoing dedication to cultural internationalism and her identification with Africa as an African American woman. She told her hometown newspaper, the *Globe-Gazette* of Mason City, Iowa, she felt a "special sense of relationship" in Africa. She would keep "seeing faces that made me think of a face at home, a face of an aunt or a cousin, and I found myself thinking, 'Could this possibly be where I came from? Might this be a tribe from which my mother's or my father's ancestors were drawn?'"[78] Speaking to Dorothy Hunt Smith, Datus's wife, for an article for the *Christian Science Monitor,* she observed that her "connection with Africa was of a texture different from yours."[79]

Walls's African American identity fed her international work, and her interest in Africa long preceded her work with Franklin. After attaining her degree from the State University of Iowa, she realized that there were "no [hometown] teaching jobs for a negro." But after finding a job as a librarian, she quickly came to believe that library work was a "public service." She earned a master's degree in library science and went to work at the New York Public Library.[80] There she became fascinated by Africa. She spent two months in West Africa in 1959 and afterward gave a public talk and slide show at the New York Public Library in which she noted the region's "change and dynamic growth." In Accra, Ghana, she was struck by the color and dynamism of the city; she observed how friendly people were and how interested they were in the United States. In a later speech at the Milwaukee Public Library about the same trip, she called on the United States to "catch up" with Africa and to engage more with its literature. She spoke of her work with an American Library Association project promoting books about Africa that were suitable for young adults.[81] These books focused on conditions in Africa (including its ongoing racial issues) but also demonstrated the commonality of youth across the world and the importance of cultural understanding.

In 1964, Walls traveled to Nigeria to survey its library facilities. She noted an interest in books and education and argued that the country needed more libraries and trained professional staff members.[82] In 1967, now working for Franklin, she went to Uganda to investigate the possibility of opening an office there. She reported to New York that, while the country was "lovely," some of the people she had encountered (probably U.S. officials) "must have been recruited from the 'Theatre of the Absurd.'"[83] During a 1968 trip to Africa, her "most hectic," she met up to twenty publishers, printers, librarians, and other industry personnel every day. At this time, Franklin was starting to wrap up its work in Nigeria, and she heard many comments from Nigerians who were appreciative of the program's work and expressed regret that it was pulling out.[84]

But Franklin was struggling in Africa, and some staff members believed the whole endeavor was just "too ambitious."[85] There were ongoing problems of book distribution, as stakeholders noted during a 1966 meeting of the U.S. Government Advisory Committee on International Book and Library Programs, which created significant obstacles for U.S. book programs. The committee considered using the distribution model of the South African magazine *Drum* but continued to worry about the difficulties of getting material to African readers.[86] Franklin also acknowledged that it had underestimated British influence in Africa.[87] During her 1967 visit to Nigeria, Walls heard from "a reliable source" that the resident Ford Foundation representative, David Heaps, believed Franklin to be something of a con job because it had achieved so little. She acknowledged that the organization's record in Nigeria had yet to amount to much and that its hopes for Africanizing American textbooks and supplementary materials had largely evaporated. But she argued that Franklin lacked the basic expertise needed to do the work and was confronting resistance from Nigerian nationalists.[88]

Clearly, American government and foundation officials in Nigeria had little faith in Franklin, and British publishers were hostile. Nigerians, too, saw little reason to support the organization. In 1967, members of the Nigerian Publishers Association expressed their doubts and suspicions. A number of them accused Franklin of being a stand-in for the U.S. State Department, and others believed that it was interested only in promoting the interests of American publishers.[89]

In addition, by the later 1960s, Franklin's approach was starting to look old-fashioned. The cultural internationalism that had animated the 1950s had little place in a rapidly decolonizing world. *Little Women* was largely irrelevant to populations that preferred more radical views of the world and wanted to read publications that focused on everyday dilemmas and challenges. Moreover, some Franklin employees were uncomfortable with the rising tide of radicalism in Africa and at home. In October 1964, Clark, who was traveling in East Africa, wrote to New York about the great popularity of Malcolm X, who had recently visited a number of African countries and addressed the Organization of African Unity. In Clark's view, Malcolm X posed a threat. "Over here he has to be taken seriously as a dangerous guy," he wrote, and he complained that the leader had said "vile and vicious things."[90]

A more immediate problem was the increasing political and regional tension that would eventually lead Nigeria into civil war. In 1967, Clark wrote from the Enugu office to comment on recent massacres and a "beleaguered feeling" in the city.[91] Biafra, a state in southeastern Nigeria, seceded that year, sparking a conflict that would kill millions. The war proved to be divisive in the West, where many people sympathized with the Biafrans, although the governments of both Britain and the United States refused to recognize or support the region's independence. Once the war broke out, Franklin's activities in Nigeria essentially ceased. The war also affected British publishing operations in the country. Although they managed to hang on, in Nigeria they had to sell most of their assets during the 1970s after the new government introduced rules that limited foreign ownership. The publishing market was already weak by this stage, and economic problems in the country escalated in the 1980s.[92] Financial problems also plagued other African publishing operations during the 1970s and beyond. The bright promise of African publishing had faded.

In 1970, Franklin briefly floated plans to revive its Africa program, and Harold Munger wrote to Ronald Barker to suggest that the organization could ally with the Publishers Association to send a two-person team to survey Nigeria and Ghana. However, the Publishers Association had established a Book Development Council to function as its commercial export division. Its goals were not philanthropic, and it regarded the United States as a rival. Barker's response to Munger's suggestion reveals the British publishing industry's ongoing attitude toward Franklin. He stated bluntly that he thought Franklin was disingenuous in asserting that its assistance to developing countries was anything other than "the essential precursor to trade expansion." He told Munger that Franklin should "accept that British publishers are fully able to meet the needs of these West African countries."

> We have assisted their book development as no-one else could possibly have done. British publishers have established local offices and trained local people to become publishers in their own right. British publishers' representatives are frequently covering both Nigeria and Ghana, and to suggest to them that they need to send someone out, together with an American, to assess the present situation is to imply that they do not know their business. I assure you that they do. . . . I am afraid, therefore, that we cannot accept your proposal that we join with Franklin in making these investigations. There is a whole wide world outside those countries which are traditionally British publishers' markets because of present and former Commonwealth ties. You really cannot expect us to assist Franklin in spear-heading American publishers' incursion into these markets. Obviously, we cannot prevent you or them from trying; but please do not ask us to help.[93]

Franklin decided not to try to revive its African operations.

Franklin in Latin America

In the early 1960s, Franklin considered setting up programs in Latin America, which had become an area of increased U.S. interest under the Kennedy administration. The government had established the Alliance for Progress and was focusing on foreign aid and assistance programs in the region. In 1964, the USIA began to expand its book translation programs to produce Spanish and Portuguese books for Latin America.[94] A variety of programs also sought to boost the circulation of Latin American texts in the United States.[95] The region was, Datus Smith believed, something of an unknown quantity; "Africa," he said, "offers a cleaner slate on which to write."[96] Nonetheless, as per the usual Franklin approach, a survey team composed of Curtis Benjamin, Dan Lacy, and Francisco Aguilera made a preliminary visit in 1961.[97]

The team's 1962 report addressed the issue of whether Americans should be working to increase the availability of books in Latin America. Markets were limited, the men wrote, due to illiteracy, poverty, and state interests. Book distribution was generally slow and expensive. They observed that the major U.S. book program was the USIA's but that Latin American publishers generally disliked the agency and what they perceived as American propaganda. The report argued that there was a real need for educational books and for help in local industry development. Such assistance could, the team contended, benefit the U.S. book industry and boost U.S. commercial and industrial interests, for "ideas, methods, materials, services, all translated into 'trade' will surely follow the books." If Franklin became involved in Latin America, they wrote, it would be doing so in the spirit of Kennedy's Alliance for Progress. The men also noted that their use of the word *underdeveloped* was a source of much "resentment, or amusement" in many of the countries they visited and required much explaining on their part. They recommended setting up offices in Latin America and asserted that these centers would be responsible for arranging translation rights and providing "informational, advisory and technical assistance services between the book interests of the USA and Latin America."[98]

Franklin approached American publishers, especially Blanche and Alfred Knopf, for comments on the survey and for recommendations about Latin American involvement. Even before World War II, the Knopfs' publishing firm was introducing important Latin American writers to American audiences, and both Blanche and Alfred were knowledgeable and enthusiastic about Latin American literature. In a letter to her husband in February 1962, Blanche thanked him for letting her see Franklin's report and said that the organization should work toward the publication of children's books and medical books. She believed that libraries in Latin America "need building up very badly" and thought Franklin's ideas were worthy of support.[99] Another response to Alfred Knopf from his staff in regards to Franklin's plan expressed concern about its failure to confront the lack of library facilities. Staff members also saw the plan as "very cumbersome with enormous amounts of money expended on personnel."[100] Thus, while American publishers supported the idea in principle, they also cautioned that success would be difficult and expensive.

Eventually, Franklin decided to adopt a new operating method for the Latin American program: it would work out of the New York office rather than set up regional offices in target countries.[101] The Ford Foundation provided a $1 million grant to Franklin for the work. Although the amount was generous by Franklin standards, Knopf called it "stingy" and wrote to Edward R. Murrow, then the director of the USIA, to complain.[102] Knopf felt that U.S. government support for Latin American publishing and literature was poor. In his letter, he emphasized his own long-standing commitment to book programs in Latin America: "I feel passionately involved with Latin America—discouraged as hell, naturally, by what is going on down there but still somehow very hopeful about Brazil and Argentina. We are working like the devil to try to do our part by developing a fairly substantial program of publishing books by Latin Americans and about Latin America."[103] In a letter to Arthur Schlesinger, Jr., then a special assistant to President Kennedy, Knopf accused the government of doing little in terms of actual assistance, despite Assistant Secretary of State Philip Coombs's lip service to the importance of books in Latin America. Knopf noted that Franklin had requested funding from AID for support for its Latin American book program but had heard nothing. As in his letter to Murrow, he emphasized his personal belief in the value of books and the book industry in the region.[104] In response, Schlesinger said that things were starting to happen but that part of the challenge was working in a way that would not disrupt the local book trade.[105]

In January 1963, Wilbur "Buzz" Knerr was appointed to oversee Franklin's Latin American program, a position funded by the Ford Foundation grant. Knerr had been the director of publishing in Macmillan USA's international division. A former resident of Puerto Rico, he was familiar with many Latin American countries and had once owned the American Bookshop in Caracas, Venezuela. In addition, he had served on the Latin American panel of the U.S. Government Advisory Committee on International Book Programs.[106] He thus brought a great deal of experience to his role.

Franklin backed a number of book development activities in Latin America. In 1964, for instance, it created an Argentinean nonprofit, Fundacion Interamericana de Bibliotecologia Franklin (FIBF), which worked on publishing and library development.¹⁰⁷ The Ford Foundation wrote that the nonprofit's goal was "to promote the concept of the 'book' as an educational and cultural medium of great value and high priority in the socio-economic development of Latin America."¹⁰⁸ The FIBF was to be a "catalyst" for various university library-level projects.¹⁰⁹ Its staff also conducted training courses for librarians, preparing them for work in children's hospitals, and helped establish two small model school libraries.¹¹⁰ In a 1967 report, Franklin concluded that the FIBF was a generally successful project.¹¹¹

Other work in Latin America included translating and producing medical textbooks. With support from the Commonwealth Fund, which focused on supporting health and medical projects, and the W. K. Kellogg Foundation, which focused on child welfare, Franklin launched a "comprehensive, continent-wide three-year program for medical books." The organization would facilitate the translation of medical textbooks and help train people in scientific publishing and bibliographical work. The program aimed not only to produce specific books but also to improve medical publishing overall.¹¹² It received aid from medical schools and associations as well as medical librarians, and the Population Council helped fund the translation and publication of books in demography and family planning.¹¹³ The program clearly tied into modernization efforts, especially in its promotion of American family planning and health texts.

A Rockefeller Foundation grant supported projects focused on library development and bibliography. They included a feasibility study of cooperative cataloging for Spanish-speaking America, intended to directly benefit libraries and the exchange of scientific knowledge.¹¹⁴ In Brazil, Franklin worked to develop libraries, with a particular focus on children's libraries.¹¹⁵ Brazil was also the location for a small project centering around the creation of a bibliography of children's books in Portuguese.¹¹⁶

Franklin also offered training programs and seminars for book industry professionals from Latin America and elsewhere. In March 1965, it ran a book industry seminar in New York for publishers from Brazil, Colombia, India, Laos, Nigeria, the Philippines, Tanzania, Turkey, and Uganda.¹¹⁷ One Brazilian participant wrote to Franklin to say that the seminar "opened my eyes and strengthened my publishing convictions." He planned to develop a series of books on business administration to help Brazilians address their economic problems.¹¹⁸ In January 1968, Franklin offered a book seminar in Costa Rica, with ninety participants from several Central American countries.¹¹⁹

In 1970, Esther Walls traveled to Latin America to survey Franklin activities and progress. She visited Mexico, Brazil, and Chile and met with AID and State Department personnel about book development projects. She concluded that Franklin's role as a consultant for some of these projects was unclear and said that the organization needed more clarification about what it was supposed to be doing in Latin America.[120] Her observation suggests that Franklin could not find an effective way to approach book work in the region and that its impact was minimal at best, probably because the publishing industry and library field, while in need of development, were already well established and because Franklin's small project-based approach could only have a limited impact.

Throughout the 1960s, the United States sought to get involved in Africa and Latin America, perhaps with the hope of reproducing its successes in Iran. But when Franklin became involved in these regions, it struggled in part because it articulated its aspirations in continental terms. In the late 1950s, the organization had envisioned a world united by books, but realization of this dream seemed far away by the end of the 1960s. Africa certainly needed assistance with books, education, and a book industry infrastructure, but Franklin lacked the financial support that would have helped it combat the suspicions of British publishers and the local population. In Latin America, existing book industry people greeted Franklin's work with skepticism, and its opportunities for impact were limited to small-scale projects in library development and educational translations. The African and Latin American ventures had highlighted the limits of empire building, and Franklin staff entered the 1970s in an ambivalent frame of mind. American global involvement—now increasingly signified by the U.S. war in Vietnam—was no longer a story of helping the world. It was raising serious moral questions. And as America's foreign policy came under scrutiny, so did Franklin's global aspirations.

6
The Decline and End of Franklin Book Programs

In 1966, the remaining assets from the Council Books in Wartime, which totaled about US$17,000, were transferred to Franklin, with the rationale that its "traditions and aims were compatible with those of the wartime group."[1] But much had changed since the end of World War II. Most notably, perhaps, there was a growing suspicion of cultural organizations, fueled by a 1967 *New York Times* article revealing that the CIA had been covertly funding a number of them for years.

The mid-1960s was the zenith of Franklin's global programs. The organization's annual report for 1965 noted new offices in Kabul, Lagos, Enugu, and Nairobi and mentioned that the publication program now included Pashto, Spanish, Portuguese, Yoruba, Igbo, Hausa, and Swahili.[2] Yet during the second half of the decade, Franklin became increasingly overextended and the countries in which it worked continued to experience political and social unrest. By the 1970s, the organization had slipped into the quagmire associated with so many American projects abroad: offices were shut down and programs abandoned.

In 1967, Datus Smith stepped down as Franklin's president, and the organization struggled without his driving force and enthusiasm. Not long before he left, he outlined Franklin's "Challenges for the Future" and admitted that the program had had its share of failures. He believed, however, that it had "unfinished business," but this work would not be led by him.[3] He noted that Franklin's ultimate aspiration was *not* to exist—that is, to cease operations after effective book industries had been established—and he urged his successors to continue to work toward that goal.

Franklin's difficulties during this period reflected the fragmentation of American culture, society, and politics as well as a shift in the way in which people thought about government's role in modernization and progress. Economic crises and stagnation increased during the 1970s, as did a broad sense of disillusionment and uncertainty. Thomas Borstelmann describes the decade as a "crucial period of change and adjustment," a time when Americans were turning inward.[4]

In 1970, Edward Booher, a publisher with McGraw-Hill, spoke of Americans' "gloomy" mood about international work, which he attributed to the destructive impact of the Vietnam War. The war had, he believed, changed domestic attitudes to involvement overseas.[5] People were disillusioned and had little faith in the power of the United States to make a positive difference. President Nixon's administration had reoriented American foreign policy along realpolitik rather than idealistic lines.[6] The rise of radicalism and youth culture and the fallout from the Watergate scandal added to a general mistrust of government and public authority.

Modernization theory became less popular during the 1970s, and new theories for development began to emerge. One of them, dependency theory, argued that core developed nations took resources from and exploited less developed areas of the world, fundamentally challenging the optimistic faith that had marked modernization. Policymakers now rarely agreed about the best approach to development and aid. They also had less money to put into such programs and less faith in the possibility of rapid development and positive change. David Ekbladh writes that the concept of "sustainable development" became popular as the term *modernization* fell into disuse.[7] Nils Gilman agrees that "the early 1970s witnessed a loss of faith in the social modernist idea that a meliorist, rationalizing, benevolent, technocratic state had the capacity and duty to solve social and economic ills." He points to the era's "deep sense of cynicism and pessimism about the future."[8] Daniel Immerwahr comments on the "crumbl[ing]" of the "grand edifice of modernization."[9] In such a context, programs such as Franklin's, which relied on a progressive view of modernization, had to battle to justify their existence ideologically.

Another contributor to the decline of such programs was the rise of "human rights discourse" and its impact on American foreign policy and the way in which people perceived American involvement abroad. Increasingly, the American public was questioning the government's support of regimes that engaged in human rights abuses, even when this support involved development rather than military aid.[10] For example, in both Europe and the United States, there was a significant shift in public perceptions of the shah's regime in Iran, which many observers now openly criticized for its human rights abuses and lack of democracy. Datus Smith's decision to work with such regimes, while effective insofar as it had improved Franklin's fortunes, began to look morally dubious; and this limited the organization's ability to appeal to potential funders, who were already constrained by a challenging economic climate.

Franklin's demise was also tied to changes in the book and publishing industry. Publishing went through an accelerating period of consolidation during the 1970s, when its traditional style of operations gave way to a more corporate and marketing-driven model.[11] In 1970, the American Textbook Publishers Institute and the American Book Publishers Council merged to form the Association of American Publishers (AAP), which, as John Tebbel writes, came to resemble a business lobbying group.[12] In addition, a new generation of publishers had arrived, and they brought with them new views on working with government and American foreign policy. For instance, in keeping with the growing focus on human rights, especially in Eastern Europe and the Soviet Union, the AAP formed its International Freedom to Publish Committee to fight censorship. The Nixon administration drastically cut appropriations for book and library activities, an indication of the government's reduced belief in the power and significance of the book.[13] The decade's straitened economic circumstances also had a considerable impact on publishers: jobs were eliminated, firms merged, and book production declined.[14] Many in the industry also sensed that serious and academic books should now be relegated to niche publishers, and paperbacks and blockbuster bestsellers came to dominate the market.

While Franklin continued to harbor great aspirations, it no longer had the money to accomplish its global projects. USIA and AID funding now formed only a small amount of its overall income, and it had to rely on grants, local government support, and donations to survive. In a struggling economy there were no guaranteed funds from either official or private sources, and by the later 1970s Franklin had been left high and dry financially and was struggling to find reasons, ideological or otherwise, to continue its work.

Propaganda or Aid?

During the 1960s, Franklin shifted its focus from propaganda and information (book diplomacy) to education and development (book modernization). In doing so, staff members knew they were risking their ability to secure USIA funding, and they were not necessarily sorry about that. In June 1966, Smith complained that agency official Reed Harris was not "with it" on Franklin's work and was "pedestrian" in his approach to books.[15] Such comments were typical of Franklin staff members, who had long disliked USIA approaches to book operations. By the 1970s, even some of the agency's own staff were unhappy, especially after Frank Shakespeare took over as USIA director under Nixon.[16]

By the mid-1960s, publishers' attitudes toward U.S. foreign policy were divided, even within organizations. In 1965, for example, Franklin's Shirley Smith wrote to Datus Smith to tell him that an editor friend who worked at Doubleday had sent her some manuscript pages of *The Radical Papers,* an essay collection edited by Irving Howe and including pieces by left-leaning intellectuals such as Daniel Bell and Michael Harrington. Datus responded to her memo with the comment that he thought the excerpt was a "most thought-provoking piece." He lamented what he called the "American idée fixe about 'communism' (real or imagined)" and the way in which this obsession had challenged Franklin's work. He believed that the United States had failed to recognize that the developing world was entitled to embrace "social revolution."[17] His comments demonstrate that his view of foreign policy was shifting, now that the Cold War had entered a new phase, although he continued to avoid expressing his opinions openly in order to keep Franklin out of politics. Yet other Franklin bookmen, especially those who had supported it early on *because* of its part in fighting Soviet influence, were uncomfortable with a shift in attitudes. In 1977, George P. Brett, the former president of Macmillan and now eighty-four years old, resigned from Franklin's board of directors. Although he had been one of the first publishers to support the organization and had remained an advocate for many years, he had come to believe that its fight against communism had not achieved "the effects that we all wanted." He thought President Carter and many others were "going soft on Communism" and that the world was "in greater danger today" than it had been at the beginning of the Cold War.[18]

In 1967, Franklin discovered that it did not have enough money to keep all of its programs going. The Ford Foundation grant that had supported its

New York office had run out, and the organization was suffering from various budget complications arising from the need to fund programs from year to year. Moreover, the money granted by local governments was not always convertible into U.S. dollars, and this could lead to miscalculations.[19] The USIA offered Franklin more funding but stipulated that it wanted greater control over the selection of book titles. Some staff members saw this as blackmail, and Smith wrote that the USIA was "determined to take advantage of our financial difficulty to force a change in the ground rules."[20] The government, however, was adamant. From its point of view, Franklin continued to show poor performance relative to the USIA's "mission and responsibilities."[21] Why continue to support an organization that refused to meet the agency's performance requirements?

Despite these ongoing tensions, Smith's successor, Mike Harris, continued to work to secure USIA funding for Franklin's translation projects. In a letter to the agency's deputy assistant director, Parker May, in May 1969, Harris reminded him of the long relationship between the USIA and Franklin and argued that "the importance of a private institution to initiate and facilitate the translation of American books into local languages . . . is a concept that has been warmly endorsed by the USIA from the time Franklin was formed."[22] Harris pointed out that Franklin was still not getting enough government support despite its contributions to ensuring that American books would be read globally, and he reiterated the organization's core principle of local selection. This was, as ever, the sticking point, and May's answer was uncompromising. In his opinion, Franklin was doing nothing that USIA offices could not do themselves, "with 100 per cent Agency choice in the determination of book titles to be published." If Franklin wanted support, it had to agree that the USIA would control title selection "from definitive lists . . . which would of course be chosen with full awareness of the practical situation under which you are operating."[23]

By 1969, the USIA had a new director, Frank Shakespeare, a former television executive. Shakespeare wanted to present the world with what he saw as a more balanced picture of the United States by including more conservative material in USIS libraries and book programs, and he appointed conservative writer William F. Buckley Jr. to the U.S. Advisory Commission on Information.[24] Shakespeare announced that books would henceforth be selected to reflect both liberal and conservative views and that educational value would be less important than informational value.[25] Ladder editions, for example, would be "conveyors of program information, not teaching tools."[26] In a

1972 letter, Shakespeare wrote that books were "essential to Agency efforts to achieve increased mutual understanding and support for U.S. foreign policy."²⁷ This instrumentalist view of books outweighed any other perceptions of their purpose or value.

Franklin found the USIA's governmental control and underlying attitudes unacceptable, and Kyle decided that Franklin should focus its requests for funding on other sources.²⁸ The long relationship had ended. Unfortunately, however, AID support did not take its place. Despite a shift in its focus toward education and development, Franklin never had very good relations with that agency. Staff members frequently complained about AID's attempts to control hiring and salaries for Franklin projects, its claim of ownership over works produced with agency money, and its refusal to cover consultant expenses such as travel insurance.²⁹

As Franklin struggled to find sustainable funding and keep its regular programs afloat, it turned increasingly toward corporate donations. The organization's corporate pitch emphasized its educational work, claiming that the "economic stability and political maturity of the people of the developing nations of Asia, Africa, and Latin America are goals of major concern to all Americans." Educational advancement, it declared, was the best way for these countries to reach their goals, and books had a role to play. The pitch emphasized that "Franklin's approach and purpose . . . are entirely in the interests of American corporations having a stake in the developing countries," which was why "Franklin earnestly seeks the[ir] financial support."³⁰ Beginning in the mid-1960s, the organization focused on large corporations that were not in the "book business but are anxious to serve the national interest and their own long-term economic interest through assistance to international educational projects."³¹ A number of them responded favorably, including Aramco, Xerox, Trans World Airlines, General Motors, Morgan Guaranty Trust Company, Pan-American World Airways, IBM, Shell International, PepsiCo International, and Newsweek, Inc.³² In 1973, Franklin approached several major oil companies, including Texaco, to secure funding for its programs in countries with oil interests, such as Nigeria and Indonesia.³³

In the early 1970s, Franklin organized a big publicity campaign targeting potential corporate and individual donors and focusing on its work in education. In one advertisement, Walter Cronkite, the anchor of CBS Evening News and a long-time member of the board of directors, is asked, "Why is it good business for a U.S. Corporation to help in the education process of people in less developed countries?" Cronkite responds that Americans need to recognize their common future with people across the planet; it is therefore necessary to help less developed countries grow, and education is central to that task. The advertisement continued: "The cooperation of U.S. Corporations is needed in this educational process to create a better informed world. Through education the standard of living of people in developing countries can be raised, with far-reaching results for them and indirectly for all of us."[34] It appeared in magazines such as *Business Weekly*, *Scientific America*, *Harper's*, *Atlantic Monthly*, and *Fortune*.[35]

In 1973, Franklin established a Friends of Franklin program to attract wealthy supporters, who paid $1,000 to join. One of the program's main functions was to provide awards for achievement in educational development; and as I will discuss, it also supported Franklin's gifts of books to Bangladesh.[36] The first award went to A. Babs Fafunwa, who had worked with Franklin in Nigeria and was a senior figure at the University of Nigeria.[37] The second went to John Spaulding and Iraj Jahanshahi, both involved in Iranian educational publishing.[38]

In a 1974 speech at a Chicago fundraising luncheon, Jack Kyle, then Franklin's president, articulated his views on why the organization's work was so important. He believed that the late-1960s shift in attitudes toward foreign aid was linked to the disillusionment created by the Vietnam War, "a growing realization that America had not squarely faced its domestic problems, . . . plus dissatisfaction with the quality of economic and political development in the Third World." By 1970, he said, "foreign assistance" was seen as inherently suspect. But, as Kyle told the attendees, overpopulation— what he called "the Malthusian nightmare"—now threatened the globe. "In this our enemy is not communism or any other un-American ideology. It is ignorance, poverty, selfishness and senseless human reproduction."[39] His concerns about overpopulation became the basis for his appeal for support to help produce educational material for developing countries. In this way he tapped into existing anxieties about overpopulation and finite resources, which were crowding out concerns about the Cold War and communism, and earlier optimism about development.[40]

Franklin continued to seek funding from philanthropic foundations, and the Ford Foundation remained an important support. A newer source was the W. K. Kellogg Foundation, which had funded Franklin's program to translate and supply medical textbooks in Latin America.[41] Other foundations offered small amounts of money, including the Commonwealth Fund, the JDR 3rd Fund, the Old Dominion Foundation, the Twentieth Century Fund, and the

Schumpeter Fund.[42] Much of this aid was project-based, however, and rarely lasted for long or covered much of Franklin's day-to-day operations, especially the costs of its New York office.

Cultural Politics and the Book Industry

In the 1960s, Franklin's staff members began periodically discussing the idea of closing down operations, and in 1967 Curtis Benjamin of McGraw-Hill reacted to that idea by declaring that it needed to gain more support from American publishers. He said that the book industry tended to view Franklin as a "do-good" organization but still did not know enough about its work.[43] Yet his comment also suggests that the industry was no longer convinced of Franklin's ability to further publishers' interests, if they were even aware of its existence. By the 1970s, American publishers were also questioning its involvement in authoritarian regimes such as Iran's. But the first real problems arose in the 1960s, on the domestic front.

Early in 1967, a story in the *New York Times* claimed that a number of American cultural organizations and foundations had covertly received funds from the CIA. Datus Smith quickly told his board of directors,

> Franklin has never received funds from any of the real or pseudo foundations mentioned in recent newspaper stories as conduits for CIA money. We innocently applied to one or two of them, along with hundreds of other foundations, from which we regularly seek help, but they turned us down! . . . No approach to Franklin has ever been made by the CIA or, as far as I know, by anyone on their behalf.[44]

In fact, Franklin had received money from the Asia Foundation, whose management confessed to having accepted funds from the CIA. In May, two months after his original statement, Smith admitted that the organization had received roughly US$179,000 from the foundation (out of a total of approximately US$26 million in funding from all sources). Franklin had used the Asia Foundation money primarily for work in Afghanistan and Malaysia, and Smith asserted that the foundation had not interfered in any way and that all funds had been publicly reported. He defended his initial response to the article by asserting that Franklin had not *knowingly* received CIA funding.[45] The board of directors quickly decided to stop taking funds from the Asia Foundation, but the CIA revelations had done lasting damage to cultural organizations that operated abroad.[46] Similar accusations resurfaced in the 1970s, and Franklin continued to reiterate Smith's statement that it had never knowingly received CIA money. The Senate investigated a number of American publishers who were accused of having received CIA subsidies for publishing certain books. They denied any such involvement: if there had been any interference with manuscripts, they argued, it had been done without the editors' knowledge.[47]

The Vietnam War affected the publishing industry as it did every other sector of American society and culture. In 1967, a *Publishers Weekly* editorial commented on the "problem" of Vietnam and said that the war was taking much-needed funds from education programs (which threatened publishers' commercial profits). The article noted publishers' "deep distress" with "the war policy and American priorities."[48] A number of publishers actively supported the antiwar cause, including Alfred A. Knopf, a Republican and certainly not a political radical. Knopf, who had heretofore supported the USIA's work in the Cold War, told a Brazilian friend in December 1969 that the United States was getting its "just deserts" in Vietnam: "We had no right ever to go in and there is no conceivable way in which we can avoid getting out."[49] He believed that the war had taught the United States "that American omnipotence is and always has been a myth."[50]

Knopf's firm supported Publishers for Peace, formed in the late 1960s to represent industry members who supported the U.S. withdrawal from Vietnam. In 1968, the members of Publishers for Peace signed an open letter asking Nixon to stop the bombing of the country.[51] In 1970, the organization held a fundraising auction of manuscripts, letters, and galley proofs that was sponsored by numerous publishers, including Chester Kerr, the director of Yale University Press; Roger W. Straus, Jr., the president of Farrar, Straus, and Giroux; and W. Bradford Wiley, the president of Wiley.[52] Knopf also supported the auction. The 1970 annual meeting of the ABPC included a debate over whether the council should pass a peace resolution (an argument led by Edward Booher and Chester Kerr), but not all publishers agreed.[53] Despite the dissent, however, it was clear that many in the industry opposed the war.

Such tensions made things difficult for Franklin. The American public was losing tolerance for rightwing dictatorships, and American publishers were struggling to decide if they should continue to deal with them. Such relationships were likely to create bad publicity and to conflict with their own personal politics. As early as 1965, Knopf wrote to Dan Lacy, the president of the ABPC, to question the actions of the Brazilian regime because one of his Brazilian publishers wanted the ABPC to protest it.[54] Lacy expressed his concern about the dictatorship and acknowledged censorship problems in the country; however, it would be, he argued, "rather quixotic" of the ABPC to try resolve such issues.[55]

As the decade advanced, it became more difficult to stay silent, yet Franklin managed to retain a portion of its cultural internationalist reputation within the industry. Bruce Wilcox, who went on to become the director of the University of Massachusetts Press, worked with the organization between 1972 and 1975, primarily on projects in Bangladesh. Wilcox had been with the Peace Corps in Senegal and had worked at the University of Washington Press, and he was attracted to Franklin because of its reputation for seeking to do good in the world. Wilcox remembers that he and the other young publishers were "all vividly aware of the 'ugly American' image and were strongly opposed to the horrific war being waged by the United States in Vietnam. We imagined that Franklin could represent a different vision of the U.S.'s role in the world." He also "knew and admired Datus Smith." Even though Smith was no longer president, his reputation was still inspiring some of the publishers of the next generation.[56]

Whenever possible, however, American publishers were moving into international markets on strictly commercial terms rather than seeking to work with the government. In 1970, for example, McGraw-Hill was looking to move into the Indian market through a deal with Tata, an Indian industrial conglomerate. Echoing Franklin rhetoric, Booher stressed the importance of publishing as "internationalism," not just as a commercial export, but the deal was largely commercial in its aspirations.[57] The AAP's International Trade Committee was leading the way on these issues, and Franklin's vision of how American publishers could and should engage with the world increasingly seemed to belong to a bygone era.[58]

Leadership Problems

In May 1967, Smith announced that he would postpone his resignation from Franklin because the board was having difficulty finding a replacement and was also dealing with a financial crisis.[59] Eventually, in November of that year, he turned the leadership over to Mike Harris, who said that he planned to maintain continuity and praised Smith "for the ingenuity with which Franklin has attacked book problems in its areas of operations."[60] Smith maintained his interest in Franklin, returning to serve on its board of directors between 1971 and 1977, but he believed that a change of leadership was good for every nonprofit organization. In his opinion, "doing the same old things in the same old ways" meant "declining usefulness" whereas fresh leadership meant a "new vision." He moved on from Franklin to become a vice-president at the JDR 3rd Fund, which he believed would enable him to continue "to serve many of the same objectives and same ideals of public service."[61] His new job involved helping to develop and teach the idea of social responsibility in the corporate world.[62]

Harris was the former deputy secretary-general of the Organization for Economic Cooperation and Development. He had a background in the labor movement and extensive experience in Europe, having been in charge of the execution of the Marshall Plan in West Germany from 1951 to 1954. Harris had subsequently worked with the Ford Foundation in Indonesia, where he met Smith. Smith believed that Harris would bring new ideas to Franklin while maintaining its basic principles.[63] In practice, Harris concentrated on furthering Franklin's orientation toward education and thus its focus on book modernization programs. Indeed, he thought translation, while having some positive effect on texts' availability, had little actual influence on the development of "indigenous publishing" and was "not a significant factor in educational and economic development." It was also expensive.[64]

A number of changes took place after Harris assumed the presidency, including staff cutbacks at the New York office at the end of the 1960s. He and the board of directors decided to focus on the most successful aspects of Franklin's work, such as the training of book industry personnel, technical assistance to local book industries, organizing and carrying out regional book-development surveys, and preparing and distributing material for new literates.[65] One of Harris's main concerns was to make regional offices aware that they needed to be as self-supporting as possible, but he struggled to convince program directors of this necessity.[66] He also identified problems in financial accountability and believed that regional offices were not properly returning all of the royalty money to the New York office.[67]

Harris's tenure did not last long: he resigned in 1969, partly, as I will show, because of a crisis in the Tehran office. A year before he left, he shared some devastating criticisms of Franklin's contribution to the development of global publishing. While he believed that the organization had contributed to "the publication of many good books and to an improvement in technical standards," he did not think it had had "a substantial effect on sales and distribution, size of markets, or professional publishing practices."[68] Harris's approach was undoubtedly more hard-nosed and realistic than Smith's had been, and he found Franklin wanting. The fact that he was not a book publisher probably

Mike Harris in Franklin's New York office. A row of Franklin books lines the shelf behind him.

also made his job difficult because he had few connections within or familiarity with the industry. Nor did he come to the job with a view of publishing as a vocation.

Carroll "Curly" Bowen, Franklin's next president, did come from a publishing background, but he, too, had limited success in the role. Bowen, who was the former director of the MIT Press, took over in December 1969 and was fired in August 1971. Like Harris, he argued for a focus on education and believed that Franklin should concentrate on countries that sought to prioritize education in their national programs. He articulated his thoughts in a 1969 address:

> I believe that free and universal education has in principle been accepted as a basic human right. I believe, second, in the necessity of print in this process. Third, I believe that the educationally related book, curricular or extra-curricular, used at whatever age levels, is the prime device of Franklin's mission. Fourth, I believe devoutly that Franklin should help first those countries who are making extraordinary efforts educationally to help themselves. Fifth, I believe further that we industrial idealists in American book publishing correctly perceive that there is an exportable entrepreneurial competence in those processes of publishing and printing which the developing world needs to learn, and once learned, will use. Sixth, I believe that Franklin must work harder to find larger roles for American-published English-language books to play, everywhere the language is used. Seventh, I believe that Franklin, while exceptional, is not unique; and that it must try never to work alone, but should seek cooperation with its foreign counterparts.[69]

Despite his attempt to plan a way forward for Franklin, Bowen soon came under fire. Raymond Harwood, the chairman of the board of directors, wrote to the executive committee in August 1971 to resign from his position, saying that Bowen had "been unable to provide the kind of leadership Franklin desperately needs in these desperately difficult times." He criticized Bowen's poor financial decisions and the fact that he was not spending enough time in the New York office and therefore creating administrative and communication problems. Staff morale was generally poor, and book industry support had eroded. Harwood recommended that Bowen resign before he was asked to leave and that Jack Kyle, the current vice-president, be made acting president.[70] Bowen agreed not to oppose the decision but told Harwood that "since the separation was involuntary it should not be described as a resignation."[71] Anders Richter, a Franklin employee who later worked at the Johns Hopkins University Press, said that he was sorry to see Bowen go but observed that his differences with the executive committee were "long-standing" and "seemingly irreconcilable."[72]

On August 20, 1971, Jack Kyle was made acting president. Kyle had been a vice-president at Franklin since December 1970; he was also the founding director of the East-West Center Press in Honolulu. He had been active in Franklin's Asia activities since 1968 and had headed the Franklin-initiated International Copyrights Information Center that aimed to assist small publishers obtain information about copyright issues.[73] After his time with

Franklin, he became the director of the University of Texas Press.[74] Not long after Kyle assumed Franklin's leadership, stakeholders discussed the possibility of merging with another organization. The Asia Foundation, the East-West Center, Freedom House, and the National Book Committee were all considered as candidates. Eventually, however, they decided that a merger did not offer the potential for better financial support and "would probably decrease the book industry's feeling that Franklin is 'their' project." In addition, it might compromise the organization's hard-won reputation abroad.[75]

Kyle sought to reformulate Franklin's objectives. He identified a new focus: to increase local capabilities in book publishing; to increase the international exchange of books, translations, and book publishing experiences; to strengthen book marketing and distribution; and to develop the reading habit in countries in which the organization operated programs. These objectives were to be translated into Franklin projects and programs around the globe. A key concern was to develop "non-formal education"—that is, to create materials for improving literacy and skills outside the formal education system.[76] Kyle also emphasized the importance of "do[ing] a better job of familiarizing the book industry with what we are doing and to seek more support and involvement from that important sector."[77] In response, Franklin undertook a 1973 campaign to publicize its work, putting out news releases, distributing fact sheets, and contacting radio and television stations.[78]

Existing Programs and Challenges

Franklin operated its existing offices with diminishing funds and often in challenging environments. For instance, the Cairo office was Franklin's oldest and one of its more successful operations. But in the late 1960s, Nasser's government took control of most of Egypt's printing and media, and Franklin had little recourse, especially in the face of continuing opposition and criticism from Egyptians who were deeply suspicious of the United States as an imperial power.[79] A 1967 article in the Egyptian magazine *Al Kateb* condemned Franklin for plotting "domination over thought, brains and sentiments to pave the way for neo-colonialism to exploit the third world economies." It was accused of being funded by the U.S. embassy in Cairo and of being a front for CIA cultural infiltration. Its books were branded as "direct propaganda for the capitalist system," and the article's author claimed that they promoted the view that American and Western cultures were superior to Middle Eastern ones. Franklin's Egyptian employees were accused of "exploiting in the worse sense of the word their supervisory and leadership positions and their authority" and of being "paid vast and fantastic sums of money for their services."[80] Datus Smith's wife, Dorothy, thought the article must be the work of Communists, but Smith himself believed that the author was an Arab nationalist with socialist sympathies. He even said that he admired the author's thinking, although he thought him "dead wrong" in his conclusions.[81] Smith asked the Cairo office staff to respond if they wanted to, suggesting that they should emphasize the difference between USIA publications and Franklin productions. Indeed, he thought it was reasonable to criticize the "Americanism" of the USIA publications.[82]

In June, a few months after the article appeared, the Six Day War between Egypt and Israel broke out. The conflict led to the temporary suspension of many American cultural activities in the area, including Franklin's.[83] A few of its Cairo programs continued into the 1970s, such as a science translation program funded by the National Science Foundation.[84] It also undertook French translations funded by the Association Nationale du Livre Français à l'Étranger and several translation projects for private customers such as Wiley.[85] But overall, translation numbers were much reduced in comparison to the office's heyday in the 1950s and early 1960s. In 1976, Franklin helped produce a pilot school magazine in Arabic.[86] But its activities during the decade were limited in scope and had little impact on the local publishing scene.

Franklin's activities in Indonesia became difficult as relations between Indonesia and the United States deteriorated during the 1960s. At one point, the board of directors commented that its ability to stay in business there was "barely short of a miracle."[87] In August 1964, the Jakarta office manager, Hassan Shadily, wrote to Don Cameron about attacks on the Franklin office and growing anti-American sentiment, especially after the United States became more heavily involved in Vietnam: "My belief is that Indonesia is not a communist country (yet) and that our foreign policy is free and active and not to tag along with either east or west, but my goodness, one feels so little production when the color is not reddish."[88] A Jakarta staff member told Cameron in April 1965 that "every American name has become a target of political mobs." He suggested changing the name of the office to something Indonesian that showed no connection to anything American: "The condition has become such that for the sake of the continuation of Franklin's good purposes we should give it a non-American name."[89]

In 1966, the Sukarno regime was ousted, and Suharto took over, with

U.S. support.⁹⁰ In 1969, Franklin accepted contracts from AID to translate university textbooks and to create a center to train Indonesian writers of secondary-school textbooks, but these programs had limited impact on the overall publishing scene.⁹¹ In 1972, Shadily resigned, and was replaced by Robert Sheeks, a former Asia Foundation staff member who had once worked for the Committee for Free Asia.⁹²

Attitudes in Malaysia, too, were becoming increasingly anti-American. By the middle of the 1960s, locals were waging political campaigns against anything "imperialist American."⁹³ In March 1968, Harris visited the Malaysia office and noted that ethnic tensions were limiting the success of the book program. The U.S. ambassador in Kuala Lumpur wanted the office to continue its work given the country's need for textbooks, but Harris thought the financial outlook was grim. In 1968, he and the board decided that their only choice was to terminate the program.⁹⁴

The Indo-Pakistani War of 1965 had a major impact on Franklin's work in Pakistan, problems that were was compounded by management troubles.⁹⁵ Dariush Homayoun of the Tehran office wrote to Cameron about the Lahore office, commenting that the "whole operation lacks the drive and efficiency which could be desired." He concluded that the office had potential but needed reorganization to survive.⁹⁶ Meanwhile, it was facing constant opposition and hostility from various quarters.

Franklin's activities in West Pakistan included two library projects: one focusing on school libraries, the other "established to provide books to libraries maintained by town communities, district councils and municipal committees through the purchase and/or reprint of Urdu translations of American books."⁹⁷ At the end of the 1960s, those books included Allan S. Downer's *Recent American Drama,* Theodore Hornberger's *Benjamin Franklin,* Alexander Nazaroff's *The Land of the Russian People,* and William S. Shirer's *The Rise and Fall of the Third Reich.*⁹⁸ In the early 1970s, Franklin was also overseeing a low-cost textbook program, funded by an AID contract, but it was not particularly successful. A final report on the project noted that it had produced 152,700 copies of 87 books but had distributed only 41,800 copies. Anders Richter, who wrote the report, concluded that the project had increased the availability of affordable upper-level textbooks yet, "as an import substitution activity, it could hardly capture the enthusiasm of American publishers."⁹⁹

A report summarizing Franklin's activities in West Pakistan in 1971 noted that the school library project had been one of the organization's most useful, resulting in the donation of more than 62,000 books to 826 libraries in high schools, intermediate colleges, and universities. According to the report, all of Franklin's library projects "have been highly appreciated by the ministries of education and of the basic democracies as well as by principals and headmasters."[100] Nonetheless, the organization reported ongoing problems with the Pakistani government, which was, it felt, trying to use the textbook program for "political purposes rather than development purposes." In addition, West Pakistan was threatening to pull out of international copyright conventions and planning to publish works without requesting permission from American publishers. Already, the government was pressuring Franklin to persuade American publishers, quickly and aggressively, to agree to textbook permissions; "complaints have been made that our presentations to the American publishing industry were a bit too strong, that we were recommending blackmail payments to the Government of Pakistan." Ultimately, Franklin ensured that no books were published illegally, and the program continued.[101] But the situation in West Pakistan became untenable, and in 1972 Jack Kyle recommended the closure of the Lahore office.[102]

In East Pakistan, Franklin's office manager, A. T. M. Abdul Mateen, had been elected to the national assembly and in 1965 was replaced by M. A. Azam, an American-trained engineer, educator, and writer. Despite the managerial change, the Dacca office continued to struggle, and during the late 1960s it lost large amounts of money.[103] Franklin's work had little impact on the local book publishing industry, though it did produce a small number of books in translation.[104] Yet after Harris took over the organization's leadership, he said that he believed the office still had potential. Franklin had good relations with the local USIS personnel, and during a March 1968 visit Harris reported that many American officials in the region held the organization in high esteem. He regretted that their counterparts in Washington did not feel the same.[105]

During the early 1970s, East Pakistan was beset with tremendous problems. In 1971, state forces murdered hundreds of thousands of Bengalis and displaced many more. In the subsequent fight for independence, a number of people associated with Franklin's Dacca programs were killed, though the office staff survived.[106] The country took a new name, Bangladesh, and 1972 became Franklin's "Year of Bangladesh." As the new nation tried to move forward, the organization signed an eighteen-month contract with the Ministry of Education to help create and procure textbooks: Bengali textbooks would be produced for primary and secondary students, and U.S. textbooks would be made available at the university level.[107] AID was particularly interested in developing programs for Bangladesh and invested large sums of money in them.[108] Franklin hoped to revive its translation program in the region, with a focus on what it called "nation-building" books on economic development, political science, demography, and public administration.[109]

In 1972, Franklin also founded what it called the Franklin Community Library:

> a small mini-library, self-contained in its own shipping carton which becomes its own display stand when opened at its destination. This size [of] library can easily fit into any primary or secondary school and can be purchased, delivered, and administered for about $1,000. With this kind of visible and impressive package at this "attractive" price, we have what we believe to be a first-rate fund-raising project, as well as a sound educational materials program.[110]

The first of these mini-libraries opened in Bangladesh, and the plan was to try them out elsewhere, although it is unclear whether any others were created or how successful they were.

In 1973, as per an agreement between Franklin and the Ministry of Education, two hundred American publishers sent an airlift of about 40,000 books to Dacca to be presented to six Bangladeshi universities.[111] Franklin used the airlift to promote its work and raise public awareness about the country's struggles. Already, Americans were aware of the issue, which had been publicized in the popular Concert for Bangladesh in 1971. Thus, supporting work there may have seemed less morally problematic than supporting work in Iran or Pakistan. But despite Franklin's best efforts, many of the organization's problems remained unresolved.

The Tehran Problem

Even at Franklin's Tehran office, its most successful operation, there were serious issues. After the manager, Homayoun Sanati, resigned at the end of 1968, Franklin's leadership passed a resolution declaring that his work had been "a major force in educational development in Iran" and affirming that his office had "helped to improve the quality of education and to increase greatly the numbers of people benefiting from it."[112] But soon his successor, Ali Asghar Mohajer, was making accusations of financial irregularities in the Tehran office's accounting. Mohajer contended that Sanati had transferred a 10 percent rebate from an office paper purchase into his own Swiss bank account. He also accused Sanati of taking expensive trips using, but not accounting for, Franklin funds. Sanati, he claimed, was "many times a millionaire, with most of his wealth invested in paintings and stock in London and real estate in Tehran." Reviewing the evidence, Harris agreed: "There is no doubt at all that Homayoun is a thief and has stolen a large but unquantifiable amount to enrich himself."[113] A subsequent audit of the office books verified the existence of numerous financial problems.[114]

Richard Arndt, who was serving as a U.S. cultural affairs officer in Tehran at the time, told Harris that he believed Sanati was a "good fellow" but that he knew many Iranians who thought the manager was a "crook." Noting Iran's endemic corruption, he added that it was customary in the country to "pay influential people under the table."[115] In his later reminiscences about Iranian society and life under the shah, Arndt observed that many Americans assumed that Iranians were lying and corrupt and were shocked by the level of nepotism that existed in the country.[116] In early 1968, while Sanati was still director, Harris had visited Iran and had reported to New York that the manager had "fingers in many pies." It was unclear, wrote Harris, what work he did for Franklin and what work he did for himself.[117]

Given the sparseness of the evidence, I find it difficult to judge the actual illegality of Sanati's behavior, especially in the context of Iran during those years. But it can be noted that the Americans had helped to create the conditions for corruption, and Franklin was directly implicated. While the New York office did not receive many of the Tehran profits, it did benefit from the status of having a successful office, and staff members had long turned a blind eye—at the very least—to its questionable practices. As early as 1959, Datus Smith had expressed concern about the office's accounting practices and suggested areas for improvement, but he was reluctant to push the issue because of Sanati's great local success.[118] In 1963, a USIA audit of Franklin's accounts revealed that Tehran staff members believed that local-currency grants were theirs to manage as they wished.[119] Again, Smith defended the office on the basis of its achievements.

Harris met with Sanati in February 1969 and proposed that he repay the money he owed to Franklin. Harris declared that "the whole matter was a mess" and explained that Franklin "had to keep honest accounts and hold people responsible for accurate accounts." According to him, Sanati responded by saying, "There must be a way out—there is a way out of everything."[120] In the meantime, Sanati, according to Mohajer, was trying to set up a rival cultural organization that would have "a complete monopoly on the publication of all elementary and secondary textbooks in Iran."[121] A small group within the government and the elite, including Princess Ashraf, the minister of science, and the prime minister's brother, were involved, and they justified the project by citing the importance of Iranian cultural independence. Harris, too, reported that Sanati believed that Franklin's Tehran programs were no longer necessary.[122]

Later that year, however, Sanati agreed to stop working to form the new organization on the understanding that Franklin's Tehran office would become an independent entity within two years.[123] He also agreed to pay what he owed to Franklin.[124] Their rapprochement meant that the Tehran office was able to stay open, and Franklin managed to maintain control over its work for another three years (primarily to engage in textbook translation and production) before the operation became fully independent. Sanati continued to be successful in business. Although he was imprisoned for five years after the revolution, he retained his wealth and kept developing his business interests in Iran.[125] Mike Harris, writing to Carroll Bowen in 1970, noted the legal difficulties thrown up by the whole affair. He had thought it best to try to avoid a lawsuit, which might lead to the divulging of facts "highly embarrassing to him and to others."[126] Indeed, the incident not only highlighted Franklin's questionable financial practices but also suggests the consequences of compromising on business practices to work in a country with a corrupt and authoritarian regime.

The Iranian office continued to operate successfully for several more years, and in 1974 it brought in US$11 million.[127] It managed the new Franklin Center for Educational Technology, described as a "rather highly advanced audio-visual center" that offered educational materials on family planning, nutrition, literacy, agriculture, home economics, and community development.[128] Franklin continued to support, directly or indirectly, most textbook publishing for Iranian students. In 1976, J. M. Filstrup noted that the organization had monopolized the country's textbook field, which he regarded as problematic: "How can a general publishing industry flourish without a market-place atmosphere and the concurrent opportunity to publish books? A monopoly, though benevolent, risks stifling opportunity."[129] His observation suggests that Franklin's success in Iran was tainted by the way in which it had achieved that success. The 1960s was a turbulent period for the country. The shah's White Revolution was having mixed effects, including socioeconomic dislocation related to land reform. When economic growth began to slow in the early 1970s, the regime increasingly came under pressure as popular opposition grew.[130] Franklin's work was, of course, only peripheral to the government's many activities, yet its links to that government was emblematic of a greater American involvement and investment in Iran and the compromises that such work required. By succeeding in Iran, Franklin had become exactly what it had always meant to avoid: ethically compromised.

Early in 1976, the Tehran office became an independent entity. Franklin had always hoped that its offices would achieve independence, but in this case it agreed to the outcome in part because of U.S. tax implications. As the organization's attorney explained, the Tehran office was operating more in a "commercial manner than a charitable and educational manner."[131] The office remained responsible for a variety of activities, including producing school textbooks and the literacy magazine *Peyk* and working with Iran's Free University to establish a new printing press.[132] The timing of its independence is worth noting, for it was clear that Iranians had long wanted their own independent operation while the Americans had postponed giving it to them. Presumably the reasons were mostly financial (or perhaps not wanting to give in to Sanati), but it does suggest that the Americans retained control of the decision. Yet the independent Tehran office did not survive the 1979 revolution, which ended the shah's regime, rejected Western influence, and established an Islamic state.

The Final Years

Despite overwhelming problems, Franklin struggled on for a few more years, undertaking a variety of programs across the globe. Many of its 1970s initiatives reveal the compromises that it made to work with regimes, as it had done in Iran. And pressure from those governments, as well as reduced U.S. private and government support, damaged the programs' potential effectiveness.

Franklin did not entirely abandon the idea of expanding into new territories. In 1972, for instance, staff members discussed a possible program for Nepal after AID reported that its own textbook program there, which included creating primary and secondary textbooks, investing in a printing plant, and promoting textbook writing, had not accomplished much. The agency blamed a "lack of modern management and lack of co-ordination between the Government of Nepal and USAID." In response, Franklin sent Edward J. Triebe, Jr., to Nepal in hopes that he could find a way for the organization to share its expertise. Triebe, who was a member of the production development staff, spent four months in the country and drew up a draft plan for two Americans to work there for two years.[133] But the program was never established.

In 1973, Franklin surveyed Chile's book needs with a view to beginning an operation there. To fund this and other projected surveys in Latin America, it applied to United Brands (for Central America) and the Johnson Wax Foundation (for Brazil). Its focus would be on what it called "non-formal education" for those with little or no literacy skills, and these programs would be delivered through Franklin Learning Centers similar in style to the Iranian one. They were described as "modest-sized institutions that would have the appearance of small libraries or reading rooms, but that would also offer audio-visual presentations in the fields of family health and planning, nutrition, [and] home-making" and on a variety of vocational subjects. Franklin also hoped to offer literacy classes and produce materials for literacy training. Its reports asserted that the organization would continue to be primarily concerned with producing educational materials: "We have no particular interest in creating the centers for the sake of education administration. However, we are convinced that these centers are essential to the *distribution* and *use* of educational materials, two of Franklin's primary objectives."[134]

Yet Franklin's move to embrace education did not prove to be a strategy for survival, and by the late 1960s and into the early 1970s, it began to close offices and abandon programs. In 1969, it halted its African programs, in large part because of the Biafran War in Nigeria.[135] In 1970, some of its bookmen considered salvaging the Nigerian office and creating a program in Ghana, but nothing changed.[136] The Kabul office also began having trouble by 1969, and Franklin reports described 1972 as a "year of crisis," with little money coming from the Afghan government to cover the costs of programs.[137] Things were no better in 1973.[138]

As I have discussed, the Lahore office closed in 1972. Arabic programs continued in the Cairo office, as did some translation contract work for the USIA.[139] But the office was losing money and failed to break even in 1974.[140] Moreover, here and elsewhere, the local office staff were increasingly eager to run things themselves. Mohajer of the Tehran office wrote in 1975 that the Americans were too likely to treat them like "latter day Gunga Dins" rather than "as partners and trusted colleagues."[141]

Despite Kyle's operational leadership, Franklin could find no solution to a lack of funding. In 1974, it analyzed the trends in its donor support between 1969 and 1974 and noted that, while the publishing industry had been reasonably generous in 1969 and 1970, their later contributions had regularly fallen below US$30,000. Corporate donations, too, had dropped—from more than US$60,000 in 1969 to slightly more than US$30,000 during each year between 1970 and 1974. Foundation support had once been a vital resource, but in 1974 Franklin received no funding at all from philanthropic foundations.[142] In fiscal year 1974–75, the organization had fallen well below its targets, and things were no better in the following fiscal year. AID was no longer providing any funding. Anders Richter, now Franklin's senior vice-president, complained in 1977 that the organization's financial problems were compounded by the fact that the "good people" who were concerned with its future were "uncomfortable" about discussing money.[143]

Franklin continued to be dogged by allegations of a CIA connection, which challenged its ability to attract corporate funding, and its leadership continued to struggle to counter these allegations. In 1975, Kyle declared that he would not put out a public disclaimer because "it would only arouse suspicion." He again formally asserted that Franklin had never received funding from the CIA nor provided any information to the agency. He emphasized that the Asia Foundation money had been the only connection and dryly commented that "he doubted that the CIA was even aware of Franklin's existence." While he could not swear that a Franklin employee had never been contacted by the agency, "there has never been the slightest bit of evidence of such 'infiltration' on the part of any regular employee—no suspicious activities, no hint of information gathering other than that required for Franklin projects, no mysterious telephone calls or absences, none of the things one might look for in the behavior of an undercover agent or reporters." He cited a story about hiring two workers for the Bangladesh project who had turned out to be alcoholics and then claimed they had once been CIA agents. However, he said, local AID officials had "attributed their remarks to a new phenomenon, namely that there is a growing number of people who claim CIA connections in order to give themselves importance."[144]

In 1975, Franklin's then-president Carroll Bowen acidly observed, "There is no money in virtue."[145] His comment summarized the organization's dire situation. That year, staff members began to close down Franklin's remaining operations. Without proper financial support, there was no real point in continuing them. The New York office moved into rent-free space in the McGraw-Hill building, and employees were laid off.[146] While cutting these expenses allowed Franklin to continue a few of its remaining projects, it merely postponed the inevitable. Yet in 1976, the organization's financial situation improved slightly, and staff considered holding on to some of their programs.[147] They even announced a new textbook project in the Philippines, with partial funding from with the World Bank; and CBS donated about

US$25,000 to help support the New York operation.[148] But the staff's optimism was short-lived. In 1977, they again determined that they could not keep the organization afloat.[149]

Datus Smith was chair of Franklin's board in 1975. During a meeting that year, he set out, as he had when Franklin was first established, an idealistic statement of purpose:

> To improve the human condition, with particular emphasis on the needs of the world's poorest people—by assisting developing nations in planning, creating, producing and using the kinds of resources that result in basic education for children and adults;
>
> To promote the growth of knowledge throughout the world by providing management and consultant services that facilitate professional conferences, teacher training, the formation and use of libraries, exhibitions of books and other learning materials, bookselling and book distribution; translations, and other related activities.[150]

But in October 1976, Francis Fox, who had been assessing all of Franklin's operations, wrote to Smith recommending that it complete all of its current programs and suspend operations by April 1978. He also suggested that the organization should redefine its goals and objectives and set out a new operating structure to see it through to the end. Yet Fox believed that Franklin might not need to fold completely:

> My study suggests that there is a great need for preserving the "spirit" of Franklin as envisioned by the founders. Some would say the need is greater than ever before. That is why I earnestly hope wise heads will assess this need and give Franklin Book Programs new life. Franklin is a totally unique concept. It is singularly qualified to join and coordinate the interests of the public and private sectors in fostering education and publishing throughout the world. Franklin should grasp the opportunity and once again lead the way.[151]

Fox's suggestions were circulated to the board, which hoped to find some way to continue.[152] They agreed, however, that if there was no progress by April 1978, they would dissolve the Franklin Corporation.[153] In the meantime, they shut down the organization's operations abroad. Some activities were transferred to other organizations. For instance, on December 29, 1977, the Cairo office's work on educational materials was handed over to a new local nonprofit agency, the Egyptian Society for the Dissemination of World Culture and Knowledge: Franklin, to be chaired by Mahmoud Mahfouz.[154] Smith, who traveled to Egypt early in 1978 to oversee the final transfer, reported, "I feel no sadness about our withdrawal from Cairo. Our objective from the beginning has been the establishment of local capability, and this is the crowning proof of our success."[155] It was fitting that he was the man to hand over the activities and assets of the Cairo office—the first of Franklin's offices, which he had established a quarter of a century earlier.

On April 28, 1978, the board of directors met for one last time and dissolved Franklin Book Programs. Its remaining assets were donated to the Library of Congress's Center for the Book.[156] The meeting adjourned just after four o'clock in the afternoon, and Franklin ceased operations.[157]

CONCLUSION
Assessing the Legacy

In November 1977, Datus Smith wrote to members of the Franklin corporation to tell them that the organization's programs were being terminated. He urged them to remember that "conditions have changed both in the American book world and in the developing countries, and we should not be unhappy if the particular kind of contribution we were making earlier is no longer needed or appropriate."[1] Yet Franklin had not achieved what it had hoped to accomplish. By the late 1970s, Americans were generally reviled abroad, not least because of the Vietnam War. Cultural diplomacy could not counter bad foreign policy decisions or U.S. government support for authoritarian regimes, nor could it save the reputation of a country notorious for Watergate, domestic dissent, and racial violence. Once the government had worked to project an image of the United States at its very best, but now there was no clear best image to project. In these years, any belief that American books could help save the nation's reputation abroad seemed naïve at best. Development efforts were faltering, and book modernization was likely to occur only through general commercialization that would ensure the global dominance of large corporations.

How, then, should we assess Franklin's legacy? When trying to match its accomplishments against its goals—putting American books into circulation and helping to develop local book publishing—I could find only fragments of evidence. Perhaps its most notable impact was in Iran. Despite the upheavals of the 1979 revolution, Franklin helped to develop some aspects of the book industry there. As I mentioned in chapter 4, Iranian publishers have acknowledged its important contributions, including its introduction of a proper editing process, its training seminars in book design and production, and its founding of the offset printing company that continues to be an important printing house in Iran.[2] Traces of Franklin's training techniques linger in the Iranian book industry, and some of former employees look back fondly on their time with the organization—among them, Majid Roshangar, who moved to the United States after the revolution, where he became the publisher of the *Persian Book Review*, but who learned his trade under Homayoun Sanati in the Tehran office.[3]

In a 1965 *New York Times* article, Mohammed Najm, who ran the Beirut office, commented that "[just] as Coca-Cola has raised the standards of the refreshment industry, Franklin has raised the standards of publishing."[4] The comparison is a telling one. Coca-Cola has long been regarded as a symbol of American cultural imperialism, and Franklin's history clearly reveals that imperialism at work. The organization operated to open up new markets for U.S. publishers, even if it was not entirely successful in forging the way for their exports. Its efforts were an element of American commercial dominance after World War II, and it participated in circulating American cultural products around the globe.

As I have discussed, Franklin had little interest in bringing international translations to Americans or in nurturing and developing local literature. Although Franklin's bookmen were aware of this problem, their decision to focus on bringing American books to developing countries had a lasting impact on both the United States and the world. The United States still publishes very little international literature in translation. In a 2010 *New Yorker* article about contemporary Arab novels, Claudia Roth Pierpont notes how few are being translated into and published in English. She asks, "Isn't it as important to listen as to speak?"[5] Today, in our present political climate, the revival of a true cultural internationalism that listens as well as speaks is surely crucial.

Franklin's legacy may lie in the insight it provides into the nature of American cultural imperialism and internationalism during a dramatic era in world history. While liberalism and internationalism inspired many Americans to work abroad, their work was almost always bound up in power differentials, racial prejudice, political intrigues, and strategic and commercial concerns. Franklin was no different. Despite its idealism, its goals and achievements were entangled with American foreign policy decisions, the interests of local regimes, and cultural colonialism.

From the point of view of the government, Franklin was not a successful player in the state-private network that was so central to American Cold War efforts, and the organization's history reveals the tensions that marked such relationships. Private programs that allowed professionals and non-government employees to "go their own way" were seen as placing their own interests and aspirations at a level that was equal with, or even higher, than the government's. For Franklin, juggling professional, philanthropic, and government interests and pressures was a near-impossible task, even without the inevitable complications of local politics and problems. But Smith was pleased that the organization had helped to train at least a few publishers around the world and had made some small contribution to developing local book industries.

Franklin's vision of the book was quite different from the government's. It sought to project books as essential cultural and intellectual objects; by focusing on academic, literary, and other serious texts, its bookmen hoped to cultivate a worldwide appreciation of them. This desire to elevate the importance and cultural value of the book dominated Franklin's programs, yet to fit into American foreign policy directives, they had to work with and support corrupt authoritarian regimes. Thus, assessing Franklin requires us to acknowledge the contradictions that were at work within the programs and inherent in the postwar American vision of cultural internationalism. On the one hand, we might admire Franklin's employees' desire to promote the book, reading, and publishing, and their choice to challenge the government's instrumentalist anti-Communist approach to culture. On the other hand, they were instruments of American imperial and commercial aspirations, promoting American texts and business practices as solutions to other countries' problems and seeing locals through the lens of their own assumptions about traditional societies and nonwhite populations. Within these contradictions lies the story of the United States and the world after World War II.

Abbreviations

AAKR   Alfred A. Knopf, Inc., Records, 1873–1996, Harry Ransom Center, University of Texas, Austin

CBWR   Council on Books in Wartime Records, 1942–47, Public Policy Papers, Department of Rare Books and Special Collections, Seeley G. Mudd Manuscript Library, Princeton University

EJWP   Esther J. Walls Papers, 1860–1997, African American Women in Iowa Digital Collection, University of Iowa

FBPR   Franklin Book Programs Records, 1920–78, Public Policy Papers, Department of Rare Books and Special Collections, Seeley G. Mudd Manuscript Library, Princeton University

FHA   Freedom House Archives, Public Policy Papers, Department of Rare Books and Special Collections, Princeton University

PW   *Publishers Weekly*

NARA   National Archives and Records Administration, College Park, Maryland.

Notes

Introduction. American Cold War Book Empires

1. "News of the Week," *PW*, March 18, 1957, 43.
2. The Franklin Book Program has been little studied to date, but limited overviews appear in Stanley A. Barnett, "American Book Aid: A Critical Assessment of Two Major Program of the 1950s–1970s," in *Publishing and Development in the Third World*, ed. P. G. Altbach, (London: Zell, 1992), 325–48; J. M. Filstrup, "Franklin Book Programs/Tehran," *International Library Review* 8, no. 4 (1976): 431–50; and Louise S. Robbins, "Publishing American Values: The Franklin Book Programs as Cold War Cultural Diplomacy," *Library Trends* 55, no. 3 (Winter 2007): 638–50.
3. "Progress Report on Franklin," *PW*, February 19, 1962, 36.
4. Nicholas J. Cull argues that the cultural Cold War "has emerged as a major concern of international history" ("Reading, Viewing, and Tuning In to the Cold War," in *The Cambridge History of the Cold War*, vol. 2, *Crises and Détente*, ed. Melvyn P. Leffler and Odd Arne Westad [New York: Cambridge University Press, 2010]), 438. Many notable works are dedicated to uncovering its various battles in Europe. See, for example, Volker R. Berghahn, *America and the Intellectual Cold Wars in Europe: Shepard Stone between Philanthropy, Academy, and Diplomacy* (Princeton: Princeton University Press, 2001); Victoria de Grazia, *Irresistible Empire: America's Advance through Twentieth-Century Europe* (Cambridge: Harvard University Press, 2005); and Richard Pells, *Not Like US: How Europeans Have Loved, Hated, and Transformed American Culture since WWII* (New York: Basic Books, 1997). A number of scholars have focused on U.S. (especially CIA) infiltration of European intellectual circles, particularly the Congress for Cultural Freedom, an organization set up to promote intellectual freedom, culture, and ideas in Western Europe that was revealed to be was funded by the CIA. See, in particular, Frances Stonor Saunders, *Who Paid the Piper? The CIA and the Cultural Cold War* (London: Granta, 1999). Cold War scholarship has also increasingly focused on the political importance of the global south, led by Odd Arne Westad's *The Global Cold War: Third World Interventions and the Making of Our Times* (Cambridge: Cambridge University Press, 2005).
5. Franklin Book Programs, annual report for the year ending June 30, 1963, 1–2, FBPR, box 15, folder 7.
6. "Volumes to Meet the World's Demand for Books," *National Observer*, November 1963, clipping in FBPR, box 24, folder 3. The emphasis is mine.
7. Thomas J. Wilson, letter to Curtis Benjamin, 1963, FBPR, box 2, folder 9.

8. A significant body of scholarship now demonstrates modernization's importance as a conceptual framework in American foreign policy thinking in the 1950s and 1960s and illustrates how the idea played out in a variety of attitudes and programs across the globe. See, for example, David C. Engerman, Nils Gilman, Mark H. Haefle, and Michael E. Latham, eds., *Staging Growth: Modernization, Development, and the Global Cold War* (Amherst: University of Massachusetts Press, 2003); and Michael E. Latham, *The Right Kind of Revolution: Modernization, Development, and U.S. Foreign Policy from the Cold War to the Present* (Ithaca: Cornell University Press, 2011). The roots of postwar modernization are effectively explored in David Ekbladh, *The Great American Mission: Modernization and the Construction of an American World Order* (Princeton: Princeton University Press, 2010). Recent scholarship has begun to consider the operation of programs on the ground. For example, see Daniel Immerwahr, *Thinking Small: The United States and the Lure of Community Perspectives* (Cambridge: Harvard University Press, 2015).
9. The workings of the state-private network is an important theme of recent scholarship in Cold War cultural history, beginning with Kenneth Osgood's *Total Cold War: Eisenhower's Secret Propaganda Battle at Home and Abroad* (Lawrence: University Press of Kansas, 2006). Laura A. Belmonte, *Selling the American Way: U.S. Propaganda and the Cold War* (Philadelphia: University of Pennsylvania Press, 2008).
10. Andrew J. Falk, *Upstaging the Cold War: American Dissent and Cultural Diplomacy, 1940–1960* (Amherst: University of Massachusetts Press, 2010), 8.
11. Alistair McCleery, "The Return of the Publisher to Book History: The Case of Allen Lane," *Book History* 5 (2002): 179.
12. Max Paul Friedman, *Rethinking Anti-Americanism: The History of an Exceptional Concept in American Foreign Relations* (New York: Cambridge University Press, 2012), 4, 8.
13. Scholarship increasingly emphasizes local agency in any understanding of how the Cold War played out in developing countries. Heonik Kwon argues that it is necessary to understand Cold War history as "a globally staged but locally diverse regime of ideas and practices" (*The Other Cold War* [New York: Columbia University Press, 2010], 32). Jeremi Suri similarly comments that it is important to see multiple layers of agency operating within the Cold War context ("The Cold War, Decolonization, and Global Social Awakenings: Historical Intersections," *Cold War History* 6 [August 2006]: 359).
14. A number of recent books discuss cultural diplomacy and exchange programs during the Cold War, often examining battles over the programs' purposes, how participants felt about working with the government in such programs, and what ideas about American culture and society were being transmitted. See, for example, Danielle Foster-Lussier, *Music in America's Cold War Diplomacy* (Oakland: University of California Press, 2015); and Clare Croft, *Dancers as Diplomats: American Choreography in Cultural Exchange* (New York: Oxford University Press, 2015).
15. On how cultural imperialism and cultural (and knowledge) transmission or transfer can be seen as part of a broader process of globalization, see Jessica C. E. Gienow-Hecht, "Shame on U.S.? Academics, Cultural Transfer, and the Cold War—A Critical Review," *Diplomatic History* 24 (Summer 2000): 465–94. On the concept of global history, see Samuel Moyn and Andrew Sartori, eds., *Global Intellectual History* (New York: Columbia University Press, 2013). The term *transnationalism* may also be applied to Franklin's work to help explain the transfer and international dimensions of ideas, institutions, and practices of everyday life and how they were mediated and adapted in new contexts. See Matthew Hilton and Rana Mitter, "Introduction," *Past and Present*, supp. 8 (2013), 7–28.
16. See Alison Rukavina, *The Development of the International Book Trade, 1870–1895* (Houndmills, UK: Palgrave Macmillan, 2010), especially 8–13. Sydney J. Shep has outlined the importance of taking an international (or transnational) perspective on book history, questioning the persistent focus on national book histories ("Books without Borders: The Transnational Turn in Book History," in *Books without Borders*, vol. 1, *The Cross-National Dimension in Print Culture*, ed. Robert Fraser and Mary Hammond (Houndmills, UK:

Palgrave Macmillan, 2008), 13–37). While it is difficult to ignore the Franklin story as at least in part an exercise in American cultural diplomacy, the organization's work assumed transnational dimensions and operated to globalize the book industry. Its operations took place in a complicated world of local and international book publishing and trade networks.

17. Penny Von Eschen, *Satchmo Blows Up the World: Jazz Ambassadors Play the Cold War* (Cambridge: Harvard University Press, 2004), 255.
18. The story of the American book industry in the postwar period is effectively overviewed in David Paul Nord, Joan Shelley Rubin, and Michael Shudson, eds., *A History of the Book in America* (Chapel Hill: University of North Carolina Press, 2009), vol. 5. However, there has been only limited attention to the role of books or the book industry in international work during this period. Greg Barnhisel's *Cold War Modernists: Art, Literature, and American Cultural Diplomacy* (New York: Columbia University Press, 2015) considers the use of literature in American cultural diplomacy and how it contributed to the construction of cultural modernism. Erin A. Smith's *What Would Jesus Read? Popular Religious Books and Everyday Life in Twentieth-Century America* (Chapel Hill: University of North Carolina Press, 2015) briefly considers the export of such books and attitudes toward them abroad. There is also good scholarship on the relationship of American publishing and Latin American literature in the Cold War period, notably Deborah Cohn's *The Latin American Literary Boom and U.S. Nationalism during the Cold War* (Nashville: Vanderbilt University Press, 2012). These works signal a growing interest in and attention to the area and is supplemented by scholarship considering the operation of the British book industry in this period, particularly in Africa. See Caroline Davis, *Postcolonial Literature: African Writers and British Publishers* (Houndmills, UK: Palgrave Macmillan, 2013); and Caroline Davis and David Johnson, eds., *The Book in Africa: Critical Debates* (Houndmills: Palgrave Macmillan, 2015).
19. Datus C. Smith, "Bowker Lecture: Moral Issues of U.S. Books in the Non-Western World," *PW,* April 14, 1958, 23–24.

Chapter 1. Books for a New War

1. Franklin Publications, certificate of incorporation, May 29, 1952, FBPR, box 23, folder 14.
2. Franklin Publications, minutes, incorporators' meeting, June 5, 1952, FBPR, box 1, folder 5.
3. Franklin Publications, certificate of incorporation.
4. Franklin Publications, minutes, incorporators' meeting.
5. Franklin Publications, minutes, board of directors' meeting, September 24, 1953, FBPR, box 1, folder 5.
6. "News of the Week," *PW,* November 15, 1952, 2022.
7. Dan Lacy and Robert W. Frase, "The American Book Publishers' Council," in *A History of the Book in America,* ed. David Paul Nord, Joan Shelley Rubin, and Michael Shudson (Chapel Hill: University of North Carolina Press, 2009), 200.
8. Louise S. Robbins, "Bringing the Mountain to Mohammed: The Franklin Book Programs and Cold War Cultural Diplomacy in the Middle East," unpublished paper, 4.
9. Emily S. Rosenberg, *Spreading the American Dream: American Economic and Cultural Expansion, 1890–1945* (New York: Hill and Wang, 1982), 7–8.
10. Frank Ninkovich, *Global Dawn: The Cultural Foundation of American Internationalism* (Cambridge: Harvard University Press, 2009), 9.
11. David Brody, *Visualizing American Empire: Orientalism and Imperialism in the Philippines* (Chicago: University of Chicago Press, 2010), 77.
12. Merle Curti and Kendall Birr, *Prelude to Point Four: American Technical Missions Overseas, 1838–1938* (Madison: University of Wisconsin Press, 1954), 22, 76.
13. Rosenberg, *Spreading,* 80.
14. Stephen Vaughn, *Holding Fast the Inner Lines: Democracy, Nationalism, and the Committee of Public Information* (Chapel Hill: University of North Carolina Press, 1980), 83.

15. Rosenberg, *Spreading*, 81.
16. Richard T. Arndt, *The First Resort of Kings: American Cultural Diplomacy in the Twentieth Century* (Washington, DC: Potomac, 2005), 40, 43.
17. Rosenberg, *Spreading*, 115, 121.
18. Akira Iriye, *Cultural Internationalism and World Order* (Baltimore: Johns Hopkins University Press, 1997), 92, 123.
19. Arndt, *First Resort*, 59, 68.
20. David Ekbladh, *The Great American Mission: Modernization and the Construction of an American World Order* (Princeton: Princeton University Press, 2010), 58, 69.
21. Dee Garrison, *Apostles of Culture: The Public Librarian and American Society, 1876–1920* (New York: Free Press, 1979), 42.
22. Thomas Augst, "Faith in Reading: Public Libraries, Liberalism, and the Civil Religion," in *Institutions of Reading: The Social Life of Libraries in the United States*, ed. Thomas Augst and Kenneth Carpenter (Amherst: University of Massachusetts Press, 2007), 174.
23. Merle Curti, *American Philanthropy Abroad: A History* (New Brunswick, NJ: Rutgers University Press, 1963), 303.
24. Maxine K. Rochester, "The Carnegie Corporation and South Africa: Non-European Library Services," *Libraries and Culture*, 24 (Winter 1999): 27–51.
25. For more on this program, see Yuan Zhou and Calvin Elliker, "From the People of the United States of America: The Books for China Programs during World War II," *Libraries and Culture* 32 (Spring 1997): 191–226.
26. Arndt, *First Resort*, 83.
27. John B. Hench, *Books as Weapons: Propaganda, Publishing, and the Battle for Global Markets in the Era of World War II* (Ithaca: Cornell University Press, 2010), 15.
28. "Pickups: Brief News of General Interest," *American Library Association Bulletin* 42 (May 1948): 237.
29. Kenneth Osgood, *Total Cold War: Eisenhower's Secret Propaganda Battle at Home and Abroad* (Lawrence: University Press of Kansas, 2006), 30.
30. Arndt, *First Resort*, 89.
31. Hench, *Books as Weapons*, 3.
32. John Tebbel, *A History of Book Publishing in the United States*, vol. 4, *The Great Change, 1940–1980* (New York: Bowker, 1981), 5.
33. Simon and Schuster and Pocket Books, press release, November 2, 1944, CBWR, box 14, folder 9.
34. Tebbel, *History of Book Publishing*, 24.
35. Clippings about Council on Books in Wartime, CBWR, box 41, folder 19.
36. Gary E. Kraske, *Missionaries of the Book: The American Library Profession and the Origins of United States Cultural Diplomacy* (Westport, CT: Greenwood, 1985), 44.
37. "Libraries and the War: A Statement of Library Policy," June 26, 1942, CBWR, box 4, folder 10.
38. Patti Clayton Becker, *Books and Libraries in American Society during World War II: Weapons in the War of Ideas* (New York: Routledge, 2005), 205.
39. Hench, *Books as Weapons*, 8, 94, 83–84, 132.
40. Philip Van Doren Stern, letter to Benjamin Stern, May 12, 1944, CBWR, box 33, folder 4.
41. Hench, *Books as Weapons*, 160, 181, 184, 189, 191, 195, 265.
42. Frank Ninkovich, *The Diplomacy of Ideas: US Foreign Policy and Cultural Relations, 1938–1950* (Cambridge: Cambridge University Press, 1981), 122.
43. U.S. Department of State, *Bulletin*, July 20, 1953, 79–80.
44. U.S. Advisory Commission on Educational Exchange, "Trading Ideas with the World: International Educational and Technical Exchange," March 31, 1949, 14, 20.
45. Osgood, *Total Cold War*, 39–40, 42.
46. Andrew J. Falk, *Upstaging the Cold War: American Dissent and Cultural Diplomacy, 1940–1960* (Amherst: University of Massachusetts Press, 2010), 147.

47. Gary D. Rawnsley, "The Campaign of Truth: A Populist Propaganda" in *Cold War Propaganda in the 1950s,* ed. Gary D. Rawnsley (Basingstoke, UK: Palgrave Macmillan, 1999), 32–33.
48. Ninkovich, *Diplomacy of Ideas,* 139.
49. Ibid., 120. See also Liping Bu, "Educational Exchange and Cultural Diplomacy in the Cold War," *Journal of American Studies* 33, no. 3 (1999): 394.
50. Robert A. Packenham, *Liberal America and the Third World* (Princeton: Princeton University Press, 1973), 43–44.
51. Rachel M. McCleary, *Global Compassion: Private Voluntary Organizations and U.S. Foreign Policy Since 1939* (New York: Oxford University Press, 2009), 78. See also Ekbladh, *Great American Mission,* 98.
52. Gilbert Rist, *The History of Development from Western Origins to Global Faith* (London: Zed, 1997), 71, 73, 77.
53. Michael Latham, *The Right Kind of Revolution: Modernization, Development, and U.S. Foreign Policy from the Cold War to the Present* (Ithaca: Cornell University Press, 2011), 10, 32.
54. For more on the committee, see Shawn J. Parry-Giles, "The Eisenhower Administration's Conceptualization of the USIA: The Development of Overt and Covert Propaganda Strategies," *Presidential Studies Quarterly* 24 (Spring 1994): 264.
55. Kenneth Osgood, "Form before Substance: Eisenhower's Commitment to Psychological Warfare and Negotiations with the Enemy," *Diplomatic History* 24 (Summer 2000): 405.
56. Kenneth Osgood, "Words and Deeds: Race, Colonialism, and Eisenhower's Propaganda War in the Third World," in *The Eisenhower Administration, the Third World, and the Globalization of the Cold War,* ed. Kathryn C. Statler and Andrew L. Johns (Lanham, MD: Rowman and Littlefield, 2006), 7.
57. Shawn J. Parry-Giles, "Propaganda, Effect, and the Cold War: Gauging the Status of America's 'War of Words,'" *Political Communication* 11 (April–June 1994): 204.
58. Edward W. Barrett, *Truth Is Our Weapon* (New York: Funk and Wagnalls, 1953), ix, x, 299.
59. Oren Stephens, *Facts to a Candid World: America's Overseas Information Program* (Stanford: Stanford University Press, 1955), 83.
60. Laura A. Belmonte, *Selling the American Way: U.S. Propaganda and the Cold War* (Philadelphia: University of Pennsylvania Press, 2008), 97, 105, 127, 50.
61. Nicholas J. Cull, *The Cold War and the United States Information Agency: American Propaganda and Public Diplomacy, 1945–1989* (New York: Cambridge University Press, 2008), 101.
62. Osgood, *Total Cold War,* 143.
63. Ibid., 107.
64. "News of the Week," *PW,* September 13, 1952, 1006.
65. Willard L. Thorp, "The Book Industry and Its Role in International Relations," *PW,* July 19, 1952, 202.
66. Arndt, *First Resort,* 156–57.
67. Cull, *Cold War,* 92.
68. Robert L. Johnson, policy statement on book and library program, U.S. Department of State, International Information Administration, Library of Congress Archives, MacLeish-Evans central file, box 871, photocopy provided to the author by Louise S. Robbins.
69. Wilson P. Dizard, *The Strategy of Truth: The Story of the U.S. Information Service* (Washington, DC: Public Affairs Press, 1961), 140.
70. Thorp, "The Book Industry," 203, 204.
71. "U.S. Translation Program Surveyed by Hodge," *PW,* March 22, 1952, 1377.
72. Thorp, "The Book Industry," 203.
73. U.S. State Department, memorandum [1952], FBPR, box 18, folder 1.
74. Theodore Waller, "Expanding the Book Audience," in *Books and the Mass Market,* by Harold K. Guinzburg, Robert W. Frase, and Theodore Waller (Urbana: University of Illinois Press, 1953), 59.

75. Tebbel, *History of Book Publishing*, 570.
76. Beth Luey, "The Organization of the Book Publishing Industry," in Nord, *History of the Book in America*, 32.
77. American Book Publishers Council, annual report, May 1, 1951–April 30, 1952, AAKR, box 563, folder 4.
78. William H. Mitchell, "Textbook Publishers Take Action on a Wide Range of Problems," *PW*, May 17, 1952, 2002.
79. Lester Asheim, "Report on the Conference on Reading Development," *Public Opinion Quarterly* 15 (Summer 1951): 315–16.
80. Allan McMahan, "Greatest Unsold Market in America Challenges Booksellers," *PW*, June 7, 1952, 2347–51, 2362.
81. "Why Reading Is Essential in a Democratic Society," *PW*, February 9, 1952, 807.
82. Tebbel, *History of Book Publishing*, 734.
83. Lacy and Frase, "The American Book Publishers' Council," 204; "News of the Week," *PW*, November 27, 1954, 2113.
84. "Programs to Help Schools Instill Love of Reading," *PW*, June 5, 1954, 2459.
85. "News of the Week," *PW*, September 11, 1954, 1118.
86. American Book Publishers Council, quarterly report, May–July 1955, AAKR, box 563, folder 4.
87. Peter S. Jennison, "How American Books Reach Readers Abroad," *Library Trends* 5 (July 1956): 7–8.
88. American Book Publishers Council, annual report.
89. Dan Lacy, "The Overseas Book Program," *Library Quarterly* 24 (April 1954): 189–90.
90. Waller, "Expanding the Book Audience," 61.
91. American Book Publishers Council, summary of proceedings, annual meeting, May 12–13, 1955, 2, AAKR, box 563, folder 4.
92. Jean Preer, "'Wake Up and Read!' Book Promotion and National Library Week, 1958," *Libraries and the Cultural Record* 45, no. 1 (2010): 92.
93. Harold K. Guinzburg, "Free Press, Free Enterprise, and Diversity," in Guinzburg et al., *Books and the Mass Market*, 1–2, 18.
94. Waller, "Expanding the Book Audience," 66.
95. Preer, "Wake Up," 95.
96. Louise S. Robbins, *Censorship and the American Library: The American Library Association's Response to Threats to Intellectual Freedom, 1939–1969* (Westport, CT: Greenwood, 1996), 189.
97. American Library Association and American Book Publishers Council, proceedings of the Conference on the Freedom to Read, May 2–3, 1953, Library of Congress Archives, Manuscript Division, photocopy provided to the author by Louise S. Robbins.
98. Dan Lacy, "Aid to National Policy," *Library Trends* 2 (July 1953): 155, 168.
99. Dan Lacy, "Freedom and Books," *Southeastern Librarian* 4 (Spring 1954): 14.
100. American Book Publishers Council, censorship bulletin, December 1955, AAKR, box 566, folder 8.
101. For a general history of UNESCO, see Michel Contil Lacoste, *The Story of a Grand Design: UNESCO, 1946–1993* (Paris: UNESCO Publishing, 1994). For a specific discussion of the role of libraries in UNESCO, see Amanda Laugesen, "UNESCO and the Globalization of the Public Library Idea," *Library and Information History* 30, no. 1 (2014): 1–19.
102. R. A. Coate, *Unilateralism, Ideology, and U.S. Foreign Policy: The United States in and out of UNESCO* (Boulder, CO: Rienner, 1988), 29.
103. Lacoste, *Story of a Grand Design*, 37.
104. U.N. Educational, Scientific, and Cultural Organization, "Agreement on the Importation of Educational, Scientific, and Cultural Materials, with Annexes A to E and Protocol Annexed 1950," Florence, Italy, June 17, 1950, http://portal.unesco.org.

105. Phillip W. Jones, *International Policies for Third World Education: UNESCO, Literacy, and Development* (London: Routledge, 1988), 47, 50.
106. Interview with Datus Smith, *Wilson Library Bulletin* (February 1966), 532, FBPR, box 47, folder 3.
107. Datus Smith, letter to his parents, January 3, 1930, and letter to his parents, April 21, 1930, both in Dorothy Hunt Smith, ed., *Journey with Joy: Letters from Datus C. Smith Jr.* (Princeton, 1972).
108. Melanie McAlister, *Epic Encounters: Culture, Media and U.S. Interests in the Middle East, 1945–2000* (Berkeley: University of California Press, 2001), 35.
109. Datus Smith, letter to family and friends, October 10, 1954, in Smith, *Journey with Joy*, 94.
110. Tebbel, *History of Book Publishing*, 648.
111. Julian P. Boyd, "Foreword," in *Putting Knowledge to Work, 1942–1952: A Tribute to Datus C. Smith Jr. on the Occasion of His Tenth Anniversary as Director of Princeton University Press* (Princeton: Princeton University Press, 1952), 11.
112. "You Meet Such Interesting People," *PW*, October 31, 1953, 1843. In an oral history interview, Stephen Paterson Belcher suggested that Smith had worked for the CIA in Iran and India ("translating name scholars") before taking up his work for Franklin. However, there is no other evidence supporting this claim. It is possible that Princeton University Press received some subsidies for publishing certain texts, although I have seen no evidence (interview with Stephen Paterson Belcher, September 29, 1988, Association for Diplomatic Studies and Training, Foreign Affairs Oral History Project, Information Series, Library of Congress, https://www.loc.gov).
113. Datus Smith, letter to Franklin Publications head office staff, April 19, 1953, FBPR, box 157, folder 9.
114. Datus Smith, letter to Franklin Publications head office staff, April 12, 1953, FBPR, box 157, folder 9.
115. Victor Weybright, *The Making of a Publisher: A Life in the 20th Century Book Revolution* (London: Weidenfeld and Nicolson, 1966), 251.
116. Smith regularly spoke before meetings of the American Book Publishers Council, the American Association of University Presses, and the American Textbook Publishers Institute. See *PW* through the 1950s and 1960s.
117. Datus Smith, "Thoughts about Franklin Publications Inc.," June 7, 1952, FBPR, box 5, folder 7.
118. Datus Smith, "Policy Memorandum for Franklin," September 18, 1952, FBPR, box 3, folder 5.
119. Smith, "Thoughts."
120. Don Cameron, letter to Datus Smith, August 22, 1952, FBPR, box 61, folder 1.
121. Smith, "Thoughts."
122. Smith, letter to family and friends, October 10, 1954.
123. For a sense of the industry at the time Franklin was operating, see Al Silverman, *The Time of Their Lives: The Golden Age of Great American Publishers, Their Editors, and Authors* (New York: St. Martin's, 2008).
124. Arthur S. Adams, letter to George P. Brett, June 13, 1952, FBPR, box 6, folder 1.
125. Douglas M. Black, letter to Datus Smith, June 24, 1952, FBPR, box 6, folder 21.
126. Joseph E. Johnson, letter to Datus Smith, October 3, 1952, FBPR, box 23, folder 8.
127. Weybright, *Making*, 172, 197, 200, 236, 251.
128. "You Meet Such Interesting People," *PW*, March 21, 1953, 1377.
129. Guinzburg et al., *Books and the Mass Market*, viii.
130. "Obituary Notes," *PW*, March 10, 1958, 41.
131. Tebbel, *History of Book Publishing*, 578.
132. "George P. Brett is Dead at 91; Headed Macmillan Company," *New York Times*, February 15, 1984.

133. "You Meet Such Interesting People," *PW,* July 9, 1955, 118. Pratt met his wife, Therese Louis, while in Beirut on Franklin business.
134. Tebbel, *History of Book Publishing,* 26.
135. "You Meet Such Interesting People," *PW,* July 12, 1952, 133.
136. American Book Publishers Council, progress report, December 11, 1952, AAKR, box 128, folder 10.
137. Guinzburg et al., *Books and the Mass Market,* vi.
138. "You Meet Such Interesting People," *PW,* April 11, 1953, 1616.
139. Malcolm Johnson, letter to Datus Smith, July 11, 1952, FBPR, box 10, folder 1.
140. Smith, "Policy Memorandum."
141. Form letter enclosure in Don Cameron, letter to William A. Koshland, November 27, 1953, AAKR, box 128, folder 2.

Chapter 2. Book Diplomacy in the Middle East

1. Steven Z. Freiberger, *Dawn over Suez: The Rise of American Power in the Middle East, 1953–1957* (Chicago: Dee, 1992), 52.
2. Michael Latham, *The Right Kind of Revolution: Modernization, Development, and U.S. Foreign Policy from the Cold War to the Present* (Ithaca: Cornell University Press, 2011), 79.
3. Douglas Little, "The Cold War in the Middle East: Suez Crisis to Camp David Accords," in *The Cambridge History of the Cold War,* vol. 2, *Crises and Détente,* ed. Melvyn P. Leffler and Odd Arne Westad (New York: Cambridge University Press, 2010), 325.
4. Freiberger, *Dawn over Suez,* 39.
5. Kenneth Osgood, *Total Cold War: Eisenhower's Secret Propaganda Battle at Home and Abroad* (Lawrence: University Press of Kansas, 2006), 131, 143.
6. Dan Lacy, letter to Datus Smith, September 5, 1952, FBPR, box 10, folder 12.
7. Don Cameron, letter to Datus Smith, August 22, 1952, FBPR, box 61, folder 1.
8. Datus Smith, letter to Dan Lacy, September 29, 1952, FBPR, box 10, folder 12.
9. Datus Smith, letter to Harry M. Snyder, October 6, 1952, FBPR, box 10, folder 12.
10. Datus Smith, letter to Malcolm Johnson, October 6, 1952, FBPR, box 10, folder 12.
11. For a discussion of Aramco's approach in Saudi Arabia, see Chad H. Parker, *Making the Desert Modern: Americans, Arabs, and Oil on the Saudi Frontier, 1933–73* (Amherst: University of Massachusetts Press, 2015).
12. Datus Smith, letter to Dan Lacy, November 3, 1952, FBPR, box 10, folder 12.
13. "News of the Week," *PW,* November 15, 1952, 2021.
14. U.S. Senate, Foreign Relations Committee, *Hearings of the Subcommittee on Overseas Information Programs of the United States,* 82nd Cong., 2nd sess., November 20–21, 1952, 319.
15. Datus Smith, "Report and Recommendations by Datus C. Smith Jr.," January 11, 1953, FBPR, box 3, folder 5.
16. Ibid.
17. Salib Botros, "Problems of Book Development in the Arab World with Special Reference to Egypt," *Library Trends* 26 (Spring 1978): 567; Nadia A. Rizk, "The Book-Publishing Industry in Egypt," *Library Trends* 26 (Spring 1978): 554.
18. Smith, "Report and Recommendations."
19. Datus Smith, "Summary of the Report Presented at the Meeting of the Board of Directors," October 8, 1952, FBPR, box 5, folder 7; Smith, "American Books in the Middle East," *Library Trends* 5 (July 1956): 45.
20. Smith, "Report and Recommendations."
21. Lewis Awad, "Advisory Memorandum for Franklin Publications," FBPR, box 92, folder 10.
22. Franklin Publications, minutes, executive committee meeting, February 19, 1953, FBPR, box 2, folder 2.

23. Datus Smith, letter to Franklin Publications board of directors, March 12, 1953, FBPR, box 3, folder 5. See also Stephen Paterson Belcher, interview, September 29, 1988, Association for Diplomatic Studies and Training Foreign Affairs, Oral History Project, Information Series, Library of Congress, https://www.loc.gov.
24. Smith, letter to Franklin board of directors, March 12, 1953.
25. Datus Smith, memorandum to Franklin Publications executive committee, February 16, 1953, FBPR, box 3, folder 5.
26. Datus Smith, "Developments in the Middle East," June 17, 1953, FBPR, box 5, folder 7.
27. Datus Smith, letter to Hassan al-Aroussy, February 13, 1953, FBPR, box 91, folder 4.
28. Hassan al-Aroussy, letter to Datus Smith, February 20, 1953, FBPR, box 91, folder 4.
29. Datus Smith, "Progress Report from Cairo," April 19, 1953, FBPR, box 3, folder 5.
30. Smith, letter to al-Aroussy, February 13, 1953.
31. Datus Smith, letter to Richard A. Humphrey, March 17, 1953, FBPR, box 68, folder 12.
32. Smith, "Progress Report."
33. Ibid.
34. Datus Smith, letter to Malcolm Johnson, May 1, 1954, FBPR, box 10, folder 1.
35. Smith, "Developments."
36. Smith, letter to al-Aroussy, February 13, 1953.
37. Smith, "Developments."
38. C. Mitry, letter to Hassan al-Aroussy, July 30, 1954, FBPR, box 99, folder 5.
39. Dar al-Maaref, advertisement, *Al Barida*, November 16, 1953, FBPR, box 99, folder 5.
40. Smith, "Developments."
41. "Pricing Policy for Franklin-Sponsored Books," February 23, 1955, FBPR, box 68, folder 1.
42. "American Books in the Middle East," September 1955, FBPR, box 38, folder 2.
43. Smith, "American Books in the Middle East," 56.
44. Franklin Publications, minutes, board of directors' meeting, September 24, 1953, 4, FBPR, box 1, folder 5.
45. Smith, "Report and Recommendations," 11.
46. "Correction for Page 11 of Memo of January 11 Report and Recommendations," January 15, 1953, FBPR, box 3, folder 5.
47. George P. Brett, letter to Datus Smith and Malcolm Johnson, January 20, 1953, FBPR, box 7, folder 6.
48. Datus Smith, letter to George P. Brett, January 21, 1953, FBPR, box 7, folder 6.
49. "Book Publishing in the Near East," NARA, RG306, box 6, Office of Research—"R" Reports 1960–1963, R70–61.
50. Malcolm Johnson, letter to Datus Smith, January 27, 1953, FBPR, box 10, folder 1.
51. Smith, memorandum to Franklin executive committee, February 16, 1953.
52. Don Cameron, letter to Franklin Publications executive committee, April 28, 1953, FBPR, box 3, folder 5.
53. Datus Smith, memorandum to Franklin Publications editors and staff, August 17, 1953, FBPR, box 222, folder 15.
54. Memorandum of agreement between Alfred A. Knopf, Publishers, and Franklin Publications, May 5, 1955, AAKR, box 167, folder 3.
55. Don Cameron, letter to William A. Koshland, November 27, 1953, AAKR, box 128, folder 2.
56. Don Cameron, letter to William A. Koshland, December 2, 1954, AAKR, box 150, folder 1.
57. Don Cameron, letter to Franklin Publications executive committee [c. 1956], FBPR, box 3, folder 4.
58. Memorandum of agreement between Knopf and Franklin, May 5, 1955.
59. Francis St. John, report on conference in Damascus, November 17, 1952, FBPR, box 149, folder 9.
60. Smith, "Developments."

61. "ATPI Annual Meeting: Publishing in an Era of Educational Expansion," *PW,* May 18, 1959, 22.
62. Jens Hanssen, "Translating Revolution: Hannah Arendt in Arab Political Culture," November 2013, http://www.hannaharendt.net/.
63. "Facts about Franklin Publications," November 1, 1956, FBPR, box 70, folder 3.
64. "Impact on Local Countries," January 7, 1957, FBPR, box 15, folder 9.
65. Hassan al-Aroussy, letter to Datus Smith, January 13, 1954, FBPR, box 92, folder 9.
66. Datus Smith, letter no. 29 [from Karachi], excerpt from trip report, May 9, 1954, FBPR, box 92, folder 9.
67. English translation of "Franklin Publications Inc. and Cultural Activity in the Arab World," *Al-Adab,* May 1955, FBPR, box 16, folder 10.
68. Today *Dawood* is more commonly transliterated as *Daoud.*
69. English translation of Samy Dawood, "We Are No Enemies of Culture," *Al-Gomhoria* October 27, 1955, FBPR, box 3, folder 4.
70. English translation of Ameed al-Imam, "Danger to Our Culture," *Al-Gomhoria,* October 30, 1955, FBPR, box 3, folder 4.
71. Dawood, "We Are Not Enemies."
72. English translation of Hassan al-Aroussy, "I Am an Enemy of Culture," *Al-Gomhoria,* November 2, 1955, FBPR, box 3, folder 4.
73. Matthew F. Jacobs, "The Perils and Promise of Islam: The United States and the Muslim Middle East in the Early Cold War," *Diplomatic History* 30 (September 2006): 712. For a contemporaneous perspective on the Middle East, see Daniel Lerner, *The Passing of Traditional Society: Modernizing the Middle East* (Glencoe, IL: Free Press, 1962 [1958]).
74. Jacobs, "Perils and Promise," 730.
75. "American Books in the Middle East."
76. Smith, "Progress Report." The emphasis is Smith's.
77. Smith, letter to Johnson, May 1, 1954.
78. Datus Smith, letter to Franklin Burdette, August 10, 1954, FBPR, box 66, folder 10.
79. Smith, letter to Johnson, May 1, 1954.
80. Don Cameron, letter to Franklin executive committee, including excerpts from the letters of Datus Smith, April 30, 1954, FBPR, box 158, folder 1.
81. Smith, "American Books in the Middle East," 52.

Chapter 3. A World of Books, an Empire of Books

1. On how maps helped Americans envision the world during the Cold War, see Timothy Burney, *Mapping the Cold War: Cartography and the Framing of America's International Power* (Chapel Hill: University of North Carolina Press, 2015).
2. Datus Smith, "Annual Report and Comment on Operations," September 4, 1956, FBPR, box 5, folder 5.
3. Datus Smith, report, September 15, 1959, FBPR, box 15, folder 8.
4. Franklin Publications, "Impact on Local Countries," January 7, 1957, FBPR, box 15, folder 9.
5. Datus Smith, "Report on Operations in Fiscal 1957," September 5, 1957, FBPR, box 5, folder 5.
6. Bill Spaulding, "Report for Board of Directors," November 19, 1957, FBPR, box 5, folder 5.
7. Franklin Publications, minutes, board of directors' meeting, September 24, 1953, FBPR, box 1, folder 5.
8. Franklin Publications, "Overseas Chinese," April 5, 1954, FBPR, box 66, folder 10.
9. R. M. McCarthy, memorandum to Datus Smith and Malcolm Johnson, January 31, 1955, FBPR, box 88, folder 9.
10. Don Cameron, letter to Malcolm Johnson, January 19, 1954, FBPR, box 10, folder 1.

11. Franklin Publications, "Projects for Future Development," August 15, 1954, FBPR, box 5, folder 7.
12. Datus Smith, letter to Henry A. Laughlin, May 10, 1960, FBPR, box 10, folder 14.
13. Datus Smith, letter to Franklin Publications executive committee, March 30, 1960, FBPR, box 3, folder 4.
14. Datus Smith, report, April 23, 1959, FBPR, box 158, folder 9.
15. Donald N. Wilber, memorandum, September 23, 1953, FBPR, box 120, folder 9.
16. Nikki R. Keddie, *Modern Iran: Roots and Results of Revolution* (New Haven: Yale University Press, 2003), 121, 125.
17. Parisa Khosravi, "Homayoun Sanatizadeh, a Well Known Writer and Translator of Mary Boyce's Books, Died," *Amordad*, September 14, 2009, http://www.amordaden.blogfa.com.
18. Michael Griffin, "Road to Damask," *Middle East*, July 1, 2006.
19. Datus Smith, letter to C. Robert Payne, February 15, 1956, FBPR, box 69, folder 4.
20. Homayoun Sanati, autobiographical essay, ca. 1953, FBPR, box 121, folder 6.
21. Smith, letter to Payne, February 15, 1956.
22. Franklin Publications, minutes, board of directors' meeting, March 4, 1954, FBPR, box 1, folder 5.
23. Wilson Dizard, memorandum, March 29, 1955, enclosed in Franklin Burdette, letter to Smith, April 19, 1955, FBPR, box 66, folder 9.
24. U.S. Information Agency, "Franklin Publications in Tehran," January 14, 1955, enclosed in Datus Smith, letter to Malcolm Johnson, August 17, 1955, FBPR, box 66, folder 19.
25. Roby C. Barrett, *The Greater Middle East and the Cold War: U.S. Foreign Policy under Eisenhower and Kennedy* (London: Tauris, 2007), 93. See also Mark T. Berger, *The Battle for Asia: From Decolonization to Globalization* (London: Routledge, 2004), 67.
26. Kenneth Osgood, *Total Cold War: Eisenhower's Secret Propaganda Battle at Home and Abroad* (Lawrence: University Press of Kansas, 2006), 136.
27. Franklin Publications, minutes, board of directors' meeting, March 4, 1954, FBPR, box 1, folder 5.
28. Franklin Publications, translation of book reviews, May 15, 1957, FBPR, box 187, folder 18.
29. Hamid Ali Khan, letter to Datus Smith, September 24, 1956, FBPR, box 205, folder 7.
30. Smith, "Report on Operations in Fiscal 1957."
31. Datus Smith and Charles Griffith, "Report on East Pakistan," January 17, 1955, FBPR, box 66, folder 9.
32. Franklin Publications, memorandum, December 5, 1955, FBPR, box 222, folder 24.
33. Franklin Burdette, letter to Datus Smith, May 26, 1955, FBPR, box 66, folder 9.
34. Franklin Publications, excerpts from several of Datus Smith's letters, February 25, 1960, FBPR, box 10, folder 14.
35. Datus Smith, letter to Malcolm Johnson, January 8, 1954, FBPR, box 10, folder 1.
36. Datus Smith, letter to Franklin Publications, December 16, 1953, in *Journey with Joy: Letters from Datus C. Smith Jr.*, ed. Dorothy Hunt Smith (Princeton, 1972), 88.
37. Richard Taplinger, "Asians Want American Books—and Aren't Getting Them," *PW*, August 27, 1955, 781.
38. "News of the Week," *PW*, April 30, 1955, 2011.
39. Robert E. Banker, "Asia Can Be a New Market for American Books: Part 2," *PW*, August 27, 1955, 788.
40. "Pakistan Will Hold Exhibit of American Books in December," *PW*, August 6, 1955, 523.
41. Alvin Grauber, "Indonesia—a New Market for American Books: Part 2," *PW*, August 9, 1952, 616–19.
42. Franklin Publications, minutes, board of directors' meeting, March 4, 1954, FBPR, box 1, folder 5.
43. Franklin Publications, "American Books in Southeast Asia," September 1955, FBPR, box 38, folder 2.

44. Andrew Roadnight, *United States Policy Towards Indonesia in the Truman and Eisenhower Years* (Houndmills, UK: Palgrave Macmillan, 2002), ix.
45. Franklin Publications, "American Books in Southeast Asia."
46. "News of the Week," *PW,* November 5, 1956, 2116.
47. "Varied Picture of Foreign Trade," *PW,* July 1, 1957, 16.
48. Charles Griffith, Francis St. John, and Datus Smith, "Indonesia: Report and Recommendations," January 26, 1954, FBPR, box 109, folder 6.
49. Tod Jones, "Indonesian Cultural Policy, 1950–2003: Culture, Institutions, Government" (PhD diss., Curtin University of Technology, Perth, 2005), 65, 72; Charles Griffith, "American Books in South-East Asia," *Library Trends* 5 (July 1956): 136.
50. Griffith et al., "Indonesia."
51. Jones, "Indonesian Cultural Policy," 60, 70.
52. Griffith, "American Books in Southeast Asia," 121.
53. "News of the Week," *PW,* October 1, 1956, 1696.
54. Robert E. Banker, "Asia Can Be a New Market for American Books: Part 1," *PW,* August 20, 1955, 702.
55. Datus Smith, letter to Franklin Publications, January 21, 1954, in Smith, *Journey with Joy,* 89.
56. Franklin Publications, "Projects for Future Development."
57. Datus Smith, "Proposal for Indonesia," September 17, 1954, FBPR, box 66, folder 10.
58. Hassan Shadily, letter to Don Cameron, January 21, 1959, and unnamed publisher, letter to Don Cameron, September 16, 1959, both in FBPR, box 193, folder 30.
59. Datus Smith, "General Information for Board of Directors," January 12, 1956, FBPR, box 5, folder 5.
60. Griffith, "American Books in Southeast Asia," 137.
61. Datus Smith, letter to Louis Fanget, February 12, 1958, FBPR, box 67, folder 4.
62. Datus Smith, letter to Dorothy Smith, July 23, 1955, in Smith, *Journey with Joy,* 103.
63. Datus Smith and Malcolm Johnson, "Report on Indonesia," 1–2, June 27, 1955, FBPR, box 109, folder 6.
64. Smith, "Report on Operations in Fiscal 1957."
65. Smith, "Annual Report and Comment on Operations."
66. Jones, "Indonesian Cultural Policy," 116.
67. Roadnight, *United States Policy Towards Indonesia,* 102.
68. Datus Smith, "Baghdad and Beirut Offices," July 19, 1956, FBPR, box 66, folder 8.
69. Franklin Publications, minutes, board of directors' meeting, January 10, 1957, FBPR, box 1, folder 5.
70. Smith, "Annual Report and Comment on Operations"; Franklin Publications, annual report for fiscal year 1964–65, 24, FBPR, box 15, folder 7.
71. Franklin Publications, "An Iraqi Book Industry," November 13, 1958, FBPR, box 123, folder 16.
72. Dana Pratt, letter to Datus Smith, October 24, 1958, FBPR, box 157, folder 3.
73. See documents in FBPR, box 123, folder 10; Franklin Publications, "Franklin in the Middle East," July 10, 1967, FBPR, box 5, folder 1.
74. Franklin Publications, annual report for fiscal year 1960–61, 8.
75. Franklin Publications, minutes, board of directors' meeting, October 12, 1962, FBPR, box 1, folder 4.
76. Franklin Publications, annual report for fiscal year 1964–65, 26.
77. Franklin Publications, "Facts about Franklin Publications," November 1, 1956, FBPR, box 70, folder 3.
78. "The Records of Translation Show More Are Needed," *PW,* April 26, 1952, 1771.
79. "The Mounting Importance of Translations," *PW,* November 4, 1957, 38.
80. Ana Ban, "Books in Translation in the United States," *Publishing Research Quarterly* 31 (September 2015): 160.

81. Smith, "Projects for Future Development."
82. Dariush Homayoun, letter to Don Cameron, December 19, 1965, FBPR, box 73, folder 11.
83. Franklin Publications, "Report on Examination of Book," and "Instructions to Translators and Revisers," FBPR, box 99, folder 12.
84. S. A. Rehman, manuscript of preface, January 3, 1957, FBPR, box 5, folder 5.
85. Franklin Publications, "Local Participation by Civic and Intellectual Leaders," January 2, 1958, FBPR, box 5, folder 4.
86. J. M. Filstrup, "Franklin Book Programs/Tehran," *International Library Review* 8, no. 4 (1976): 434.
87. Franklin Publications, "Local Participation."
88. Filstrup, "Franklin Book Programs," 437.
89. Richard F. Shepard, "U.S. Books Leading in Translation," *New York Times,* May 28, 1965.
90. "News of the Week," *PW,* November 5, 1956, 2118.
91. Franklin Publications, memorandum, April 3, 1953, FBPR, box 194, folder 2.
92. Introduction to Urdu edition, FBPR, box 194, folder 5.
93. Franklin Publications, "Local Participation."
94. Filstrup, "Franklin Book Program," 434.
95. Franklin Publications, memorandum, March 2, 1953, FBPR, box 193, folder 33.
96. See documents in FBPR, box 193, folder 33.
97. Datus Smith, letter to Franklin Publications, April 2, 1953, FBPR, box 157, folder 9.
98. Datus Smith, "Progress Report from Cairo," April 19, 1953, FBPR, box 3, folder 5.
99. Datus Smith, letter to Dorothy Smith, November 2, 1953, in Smith, *Journey with Joy,* 85.
100. "Progress Report from Franklin Publications, Inc.," *PW,* October 31, 1953, 1829.
101. Don Cameron, letter to Franklin Publications board of directors, October 21, 1953, FBPR, box 5, folder 7.
102. Datus Smith, letter to Franklin Publications board of directors, June 2, 1955, FBPR, box 5, folder 6.
103. "New Developments in the Persian Book Trade," *PW,* April 28, 1956, 1878.
104. Don Cameron, letter to William A. Koshland, April 21, 1955, AAKR, box 167, folder 13.
105. Franklin Publications, report, November–December 1961, FBPR, box 98, folder 5.
106. Shepard, "U.S. Books."
107. Najaf Darybandari, letter to Datus Smith, July 14, 1965, FBPR, box 239, folder 10.
108. Don Cameron, letter to Gerard Piel, September 13, 1963, AAKR, box 396, folder 10.
109. Hamid Ali Khan, "Address," January 1963, FBPR, box 144, folder 3.
110. Douglas W. Bryant, "Summary of Round Table Discussions—National Book Committee, Conference on American Books Abroad," October 1955, FBPR, box 38, folder 1.
111. Charles Griffith, letter to Barratt O'Hara, December 19, 1955, FBPR, box 47, folder 23.
112. Victor Weybright, *The Making of a Publisher: A Life in the 20th Century Book Revolution* (London: Weidenfeld and Nicolson, 1966), 251.
113. Stephens Mitchell, letters to Don Cameron, March 21, 1955, and February 20, 1959, FBPR, box 225, folder 38.
114. Datus Smith, letter to A. T. M. Abdul Mateen, April 9, 1959, FBPR, box 225, folder 38.
115. Hassan al-Aroussy, letter to Datus Smith, January 21, 1955, FBPR, box 225, folder 38.
116. Smith, letter to Mateen, April 9, 1959.
117. Helen Cantwell, letter to William A. Koshland, July 26, 1957, AAKR, box 206, folder 12.
118. William A. Koshland, letter to Don Cameron, May 12, 1959, AAKR, box 255, folder 8.
119. M. Elizabeth McNaull, letter to William A. Koshland, January 28, 1954, AAKR, box 160, folder 2.
120. Don Cameron, letter to William A. Koshland, May 5, 1955, and William A. Koshland, letter to Don Cameron, May 23, 1955, AAKR, box 167, folder 13.
121. M. Elizabeth McNaull, letter to William A. Koshland, May 20, 1955, AAKR, box 177, folder 1.

122. Alfred A. Knopf, letter to Arthur Larson, May 1, 1957, AAKR, box 222, folder 2. On Knopf's relationship with the U.S. government during this period, see Amanda Laugesen, "American Publishers, Books, and the Global Cultural Cold War: Alfred A. Knopf Inc. and the United States Information Agency, 1953–1970," *Australasian Journal of American Studies* 35, no. 2 (2016), 19–38.
123. "ABPC: Trends of Book Sales in Major Marketing Areas," *PW,* June 1, 1959, 25.
124. Alfred A. Knopf, letter to John J. Rooney, April 28, 1959, AAKR, box 504, folder 10. He sent the same letter to Frank Bow, Elford A. Cederberg, Glenard P. Lipscomb, Don Magnuson, Prince H. Preston, and Robert L. F. Sikes.
125. Curtis G. Benjamin, "One Battle We're Losing—and Why," AAKR, box 504, folder 10.
126. William J. Lederer and Eugene Burdick, *The Ugly American* (New York: Norton, 1999 [1958]), intro., 284.
127. Datus Smith, letter to Storer Lunt, October 2, 1958, FBPR, box 10, folder 17.
128. Datus Smith, letter to Malcolm Johnson, March 12, 1954, FBPR, box 10, folder 1.
129. Datus Smith, letter to Franklin Burdette, March 23, 1954, FBPR, box 66, folder 10.
130. Malcolm Johnson, letter to Datus Smith, July 30, 1952, FBPR, box 10, folder 1.
131. Datus Smith, letter to Malcolm Johnson, January 11, 1956, FBPR, box 9, folder 17.
132. Richard Humphrey, letter to Datus Smith, February 6, 1953, FBPR, box 68, folder 12.
133. Datus Smith, letter to Franklin Burdette, September 23, 1954, FBPR, box 66, folder 10.
134. Franklin Publications, minutes, board of directors' meeting, December 9, 1954, FBPR, box 1, folder 5.
135. Theodore Streibert, letter to Malcolm Johnson, December 30, 1954, FBPR, box 71, folder 9.
136. Datus Smith, letter to Malcolm Johnson, March 17, 1955, FBPR, box 9, folder 17.
137. Franklin Publications, minutes, board of directors' meeting, March 24, 1955, FBPR, box 1, folder 5.
138. Franklin Burdette, letter to Datus Smith, March 21, 1955, FBPR, box 5, folder 6.
139. Datus Smith, letter to Claude Hawley, March 30, 1955, FBPR, box 68, folder 8.
140. Datus Smith, "Background Information on Title Selection," April 11, 1955, FBPR, box 16, folder 10.
141. Datus Smith, letter to Claude Hawley, August 22, 1955, FBPR, box 16, folder 9.
142. U.S. Information Agency, minutes, February 10, 1956, NARA, RG306, USIA records of the Advisory Commission on Information, box 1, folder "Cultural Information Advisory Committee."
143. Datus Smith, letter to Malcolm Johnson, October 6, 1956, FBPR, box 9, folder 17.
144. Malcolm Johnson, letter to Datus Smith, November 14, 1956, FBPR, box 9, folder 16.
145. U.S. Information Agency, minutes, February 10, 1956.
146. U.S. Information Agency, minutes, November 15, 1956, NARA, RG306, USIA records of the Advisory Commission on Information, box 1, folder "Cultural Information Advisory Committee."
147. Richard T. Arndt, *The First Resort of Kings: American Cultural Diplomacy in the Twentieth Century* (Washington: Potomac, 2005), 128–30, 275, 318.
148. U.S. Information Agency, minutes, March 28, 1957, NARA, RG306, USIA records of the Advisory Commission on Information, box 1, folder "Cultural Information Advisory Committee."
149. Datus Smith, letter to Bill Spaulding, August 17, 1958, FBPR, box 65, folder 16. Dorothy Hunt Smith, in her collection of letters to and from Datus Smith, published as *Journey with Joy,* writes that Franklin's work involved considerable secrecy—from burning scrap paper, to making calls from pay phones, to not being open about Smith's activities in general conversation. "It was nevertheless," she noted, "glorious fun." (139–40)
150. Filstrup, "Franklin Book Program," 432.
151. Datus Smith, letter to James Halsema, July 5, 1961, FBPR, box 94, folder 7.
152. Wilson Dizard, *The Strategy of Truth: The Story of the U.S. Information Service* (Washington, DC: Public Affairs Press, 1961), 149.

153. U.S. Information Agency, minutes, November 22, 1954, NARA, RG306, USIA records of the Advisory Commission on Information, box 1, folder "Cultural Information Advisory Committee."
154. U.S. Information Agency, minutes, October 4, 1956, NARA, RG306, USIA records of the Advisory Commission on Information, box 1, folder "Cultural Information Advisory Committee."
155. U.S. Information Agency, minutes, November 15, 1956.
156. U.S. Information Agency, "Books Published Abroad," July 1, 1957–June 30, 1958, NARA, RG306, USIA book program records, 1966–99, box 2.
157. U.S. Information Agency, "Books Published Abroad," July 1, 1958–June 30, 1959, NARA, RG306, USIA book program records, 1966–99, box 2.
158. U.S. Information Agency, memorandum, June 29, 1955, NARA, RG306, USIA records of the Advisory Commission on Information, box 1, folder "Cultural Information Advisory Committee."
159. American Book Publishers Council, memorandum, September 5, 1961, FBPR, box 18, folder 12; Alfred A. Knopf, letter to Arthur Larson, May 1, 1957, AAKR, box 222, folder 2.
160. Datus Smith, "The Issues Facing Franklin," February 1, 1962, FBPR, box 5, folder 3.
161. Franklin Publications, minutes, board of directors' meeting, October 21, 1959, FBPR, box 1, folder 5.
162. Datus Smith, "Bowker Lecture: Moral Issues of U.S. Books in the Non-Western World," *PW*, April 14, 1958, 26.
163. "Report on National Book Committee's Conference on U.S. Books Abroad," *PW*, November 25, 1957, 22.
164. "Spaulding's Report on Franklin: 'It Is Succeeding Beyond Belief,'" *PW*, March 24, 1958, 27.
165. Franklin Publications, "Facts about Franklin Publications."

Chapter 4. Book Work as Modernization

1. Franklin Publications, excerpts from several of Datus Smith's letters, February 25, 1960, FBPR, box 10, folder 14.
2. Franklin Publications, "Plan for Worldwide Development," January 29, 1962, FBPR, box 5, folder 3.
3. Franklin Publications, "Topics for Discussion," July 2, 1964, FBPR, box 3, folder 7.
4. Datus Smith, "The Bright Promise of Publishing in Developing Countries," *Annals of the American Academy of Political and Social Science* 421 (September 1975): 132.
5. Datus Smith, letter to Franklin Publications executive committee, January 11, 1962, FBPR, box 3, folder 4.
6. "Currents," *PW*, April 17, 1961, 23.
7. U.S. Information Agency, audit report circulated to Franklin Publications board of directors, October 16, 1963, FBPR, box 5, folder 2.
8. Franklin Publications, "Topics for Discussion."
9. Roby C. Barrett, *The Greater Middle East and the Cold War: U.S. Foreign Policy under Eisenhower and Kennedy* (London: Tauris, 2007), 191.
10. Bradley R. Simpson, *Economists with Guns: Authoritarian Development and U.S.-Indonesian Relations, 1960–1968* (Stanford: Stanford University Press, 2008), 73.
11. Phillip W. Jones, *International Policies for Third World Education: UNESCO, Literacy, and Development* (London: Routledge, 1988), 106, 111, 140.
12. Robert Jervis, "Identity and the Cold War," in *The Cambridge History of the Cold War*, vol. 2, *Crises and Détente*, ed. Melvyn P. Leffler and Odd Arne Westad (New York: Cambridge University Press, 2010), 24, 35.
13. Thomas Robertson, "Cold War Landscapes: Towards an Environmental History of U.S. Development Programmes in the 1950s and 1960s," *Cold War History* 16, no. 4 (2015): 417–41.

14. Michael Latham, *The Right Kind of Revolution: Modernization, Development, and U.S. Foreign Policy from the Cold War to the Present* (Ithaca: Cornell University Press, 2011), 3, 7.
15. Nils Gilman, *Mandarins of the Future: Modernization Theory in Cold War America* (Baltimore: Johns Hopkins University Press, 2003), 3.
16. Michael Adas, "Modernization Theory and the American Revival of the Scientific and Technological Standards of Social Achievement and Human Worth," in *Staging Growth: Modernization, Development, and the Global Cold War*, ed. David C. Engerman, Nils Gilman, Mark H. Haefle, and Michael E. Latham (Amherst: University of Massachusetts Press, 2003), 35.
17. Michael E. Latham, *Modernization as Ideology: American Social Science and "Nation Building" in the Kennedy Era* (Chapel Hill: University of North Carolina Press, 2000), 13, 59, 209.
18. Franklin Publications, "Plan for Worldwide Development."
19. Franklin Publications, report, September 15, 1959, FBPR, box 15, folder 8.
20. Nick Cullather, *The Hungry World: America's Cold War Battle against Poverty in Asia* (Cambridge: Harvard University Press, 2013), 8.
21. Latham, *Modernization as Ideology*, 19.
22. Quoted in Gilman, *Mandarins*, 69.
23. Latham, *Right Kind of Revolution*, 5.
24. Gilman, *Mandarins*, 185–86, 90; Mark T. Berger, *The Battle for Asia: From Decolonization to Globalization* (London: Routledge, 2004), 102.
25. Latham, *Modernization as Ideology*, 61.
26. Gilman, *Mandarins*, 172.
27. "American Books Abroad," *National Book Committee Quarterly* 5 (Fall–Winter 1961): 1, 5.
28. Thomas J. Wilson, Bill Spaulding, and Datus Smith, "Books in Industrial Development," May 4, 1962, FBPR, box 15, folder 1.
29. "ATPI Annual Meeting: Education and Publishing: A Growing Partnership," *PW,* May 30, 1960, 24.
30. "ABPC Annual Meeting: The Near Future," *PW,* June 13, 1966, 81.
31. Michael E. Latham, "Ideology, Social Science, and Destiny: Modernization and the Kennedy-Era Alliance for Progress," *Diplomatic History* 22, no. 2 (1998): 199.
32. Don Cameron, letter to Franklin Publications executive committee, 1957, FBPR, box 3, folder 3.
33. U.S. Agency for International Development, "The Use of Books in the AID Program," FBPR, box 61, folder 10; Stanley A. Barnett, "American Book Aid: A Critical Assessment of Two Major Program of the 1950s–1970s," in *Publishing and Development in the Third World*, ed. Philip G. Altbach (London: Zell, 1992), 336. The Central Book Activities unit was discontinued in 1969.
34. U.S. Agency for International Development, "Use of Books."
35. Franklin Publications, "Plan for Worldwide Development"; Franklin Publications, minutes, board of directors' meeting, April 30, 1963, FBPR, box 1, folder 6.
36. Datus Smith, letter to Franklin Publications office managers, August 9, 1963, FBPR, box 74, folder 12.
37. See Stanley Meisler, *When the World Calls: The Inside Story of the Peace Corps and Its First Fifty Years* (Boston: Beacon, 2011), 34; and Elizabeth Cobbs Hoffman, *All You Need Is Love: The Peace Corps and the Spirit of the 1960s* (Cambridge: Harvard University Press, 1998).
38. Don Cameron, letter to A.T.M. Abdul Mateen, June 26, 1963, FBPR, box 106, folder 5.
39. Datus Smith, "Notes on Recent Developments," June 25, 1964, FBPR, box 5, folder 2.
40. Franklin Publications, "Here to Learn," January 1965, FBPR, box 39, folder 1.
41. Franklin Publications, report, September 15, 1959.
42. Franklin Publications, "Franklin Summary of Operations," February 10, 1965, FBPR, box 140, folder 27.
43. Rowan Wakefield, letter to Bill Spaulding, October 30, 1964, FBPR, box 12, folder 9.
44. Bill Spaulding, letter to Alden Clark, November 10, 1964, FBPR, box 12, folder 9.

45. Franklin Publications, "Report on Recent Developments," December 27, 1963, FBPR, box 5, folder 2.
46. Datus Smith, letter to Charles Frankel, April 25, 1966, FBPR, box 8, folder 13.
47. Franklin Publications, minutes of board of directors' meeting, October 26, 1966, FBPR, box 1, folder 3.
48. Datus Smith, "Ten Years of Franklin Publications," *American Library Association Bulletin* 57 (June 1963): 510.
49. Jay E. Daily, "Oil for the Lamps of Knowledge," *Library Journal*, November 15, 1964, 4483–87.
50. Franklin Publications, annual report for fiscal year 1963–64, 13, FBPR, box 15, folder 7.
51. Lester Asheim, *Librarianship in the Developing Countries* (Urbana: University of Illinois Press, 1966), 64, 66, 84.
52. J. M. Filstrup, "Franklin Book Programs/Tehran," *International Library Review* 8, no. 4 (1976): 445.
53. Franklin Publications, "Library Development," [1966], FBPR, box 29, folder 11.
54. Franklin Publications, "Urdu School Library Distribution, Lahore, West Pakistan," FBPR, box 144, folder 3.
55. Datus Smith, letter to Hamid Ali Khan, July 2, 1962, FBPR, box 144, folder 3.
56. Franklin Publications, annual report for fiscal year 1963–64, 8–9.
57. Franklin Publications, annual report for fiscal year 1964–65, 12, FBPR, box 15, folder 7.
58. See Timothy Nunan, *Humanitarian Invasion: Global Development in Cold War Afghanistan* (New York: Cambridge University Press, 2016).
59. Franklin Publications, annual report for fiscal year 1963–64, 3; Filstrup, "Franklin Book Program," 446; Franklin Publications, circular, September 4, 1963, FBPR, box 73, folder 2.
60. Don Cameron, letter to Franklin Publications, November 26, 1963, FBPR, box 153, folder 7.
61. Don Cameron, letter to Franklin Publications, May 4, 1964, FBPR, box 153, folder 8.
62. Datus Smith, letter to Franklin Publications, October 1964, FBPR, box 159, folder 6.
63. Datus Smith, letter to Franklin Publications, April 2, 1964, in *Journey with Joy: Letters from Datus C. Smith Jr.*, ed. Dorothy Hunt Smith (Princeton, 1972), 126.
64. Dariush Homayoun, letter to Don Cameron, December 19, 1965, FBPR, box 73, folder 11.
65. Datus Smith, draft letter to American book publishers, August 13, 1964, FBPR, box 19, folder 11.
66. Franklin Publications, annual report for fiscal year 1960–61, 5, FBPR, box 15, folder 7.
67. Franklin Publications, "Books Are Crucial to Sound Development of Emerging Nations," October 6, 1964, FBPR, box 29, folder 11.
68. William Graebner, "The Unstable World of Benjamin Spock: Social Engineering in a Democratic Culture, 1917–1950," *Journal of American History* 67 (December 1980): 613. See also Rima D. Apple, "Constructing Mothers: Scientific Motherhood in the 19th and 20th Centuries," *Social History of Medicine* 8, no. 22 (1995): 161–78.
69. Filstrup, "Franklin Book Program," 437.
70. Robert D. Walsh, letter to Thomas B. Stauffer, April 6, 1961, FBPR, box 47, folder 23.
71. Franklin Publications, notes on *Industrialism and Industrial Man,* FBPR, box 205, folder 12.
72. Datus Smith, *A Guide to Book Publishing* (New York: Bowker, 1966), vii, 3, 33–36.
73. Gary R. Hess, "Waging the Cold War in the Third World: The Foundations and the Challenges of Development," in *Charity, Philanthropy, and Civility in American History,* ed. Lawrence J. Friedman and Mark D. McGarvie (Cambridge: Cambridge University Press, 2003), 319. Volker R. Berghahn believes that the foundations generally supported the fight against communism ("Philanthropy and Diplomacy in the 'American Century,'" *Diplomatic History* 23 [Summer 1999]: 402). On the networks among foundations, universities, and government, see Mark Solovey, *Shaky Foundation: The Politics–Patronage–Social Science Nexus in Cold War America* (New Brunswick, NJ: Rutgers University Press, 2013).

74. Akira Iriye, *Global Community: The Role of International Organizations in the Making of the Contemporary World* (Berkeley: University of California Press, 2002), 93.
75. Rockefeller Foundation, *Annual Report for 1951* (New York: Rockefeller Foundation) 13.
76. Rockefeller Foundation, *Annual Report for 1947* (New York: Rockefeller Foundation) 244–45.
77. Berghahn, "Philanthropy and Diplomacy," 402.
78. "News of the Week," *PW,* September 9, 1957, 49.
79. J. Donald Kingsley, "The Ford Foundation and Education in Africa," *African Studies Bulletin* 9 (December 1966): 1.
80. "News of the Week," *PW,* October 15, 1956, 1875.
81. Franklin Publications, minutes of the board of directors' meeting, October 19, 1960, FBPR, box 1, folder 4.
82. Datus Smith, letter to Franklin Publications board of directors, January 2, 1963, FBPR, box 5, folder 2.
83. Franklin Publications, application to Ford Foundation, February 15, 1962, FBPR, box 28, folder 8.
84. Ron Robin, *The Making of the Cold War Enemy: Culture and Politics in the Military-Intellectual Complex* (Princeton: Princeton University Press, 2001), 34.
85. Franklin Publications, minutes, board of directors' meeting, October 19, 1960.
86. Datus Smith, letter to Franklin Publications board of directors, July 22, 1963, FBPR, box 5, folder 2.
87. Franklin Publications, "Proposal, English-Arabic Dictionary," July 25, 1963, FBPR, box 93, folder 5.
88. William E. Mulligan, letter to Datus Smith, February 23, 1964, FBPR, box 135, folder 6.
89. Ali M. Ansari, *The Politics of Nationalism in Modern Iran* (Cambridge: Cambridge University Press, 2012), 156.
90. Ali M. Ansari, *Modern Iran Since 1921: The Pahlavis and After* (London: Longman, 2003), 136.
91. Ali M. Ansari, "The Myth of the White Revolution: Mohammad Reza Shah, 'Modernization,' and the Consolidation of Power," *Middle Eastern Studies* 37 (July 2001): 2, 12, 13, 3.
92. Datus Smith, "Excerpts from Letters, Trip #10, Winter 1957," FBPR, box 5, folder 5.
93. Beytolah Biniaz, "Introduction," and Farid Moradi, "History of Book Publishing in Iran," both in *Publishing in Persian Language in Iran, Afghanistan, Tajikistan, Uzbekistan, Europe, and United States,* by Farid Moradi, Laetitia Nanquette, Masoud Hosseinipour, Ali Amiri, Dilshad Rakhimov, and Beytolah Biniaz (Paris: International Alliance of Independent Publishers, 2013), 8–9, 25.
94. Datus Smith, "American Books in the Middle East," September 1955, FBPR, box 38, folder 2.
95. Biniaz, "Introduction," 14.
96. Moradi, "History of Book Publishing in Iran," 32, 34.
97. Datus Smith, memorandum to Franklin Publications board of directors, March 20, 1956, FBPR, box 5, folder 5.
98. "Shah of Iran Honors Head of Franklin Book Programs," *PW,* November 30, 1964, 32.
99. Datus Smith, letter to Franklin Publications executive committee, June 14, 1956, FBPR, box 3, folder 4; "How Book Translations Help Mideast Understand U.S.," *Chicago Sun-Times,* June 17, 1956.
100. Filstrup, "Franklin Book Program," 436, 439, 447, 435.
101. Datus Smith, letter to James L. Meader, January 11, 1957, FBPR, box 70, folder 3.
102. Datus Smith, letter to Clarence Hendershot, September 26, 1962, FBPR, box 62, folder 10.
103. Byron Buck, "New Textbooks for Iran," September 23, 1960, FBPR, box 122, folder 4.
104. Franklin Publications, annual report for fiscal year 1963–64, 16.
105. Seyed Farian Sabahi, "The Literacy Corps in Pahlavi Iran (1963–1979): Political, Social, and Literary Implications," *Cahiers d'Études sur la Méditerranée Orientale et le Monde Turco-Iranien* 31 (January–June 2001): [6, 9–10].

106. Franklin Publications, annual report for fiscal year 1964–65, 11.
107. Sabahi "The Literacy Corps," [16].
108. Filstrup "Franklin Book Program," 441.
109. Buck, "New Textbooks for Iran."
110. Don Cameron, letter to Malcolm Johnson, March 12, 1957, FBPR, box 9, folder 16.
111. Filstrup, "Franklin Book Program," 437–38.
112. Cameron, letter to Johnson, March 12, 1957.
113. "Paper and Papermaking," July 20, 2005, *Encyclopaedia Iranica,* http://www.iranicaonline.org.
114. Filstrup, "Franklin Book Program," 438.
115. Franklin Publications, "The Persian Pocket Books: A Worthwhile Experiment," FBPR, box 121, folder 4.
116. Franklin Publications, newsletter, September 15, 1961, FBPR, box 39, folder 1; Franklin Publications, annual report for fiscal year 1962–63, 12, FBPR, box 15, folder 7.
117. Franklin Publications, "Persian Pocket Books."
118. Biniaz, "Introduction," 14.
119. Moradi, "History of Book Publishing in Iran," 30–31.
120. "ABPC: Annual Meeting Highlights: Marketing and Management," *PW,* June 5, 1961, 26.
121. U.S. Information Agency, "Soviet Book Publishing in Free World Languages," May 9, 1962, NARA, RG306 Office of Research "R" reports, 1960–63, R43–62, box 3.
122. U.S. Information Agency, "Low-Priced Books from the USA," NARA, RG306, USIA Office of Private Cooperation entry 56 250/A/1/01, box 35, folder "Donated Books, ICS Review of Books."
123. U.S. Information Agency, "Books Published Abroad," July 1, 1962–June 30, 1963, NARA, RG306, USIA records relating to the book program, 1966–99, box 3.
124. U.S. Information Agency, "Books Published Abroad," July 1, 1964–June 30, 1965, NARA, RG306, USIA records relating to the book program, 1966–99, box 3.
125. U.S. Information Agency, "Ladder Editions from the USA," NARA, RG306, USIA Office of Private Cooperation entry 56 250/A/1/01, box 35, folder "Donated Books, ICS Review of Books."
126. U.S. Information Agency, study of ladder editions, September 26, 1969, NARA, RG306 USIA director's subject files, 1968–72, entry 42 350/77/27/04, box 1, folder "Books, General Reports and Statistics."
127. Richard T. Arndt, transcript of interview, May 9, 1988, 4, Columbia University, Iranian-American Relations Oral History Project, 1989, session 1.
128. U.S. Information Service, Ibadan Office, memorandum to U.S. Information Agency, April 30, 1963, NARA, RG306, USIA Office of Private Cooperation, box 46, folder "IAA Nigeria 1963."
129. U.S. Information Agency, "Donated Books—General Shipments, 1963," NARA, RG306, USIA Office of Private Cooperation entry 56 250/A/1/01, box 33.
130. Edward R. Murrow, press release, December 14, 1962, FHA, box 52, folder M2.
131. U.S. Information Agency, files of letters, NARA, RG306, USIA Office of Private Cooperation entry 56 250/A/1/01, box 34, folder "Donated Books, Effectiveness."
132. U.S. State Department, "Secretary of State Appoints Book Publishers' Committee," October 11, 1962, AAKR, box 590, folder 5.
133. Alfred A. Knopf, letter to Dan Lacy, March 25, 1964, AAKR, box 401, folder 3.
134. Franklin Publications, "New Plan for Translation Rights," AAKR, box 380, folder 1.
135. Franklin Publications, report, September 15, 1959.
136. Franklin Publications, manifesto, [1967], FBPR, box 23, folder 3.
137. Harold Munger, letter to Karim Emami, February 28, 1969, FBPR, box 225, folder 10.
138. American Book Publishers Council and American Textbook Publishers Institute, newsletter, January 30, 1967, AAKR, box 593, folder 9.
139. Franklin Publications, annual report for fiscal year 1967–68, 3, FBPR, box 15, folder 7.

Chapter 5. Book Modernization in Africa and Latin America

1. Datus Smith, letter with attached note to Franklin Publications board of directors, January 18, 1961, FBPR, box 5, folder 3.
2. Franklin Publications, "Plan for Worldwide Development," January 29, 1962, FBPR, box 5, folder 3.
3. Franklin Publications, annual report for fiscal year 1963–64, 3, FBPR, box 15, folder 7.
4. Datus Smith, report, April 17, 1959, FBPR, box 158, folder 9.
5. Frederick Cooper, *Africa Since 1940: The Past of the Present* (Cambridge: Cambridge University Press, 2002), 84.
6. Larry Grubbs, *Secular Missionaries: Americans and African Development in the 1960s* (Amherst: University of Massachusetts Press, 2009), 42.
7. On African Americans and the U.S. State Department, see Michael L. Krenn, *Black Diplomacy: African-Americans and the State Department, 1945–1969* (Armonk, NY: Sharpe, 1999). On race and the Cold War, see Philip E. Muehlenbeck, ed., *Race, Ethnicity and the Cold War: A Global Perspective*, (Nashville, TN: Vanderbilt University Press, 2012). On African Americans' attitudes to American foreign policy, see Brenda Gayle Plummer, *In Search of Power: African Americans in the Era of Decolonization, 1956–1974* (New York: Cambridge University Press, 2013).
8. Grubbs, *Secular Missionaries*, 9, 54.
9. Datus Smith, letter to Dorothy Smith, April 22, 1959, in *Journey with Joy: Letters from Datus C. Smith Jr.*, ed. Dorothy Hunt Smith (Princeton, 1972), 114.
10. Anne-Marie Angelo and Tom Adam Davies, "'American Business Can Assist [African] Hands': The Kennedy Administration, U.S. Corporations, and the Cold War Struggle for Africa," *The Sixties* 8, no. 2 (2015): 157, 162, 165.
11. Byron Buck, letter to Charles Richards, April 5, 1961, FBPR, box 125, folder 1.
12. Byron Buck, "Books in Nigeria and East Africa," February 1961, FBPR, box 75, folder 7.
13. Franklin Publications, annual report for fiscal year 1960–61, 12, FBPR, box 15, folder 7.
14. Byron Buck, "Books for Ghana and Nigeria," January 15, 1962, FBPR, box 75, folder 7.
15. Bill Spaulding, "Some Observations on Books and Publishing in Ghana and Nigeria," FBPR, box 12, folder 12.
16. Alden Clark, "The Franklin Program in Africa," April 27, 1964, FBPR, box 19, folder 11.
17. Bill Spaulding, letter to Datus Smith, February 5, 1963, FBPR, box 12, folder 11.
18. Datus Smith, letter to Franklin Publications board of directors, July 22, 1963, FBPR, box 5, folder 2.
19. Amanda Laugesen, "'An Inalienable Right to Read': UNESCO's Promotion of a Universal Culture of Reading and Public Libraries, and Its Involvement in Africa, 1948–1968," *English in Africa* 35 (May 2008): 67–88.
20. Thomas J. Davis and Azubike Kalu-Nwiwu, "Education, Ethnicity, and National Integration in the History of Nigeria: Continuing Problems of Africa's Colonial Legacy," *Journal of Negro History* 86 (Winter 2001): 6.
21. Richard Gamble, letter to Datus Smith, September 18, 1963, FBPR, box 30, folder 2. *Drum* published writers such as Lewis Nkosi, Bloke Modisane, and Can Themba and was distributed in a number of African countries in the 1950s and 1960s.
22. Buck, "Books in Nigeria and East Africa."
23. Franklin Publications, annual report for fiscal year 1963–64, 4, FBPR, box 15, folder 7.
24. Alden Clark, letter to Bill Spaulding, July 21, 1964, FBPR, box 12, folder 9.
25. Franklin Publications, annual report for fiscal year 1963–64, 4.
26. "More Text Books for Our Schools," *[Lagos, Nigeria] Morning Post*, September 19, 1964, 9; Franklin Publications, minutes, board of directors' meeting, February 16, 1966, 5–6, FBPR, box 1, folder 3.
27. Franklin Publications, "A Franklin Publications Program for Africa," September 13, 1962, AAKR, box 380, folder 1.

28. Franklin Publications, list of contributors to special Africa fund, February 25, 1963, AAKR, box 380, folder 1.
29. Alden Clark, "The Franklin Program in Nigeria," April 27, 1964, FBPR, box 19, folder 11.
30. "News of the Week," *PW,* October 14, 1963, 35.
31. A. Babs Fafunwa, letter to Datus Smith, June 20, 1963, FBPR, box 136, folder 8.
32. A. Babs Fafunwa, "Report on Second Educational Writers Workshop, University of Nigeria, Nsukka, 1–27 May," FBPR, box 139, folder 5.
33. E. A. Etudo, letter to Shirley Smith, December 23, 1964, FBPR, box 136, folder 8.
34. Franklin Publications, minutes, Midwestern Nigeria Advisory Board, May 14, 1965, FBPR, box 139, folder 3.
35. Alden Clark, "Books in East Africa: Report and Recommendations," August 1, 1964, 1, FBPR, box 75, folder 8.
36. Franklin Publications, summary of meetings, May 28, 1964, and July 29, 1964, FBPR, box 44, folder 4.
37. Franklin Publications, annual report for fiscal year 1965–66, 3, 20, FBPR, box 15, folder 7.
38. H. S. Bhola, "An Overview of Literacy in Sub-Sahara Africa—Images in the Making," *African Studies Review* 33 (December 1990): 7.
39. Franklin Publications, minutes, board of directors' meeting, October 19, 1960, FBPR, box 1, folder 7.
40. Smith, letter to Franklin Publications board of directors, January 18, 1961.
41. Franklin Publications, minutes, board of directors' meeting, January 26, 1961, FBPR, box 1, folder 4.
42. Buck, "Books for Ghana and Nigeria."
43. Ruth C. Sloan, "American Books in Africa South of the Sahara," *Library Trends* 5 (July 1956): 45.
44. Buck, "Books for Ghana and Nigeria."
45. Bill Spaulding, letter to Alden Clark, April 17, 1964, FBPR, box 12, folder 9.
46. W. P. Kerr, letter to Datus Smith, March 29, 1963, FBPR, box 43, folder 5.
47. Caroline Davis, "Creating a Book Empire: Longmans in Africa," in *The Book in Africa: Critical Debates,* ed. Caroline Davis and David Johnson (Houndmills, UK: Palgrave Macmillan, 2015), 138.
48. Gail Low, "In Pursuit of Publishing: Heinemann's African Writers Series," *Wasafiri* 17, no. 37 (2002): 32.
49. Ibid., 31–35; Becky Clarke, "The African Writers Series: Celebrating Forty Years of Publishing Distinction," *Research in African Literatures* 34 (Summer 2003): 163–74. The literature on U.S. and British publishers are usually not studied in tandem, but the parallels and contrasts are worthy of detailed study.
50. John Ardagh, "U.S. Books Invade Africa," *Observer,* December 23, 1962.
51. Datus Smith, letter to J. E. Morpurgo, March 29, 1963, FBPR, box 102, folder 5.
52. Alden Clark, report, September 13, 1963, FBPR, box 154, folder 2.
53. Bill Spaulding, letter to Alden Clark, January 7, 1964, FBPR, box 12, folder 9; Alden Clark, letter to Ronald Barker, January 2, 1964, FBPR, box 75, folder 19.
54. Alden Clark, letter to New York office, October 18, 1964, FBPR, box 154, folder 5.
55. Alden Clark, letter to Bill Spaulding, July 21, 1964, FBPR, box 12, folder 9.
56. Lee C. Deighton, letter to Bill Spaulding, July 29, 1965, FBPR, box 12, folder 8.
57. Alden Clark, letter to Franklin Publications, September 2, 1965, FBPR, box 154, folder 6.
58. "Macmillan Shock for Publishers," *Sunday Times,* April 23, 1967.
59. "Macmillan in Africa: The Plot Thickens," *Sunday Times,* April 30, 1967.
60. Franklin Publications, "Books in West Africa—Report and Recommendations," March 1, 1963, FBPR, box 75, folder 9.
61. Datus Smith, letter to Dan Lacy, February 6, 1962, FBPR, box 10, folder 12.
62. Dan Lacy, letter to Datus Smith, April 18, 1962, FBPR, box 10, folder 11.
63. Alden Clark, letter to New York staff, November 1964, FBPR, box 154, folder 5.

64. Bill Spaulding, letter to Alden Clark, November 10, 1964, FBPR, box 12, folder 9.
65. Alden Clark, letter to Franklin Publications, May 8, 1966, FBPR, box 154, folder 7.
66. Datus Smith, letter to David Heaps, September 3, 1963, FBPR, box 137, folder 9.
67. Stephen Paterson Belcher, interview, September 29, 1988, Association for Diplomatic Studies and Training, Foreign Affairs Oral History Project, Information Series, Library of Congress, https://www.loc.gov.
68. Shirley Smith, letters to Franklin Publications, January 17, 1965, and January 30, 1965, FBPR, box 160, folder 1.
69. Shirley Smith, letter to Franklin Publications, February 16, 1965, FBPR, box 160, folder 1.
70. Ibid.
71. Shirley Smith, letter to Franklin Publications, February 25, 1965, box 160, folder 1.
72. Shirley Smith, letter to Franklin Publications, March 6, 1965, box 160, folder 1.
73. Dorothy Hunt Smith, "From Mason City to Uganda," *Christian Science Monitor*, June 7, 1969.
74. "Retired Librarian Could Write Book about Life, Career," *[Mason City, Iowa] Globe-Gazette*, December 23, 1996.
75. Esther J. Walls, "Christian Women Waging the Battle for Life," n.d., EJWP, box 3, folder "Speeches, Undated."
76. Michael Harris, reference for Esther J. Walls, July 22, 1974, EJWP, box 2, folder "Correspondence: General—1970–4."
77. Esther J. Walls, letter to Curly Bowen, July 14, 1971, EJWP, box 2, folder "Correspondence: General—1970–4."
78. "Mason City's Home," *[Mason City, Iowa] Globe-Gazette*, June 6, 1969.
79. Smith, "From Mason City to Uganda."
80. Ibid.
81. Esther J. Walls, transcript of speech at New York Public Library, Mott Haven Branch, and transcript of speech at Milwaukee Public Library, 1959, both in EJWP, box 3, folder "Writings: Speeches, 1950–59."
82. Esther J. Walls, "Some Observations on Nigerian Libraries," October 1964, FBPR, box 137, folder 5.
83. Esther J. Walls, letter to Franklin Publications, May 1, 1967, EJWP, folder "Correspondence: Franklin Book Programs—Trip 3, April–May 1967."
84. Esther J. Walls, letter to Franklin Publications, May 25, 1968, EJWP, folder "Correspondence: Franklin Book Programs—Trips 4, 6, and 8, May 1968–70."
85. Franklin Publications, minutes, December 27–28, 1967, FBPR, box 3, folder 3.
86. U.S. Government Advisory Committee on International Book and Library Programs, minutes, January 12–13, FBPR, box 51, folder 3.
87. Franklin Publications, minutes, December 27–28, 1967.
88. Esther J. Walls, to Datus Smith, February 9, 1967, FBPR, box 184, folder 12.
89. Nigerian Publishers Association, minutes, April 29, 1967, FBPR, box 138, folder 9.
90. Alden Clark, letter to New York staff, October 25, 1964, FBPR, box 154, folder 5.
91. Alden Clark, letter to Franklin Publications, February 5, 1967, FBPR, box 156, folder 8.
92. Caroline Davis, *Creating Postcolonial Literature: African Writers and British Publishers* (Houndmills, UK: Palgrave Macmillan, 2013), 45.
93. Harold Munger, letter to Ronald Barker, March 27, 1970; Ronald Barker, letter to Harold Munger, April 14, 1970, both in FBPR, box 3, folder 1.
94. "The USIA's Expanded Latin American Book Program," *PW*, August 10, 1964, 29.
95. Deborah Cohn, "A Tale of Two Translation Programs: Politics, the Market, and Rockefeller Funding for Latin American Literature in the United States during the 1960s and 1970s," *Latin American Research Review*, 41 (June 2006): 139–64. Some Rockefeller Foundation funding supported American university presses that were publishing Latin American authors.
96. Datus Smith, letter to Dan Lacy, February 6, 1962, FBPR, box 10, folder 12.

97. Franklin Publications, "Books in Latin America," January 31, 1962, AAKR, box 590, folder 6.
98. "Books in Latin America."
99. Blanche Knopf, letter to Alfred Knopf, February 2, 1962, AAKR, box 590, folder 6.
100. Alfred A. Knopf Publishing Company staff, draft memorandum to Alfred A. Knopf, January 29, 1953, AAKR, box 590, folder 5.
101. Franklin Publications, "Final Report on Grant," July 10, 1962, FBPR, box 184, folder 11.
102. Alfred A. Knopf, letter to Edward R. Murrow, September 28, 1962, AAKR, box 565, folder 2.
103. Alfred A. Knopf, letter to Edward R. Murrow, August 16, 1962, AAKR, box 565, folder 2.
104. Alfred A. Knopf, letter to Arthur Schlesinger, Jr., April 24, 1962, AAKR, box 565, folder 2.
105. Arthur Schlesinger, Jr., to Alfred A. Knopf, June 12, 1962, AAKR, box 565, folder 2.
106. Datus Smith, letter to Franklin Publications board of directors, January 2, 1963, FBPR, box 5, folder 2.
107. Franklin Publications, annual report for fiscal year 1963–64, 5.
108. Franklin Publications, report, May 1965–March 31, 1966, FBPR, box 78, folder 1.
109. Franklin Publications, report, March 17, 1964–April 30, 1965, FBPR, box 78, folder 2.
110. Franklin Publications, annual report for fiscal year 1966–67, 2, 6, FBPR, box 15, folder 7.
111. Franklin Publications, report, March 17, 1964–March 17, 1967, 17, FBPR, box 78, folder 5.
112. Franklin Publications, annual report for fiscal year 1965–66, 13.
113. Franklin Publications, annual report for fiscal year 1964–65, 11, FBPR, box 15, folder 7; Franklin Publications, annual report for fiscal year 1966–67, 12; Franklin Publications, annual report for fiscal year 1967–68, 16, FBPR, box 15, folder 7.
114. Franklin Publications, annual report for fiscal year 1964–65, 30.
115. Franklin Publications, newsletter, March 1966, FBPR, box 39, folder 1.
116. Franklin Publications, annual report for fiscal year 1966–67, 8.
117. Franklin Publications, list of seminar participants, March 15, 1965, AAKR, box 517, folder 2.
118. Geraldo Jordao Pereira, "Developing a Series on Administration," February 1965, AAKR, box 518, folder 2.
119. Franklin Publications, annual report for fiscal year 1967–68, 17.
120. Esther J. Walls, report, February 18, 1970, FBPR, box 160, folder 5.

Chapter 6. The Decline and End of Franklin Book Programs

1. Franklin Publications, "Wartime Council's Assets Transferred to Franklin," January 10, 1966, FBPR, box 24, folder 2.
2. Franklin Publications, annual report for fiscal year 1964–65, 1, FBPR, box 15, folder 7.
3. Datus Smith, letter to Franklin Publications board of directors, October 31, 1966, FBPR, box 5, folder 1.
4. Thomas Borstelmann, *The 1970s: A New Global History from Civil Rights to Economic Inequality* (Princeton: Princeton University Press, 2012), 3, 12.
5. "U.S. Publishing's 'New Look' in Newly Developing Countries," *PW*, April 6, 1970, 29.
6. On this foreign policy reorientation, see Daniel J. Sargent, *A Superpower Transformed: The Remaking of American Foreign Relations in the 1970s* (New York: Oxford University Press, 2015).
7. David Ekbladh, *The Great American Mission: Modernization and the Construction of an American World Order* (Princeton: Princeton University Press, 2010), 250.
8. Nils Gilman, *Mandarins of the Future: Modernization Theory in Cold War America* (Baltimore: Johns Hopkins University Press, 2003), 204, 250.
9. Daniel Immerwahr, *Thinking Small: The United States and the Lure of Community Perspectives* (Cambridge: Harvard University Press, 2015), 168.
10. Barbara J. Keys, *Reclaiming American Virtue: The Human Rights Revolution of the 1970s* (Baltimore: Johns Hopkins University Press, 2014), 138. On the development of human rights

discourse, see Akira Iriye, Petra Goedde, and William I. Hitchcock, eds., *The Human Rights Revolution: An International History* (New York: Oxford University Press, 2012); Samuel Moyn, *The Last Utopia: Human Rights in History* (Cambridge: Harvard University Press, 2010); and Samuel Moyn, *Human Rights and the Uses of History* (London: Verso, 2014). On this discourse's effect on 1970s foreign policy, see Sargent, *A Superpower Transformed*.

11. Michael Shudson, "The Enduring Book in a Multimedia Age," in *A History of the Book in America,* ed. David Paul Nord, Joan Shelley Rubin, and Michael Shudson (Chapel Hill: University of North Carolina Press, 2009), 17. For publishers' experiences of these transitions, see Al Silverman, *The Time of Their Lives: The Golden Age of Great American Publishers, Their Editors, and Authors* (New York: St. Martin's Press, 2008). Silverman writes that ossification of the industry began when the "great old-line book people began to be replaced by bottom-line business men" (2).
12. John Tebbel, *A History of Book Publishing in the United States,* vol. 2, *The Great Change, 1940–1980* (New York: Bowker, 1981), 495.
13. "Nixon Budget Eliminates Book and Library Programs," *PW,* February 5, 1973, 55. Debates about the cuts, which the AAP opposed, continued for several years.
14. After 1972, *PW* articles frequently examined the economic problems of the publishing industry. See, for instance, "University Presses Cite Serious Financial Crisis" (May 15, 1972, 32). In "The End of a Love Affair with Publishing," Charles Rolo noted that publishing firms listed on Wall Street were increasingly seen as poor financial investments (May 7, 1973, 24–26).
15. Datus Smith, letter to Dan Lacy, June 24, 1966, FBPR, box 72, folder 2.
16. Stephen Paterson Belcher, interview, September 29, 1988, Association for Diplomatic Studies and Training, Foreign Affairs Oral History Project, Information Series, Library of Congress, https://www.loc.gov. Belcher left the USIA in 1972, disillusioned by its reactions to Watergate and Vietnam.
17. Shirley Smith, memorandum to Datus Smith, and Datus Smith, memorandum to Shirley Smith, both dated August 9, 1965, FBPR, box 76, folder 10.
18. George P. Brett, letter to Datus Smith, November 8, 1977, FBPR, box 7, folder 6.
19. Franklin Publications, minutes, board of directors' meeting, May 26, 1967, FBPR, box 1, folder 3. As I will discuss, some board members later expressed concern about "long-term problems" and "unsatisfactory budgeting procedures," primarily in relation to the Tehran office (Franklin Publications, minutes, board of directors' meeting, June 9, 1969, FBPR, box 1, folder 3).
20. Datus Smith, memorandum to Franklin Publications executive committee, July 7, 1967, FBPR, box 3, folder 3.
21. David Nalle, letter to Henry Loomis, May 16, 1969, NARA, RG 306, USIA director's subject files, 1968–72, entry 42 350/77/27/04, box 1, folder "Books."
22. Michael Harris, letter to Parker May, May 28, 1969, FBPR, box 3, folder 2.
23. Parker May, letter to Michael Harris, July 3, 1969, FBPR, box 3, folder 2.
24. Clipping, *New York Times,* December 8, 1969, AAKP, box 593, folder 8.
25. Frank Shakespeare, airgram, April 3, 1970, NARA, RG 306, USIA director's subject files, 1968–72, entry 42 350/77/27/04, box 1, folder 13.
26. Henry Dunlap, letter to Henry Loomis, June 1, 1970, NARA, RG 306, USIA director's subject files, 1968–72, entry 42 350/77/27/04, box 1, folder 13.
27. Frank Shakespeare, letter to Guy van der Jagt, January 12, 1972, NARA, RG 306, USIA director's subject files, 1968–72, entry 42 350/77/27/04, box 31, folder "INC: Books for Information Centers."
28. Jack Kyle, "Comments for the Annual Meeting of the Members of the Corporation," December 19, 1972, FBPR, box 1, folder 6.
29. Franklin Publications executive committee, memorandum to Datus Smith, May 17, 1965, FBPR, box 3, folder 4.

30. Franklin Publications, "Franklin Book Programs, Inc.," May 20, 1966, FBPR, box 29, folder 11.
31. Franklin Publications, annual report for fiscal year 1965–66, 25, FBPR, box 15, folder 7.
32. Charles F. Band, "Fund-raising Progress Report, July 1 1965 to March 31 1966," FBPR, box 5, folder 1; Franklin Publications, annual report for fiscal year 1965–66, 25; Franklin Publications, corporate donor list, August 16, 1967, FBPR, box 5, folder 1.
33. Franklin Publications, report, March 21, 1973, FBPR, box 1, folder 3.
34. Franklin Publications, advertisement, ca. 1970–71, FBPR, box 1, folder 9.
35. Franklin Publications, report, September 18, 1974, FBPR, box 1, folder 9.
36. "Franklin 'Friends' Plan Awards, Gifts of Libraries," *PW,* January 8, 1973, 48.
37. "Franklin Gives Its First Education Award," *PW,* February 26, 1973, 107.
38. "Franklin Awards Honor Spaulding, Jahanshahi," *PW,* January 13, 1975, 24.
39. Jack Kyle, "Books, Education, and the Developing World," November 8, 1964, FBPR, box 164, folder 3.
40. For a discussion of the era's population concerns, see Thomas Robertson, *The Malthusian Moment: Global Population Growth and the Birth of American Environmentalism* (New Brunswick, NJ: Rutgers University Press, 2012).
41. Franklin Publications, annual report for fiscal year 1965–66, 24.
42. Franklin Publications, foundation donor list, August 29, 1967, FBPR, box 5, folder 1.
43. Franklin Publications, minutes, members' meeting, June 27, 1968, FBPR, box 1, folder 7.
44. Datus Smith, to Franklin Publications board of directors, March 1, 1967, FBPR, box 5, folder 1.
45. Datus Smith, memorandum to all Franklin Publications offices, May 1, 1967, FBPR, box 5, folder 1.
46. Franklin Publications, minutes, board of directors' meeting, May 26, 1967, FBPR, box 1, folder 3.
47. Tebbel, *A History of Book Publishing,* 2:331. A 1976 Senate inquiry focused on Praeger, which claimed that the CIA had never interfered in its editorial process, although the publisher had produced books on communism for the agency ("Senate Group Finds CIA Now Only Active in Books Abroad," *PW,* May 17, 1976, 17). The *New York Times* continued to investigate the story, and Datus Smith reiterated that Franklin had never knowingly received any CIA money ("N.Y. Times Investigates CIA Ties to Book Industry," *PW,* January 16, 1978, 18–24). That *PW* article also named some of the publishers in question, including Ballantine and Putnam, and quoted Walter J. Minton of Putnam, who said that he had no idea how a publisher would know if there had been CIA intervention but wished he *had* known as "I'd have billed the CIA for the loss we took on [the book]" (23).
48. "Our National Priorities Are Upside Down," *PW,* November 6, 1967, 35.
49. Alfred A. Knopf, letter to José Vieitas, December 1, 1969, AAKR, box 601, folder 2.
50. Alfred A. Knopf, letter to José Vieitas, October 27, 1969, AAKR, box 601, folder 2.
51. "News," *PW,* January 1, 1968, 24.
52. Arthur Wang, letter to William A. Koshland, July 31, 1970, AAKR, box 878, folder 7.
53. "AAP Emerges: Newly Federated Organization Meets in an Atmosphere Charged by National Issues," *PW,* June 1, 1970, 39.
54. Alfred A. Knopf, letter to Dan Lacy, November 10, 1965, AAKR, box 517, folder 10.
55. Dan Lacy, letter to Alfred A. Knopf, November 19, 1965, AAKR, box 517, folder 10.
56. Bruce Wilcox, personal communication, August 26, 2013.
57. "U.S. Publishing's 'New Look,'" 27.
58. "At Home and Abroad with AAP," *PW,* May 24, 1976, 37.
59. Franklin Publications, minutes, board of directors' meeting, May 26, 1967, FBPR, box 1, folder 3.
60. Franklin Publications, minutes, members' meeting, November 1, 1967, FBPR, box 1, folder 7.

61. Datus Smith, "My Friends, and Friends of Franklin," November 7, 1967, FBPR, box 12, folder 3.
62. The JDR 3rd Fund had mixed success. See Karen Paul and Peter Dobkin Hall, "The Influence of the JDR 3rd Fund on 'Business and Society': Incorporating Social Responsibility in the Business Curriculum," *Journal of Business Ethics* 14, no. 9 (1995): 769–79.
63. Smith, "My Friends, and Friends of Franklin."
64. Franklin Publications, minutes, members' meeting, November 7, 1968, FBPR, box 1, folder 7.
65. Franklin Publications, annual report for the fiscal year 1967–68, 22, FBPR, box 15, folder 7.
66. Michael Harris, letter to Franklin Publications executive committee, September 24, 1968, FBPR, box 3, folder 3.
67. Michael Harris, letter to Franklin Publications executive committee, September 19, 1968, FBPR, box 144, folder 2.
68. Michael Harris, letter to Franklin Publications executive committee, September 26, 1968, FBPR, box 3, folder 3.
69. Carroll G. Bowen, "Address," November 19, 1969, FBPR, box 1, folder 7.
70. Raymond Harwood, letter to Franklin Publications executive committee, August 4, 1971, FBPR, box 3, folder 1.
71. Raymond Harwood, letter to Franklin Publications executive committee, August 23, 1971, FBPR, box 3, folder 1.
72. Anders Richter, letter to Hamid Ali Khan, August 25, 1971, FBPR, box 142, folder 14.
73. Raymond Harwood, announcement to Franklin Publications executive committee, August 23, 1971, FBPR, box 3, folder 1; "U.S. Publishing's 'New Look.'"
74. Datus Smith, "Franklin Book Program," *Encyclopaedia Iranica*, http://www.iranicaonline.org.
75. Franklin Publications, draft of report, October 4, 1971, FBPR, box 12, folder 3.
76. Jack Kyle, report, November 15, 1973, FBPR, box 1, folder 6.
77. Kyle, "Comments," December 19, 1972.
78. Franklin Publications, "Information and Development Report," September 10, 1973, FBPR, box 1, folder 8.
79. U.S. Information Agency, Office of Research, "The Role and Trend of Public Opinion in the Arab States 1961," February 16, 1962, NARA, RG 306, Office of Research, "R" reports 1960–63, R13–62, box 7.
80. Abdel Galil Hassan, "Franklin and the Sabotage of Arab Culture" [translation of *Al Kateb* article], FBPR, box 92, folder 9.
81. Datus Smith, letter to Don Cameron and Harold Munger, February 6, 1967, FBPR, box 92, folder 9.
82. Datus Smith, letter to Riad Abaza, February 6, 1967, FBPR, box 92, folder 9.
83. Datus Smith, letter to Franklin Publications board of directors, July 10, 1967, FBPR, box 5, folder 1; Nalle, letter to Loomis, May 16, 1969.
84. Franklin Publications, report, January 9, 1976, FBPR, box 1, folder 6.
85. Franklin Publications, "Foreign Office Highlights," November 1, 1972, FBPR, box 1, folder 3; "Franklin Programs Expanding," *PW,* March 6, 1978, 50.
86. "FBP Consultants Assist Projects in Three Nations," *PW,* July 26, 1976, 24.
87. Franklin Publications, minutes, board of directors' meeting, February 16, 1966, FBPR, box 1, folder 4.
88. Hassan Shadily, to Don Cameron, August 13 1964, FBPR, box 109, folder 6.
89. Franklin Publications, Jakarta office, letter to Don Cameron, April 7, 1965, FBPR, box 109, folder 6.
90. Bradley R. Simpson, *Economists with Guns: Authoritarian Development and U.S.-Indonesian Relations, 1960–1968* (Stanford: Stanford University Press, 2008), 207.
91. Franklin Publications, minutes, members' meeting, April 11, 1969, FBPR, box 1, folder 7.

92. "Franklin Reorganizes Southeast Asia Office," *PW,* May 1, 1972, 34.
93. Hassan Shadily, letter to Datus Smith, August 18, 1965, FBPR, box 106, folder 16.
94. Michael Harris, letter to Franklin Publications, March 14, 1968, box 155, folder 1.
95. Franklin Publications, annual report for fiscal year 1965–66, 4.
96. Dariush Homayoun, letter to Don Cameron, March 17, 1966, FBPR, box 142, folder 5.
97. Franklin Publications, "Description of Special Franklin Projects under Contract with USIA," July 31, 1969, FBPR, box 3, folder 2.
98. Hamid Ali Khan, letter to Harold Munger, September 29, 1969, FBPR, box 68, folder 3.
99. Franklin Publications, "Pakistan Low Cost Textbook Project: Final Project Report," June 30, 1974, FBPR, box 142, folder 1.
100. Franklin Publications, "Summary of Activities Year Ended June 30, 1971," FBPR, box 142, folder 4.
101. Franklin Publications, "Foreign Office Highlights."
102. Jack Kyle, "Recommendations for the Lahore Office," May 1972, FBPR, box 142, folder 5.
103. Harris, letter to Franklin Publications executive committee, September 24, 1968.
104. Harris, letter to Franklin Publications executive committee, September 26, 1968.
105. Michael Harris, letter to Franklin Publications, March 11, 1968, FBPR, box 155, folder 1.
106. "Franklin Plans Book Aid Programs in Bangladesh," *PW,* May 15, 1972, 32.
107. Kyle, "Comments," December 19, 1972.
108. Franklin Publications, "Remarks on Bangladesh," November 1, 1972, FBPR, box 1, folder 3.
109. "Franklin Plans Book Aid Programs in Bangladesh," 32.
110. Kyle, "Comments," December 19, 1972.
111. Jack Kyle, letter to Hosen Ali, FBPR, box 164, folder 2.
112. Franklin Publications, minutes, board of directors' meeting, November 7, 1968, FBPR, box 1, folder 3.
113. Michael Harris, letter to Harold Munger, March 14, 1969, FBPR, box 3, folder 8.
114. Michael Harris, letter to Harold Munger, March 15, 1969, FBPR, box 3, folder 8.
115. Ibid.
116. Richard T. Arndt, transcript of interview, May 9, 1988, 67–69, Columbia University, Iranian-American Relations Oral History Project, 1989, session 1.
117. Michael Harris, letter to Franklin Publications, February 21, 1968, FBPR, box 155, folder 1.
118. Datus Smith, letter to Homayoun Sanati, August 19, 1959, FBPR, box 3, folder 8.
119. Franklin Publications, "USIA Audit Report," October 16, 1963, FBPR, box 5, folder 2.
120. Harris, letter to Munger, March 15, 1969.
121. Harris, letter to Munger, March 14, 1969.
122. Harris, letter to Munger, March 15, 1969.
123. Michael Harris, letter to Franklin Publications executive committee, April 29, 1969, FBPR, box 3, folder 3.
124. Franklin Publications, minutes, board of directors' meeting, April 11, 1969.
125. Michael Griffin, "Road to Damask," *Middle East,* July 1, 2006.
126. Michael Harris, letter to Carroll Bowen, December 15, 1970, FBPR, box 9, folder 1.
127. Franklin Publications, minutes, members' meeting, December 11, 1974, FBPR, box 1, folder 6.
128. Kyle, "Comments," December 19, 1972.
129. J. M. Filstrup, "Franklin Book Programs/Tehran," *International Library Review* 8, no. 4 (1976): 440.
130. Ali M. Ansari, *Modern Iran Since 1921: The Pahlavis and After* (London: Longman, 2003), 150, 152, 171.
131. Arthur Goldschmidt, John Keane, and Cheryl Johnson, memorandum to Franklin Publications, August 8, 1974, FBPR, box 122, folder 3.
132. Franklin Publications, report, January 9, 1976, FBPR, box 1, folder 6.
133. Kyle, "Comments," December 19, 1972.

134. Jack Kyle, report to Franklin Publications board of directors, June 27, 1973, FBPR, box 1, folder 3.
135. Harold Munger, letter to Ruth Sloan, February 7, 1969, FBPR, box 74, folder 13.
136. Harold Munger, letter to Ronald Barker, March 27, 1970, FBPR, box 3, folder 1.
137. Michael Harris, letter to Franklin Publications New York office, February 16, 1969, FBPR, box 3, folder 2; Franklin Publications, "Foreign Office Highlights."
138. Franklin Publications, report, March 21, 1973, FBPR, box 1, folder 3.
139. Kyle, report, June 27, 1973.
140. Franklin Publications, minutes, members' meeting, December 11, 1974, FBPR, box 1, folder 6.
141. Ali Asghar Mohajer, letter to Datus Smith, October 13, 1975, FBPR, box 122, folder 1.
142. Franklin Publications, "Analysis of Donor Support," March 13, 1974, FBPR, box 1, folder 9.
143. Anders Richter, letter to Datus Smith, November 9, 1977, FBPR, box 12, folder 2.
144. Jack Kyle, letter to Robert J. Callender, February 4, 1975, FBPR, box 12, folder 2.
145. Ibid.
146. Franklin Publications, minutes, executive committee meeting, December 16, 1975, FBPR, box 1, folder 8.
147. Franklin Publications, minutes, executive committee meeting, July 27, 1976, FBPR, box 1, folder 8.
148. "Franklin Book Programs Expands Worldwide Activities," *PW,* March 7, 1977, 34.
149. Franklin Publications, minutes, board of directors' meeting, July 27, 1977, FBPR, box 1, folder 1.
150. Ibid.
151. Francis Fox, letter to Datus Smith, October 6, 1977, FBPR, box 12, folder 2.
152. Datus Smith, letter to Franklin Publications board of directors, October 10, 1977, FBPR, box 1, folder 8.
153. Franklin Publications, minutes, board of directors' meeting, October 27, 1977, FBPR, box 1, folder 1.
154. Ibid.; Franklin Publications, minutes, board of directors' meeting, December 29, 1977, FBPR, box 1, folder 6.
155. Datus Smith, letter to Franklin Publications members' meeting, March 17, 1978, FBPR, box 5, folder 8.
156. Datus Smith, letter to Franklin Publications members' meeting, May 1978, FBPR, box 1, folder 6.
157. Franklin Publications, minutes, board of directors' meeting, April 25, 1978, FBPR, box 1, folder 1.

Conclusion. Assessing the Legacy

1. Datus Smith, letter to Franklin Publications corporation members, November 1, 1977, FBPR, box 5, folder 8.
2. Farid Moradi, "History of Book Publishing in Iran," in *Publishing in Persian Language in Iran, Afghanistan, Tajikistan, Uzbekistan, Europe and United States,* by Farid Moradi, Laetitia Nanquette, Masoud Hosseinipour, Ali Amiri, Dilshad Rakhimov, and Beytolah Biniaz (Paris: International Alliance of Independent Publishers, 2013), 30. In "Bringing the Mountain to Mohammed: The Franklin Book Programs and Cold War Cultural Diplomacy in the Middle East," Louise Robbins details the traces she found of Franklin-trained editors and book illustrators (unpublished paper, 14).
3. Ben Pleasants, "Heart of Teheran," *Malibu,* February 15, 2011.
4. Clipping, *New York Times,* May 28, 1965, FBPR, box 5, folder 2.
5. Claudia Roth Pierpont, "Found in Translation," *New Yorker,* January 18, 2010.

Index

Adams, Arthur S., 9, 34
Afghanistan, 60, 62, 73, 97–99, 137
Africa, 86, 101–2, 113–25, 151. *See also* Kenya; Nigeria
Aguilera, Francisco, 115
Alcott, Louisa May, *Little Women,* 48, 50, 65, 72
Alfred A. Knopf, Inc., 37, 49–50, 80, 81, 117, 138
Alliance for Progress, 92, 125–26
American Association of University Presses, 117. *See also* university presses
American Book Council, 16
American Book Publishers Council (ABPC), 10, 25–27, 28–29, 35, 81, 94, 108, 132, 138–39. *See also* book exhibits
American Booksellers Association, 26
American Book Shop, 68
American Library Association, 15, 17, 26–27, 29, 101, 123
American Textbook Publishers Institute (ATPI), 17, 26, 34, 68, 94, 115, 116, 132
Amin, Mohammed el-, 71
anti-Americanism, 5, 23, 42–44, 47, 71, 143–45
anti-communism, 19, 25, 38, 93
Arabic (language): book design, 51, 111; Franklin's publications in, 39, 47–51, 55, 56, 60–61, 76–78, 80, 88, 100, 144, 151; sales of books, 60; translation of books into, 10, 50; USIA publications in, 87, 108–9. *See also* Egypt; Middle East; translation
Aramco, 41, 102, 135
Argentina, 127
Armour, Norman, 9
Arndt, Richard T., 109, 148
Aroussy, Hassan Galal al-, 44–45, 52, 54–55, 80
Asheim, Lester, 26, 97
Asia Foundation, 27, 65, 67, 71, 98, 137, 143, 152
Association Nationale du Livre Français à l'Étranger, 144

Association of American Publishers, 132, 139, 184n13
Awad, Lewis, 44
Azam, M. A., 146

Baghdad Pact, 40
Bahasa Indonesia, 61, 68, 74, 88, 100
Bangladesh. *See* Pakistan, East
Banker, Robert E., 67, 69
Barker, Ronald, 119, 125
Battle, Lucius, 110
Beers, Robert, 108
Belcher, Pat, 121, 167n112, 184n16
Bengali, 50, 65, 66, 88, 146
Benjamin, Curtis, 81, 110, 115, 126, 137
Biafran War, 151
Black, Douglas M., 9, 34
Bolton, Sarah K.: *Lives of Girls Who Became Famous,* 76; *Lives of Poor Boys Who Became Famous,* 48, 75, 77
Booher, Edward, 131, 138, 139
book development, 8, 28, 97, 129, 140
book distribution, 10, 22, 28, 37, 51, 61, 69, 71, 79, 86, 97–98, 123, 140, 143, 153
book exhibits, 19, 67, 80
book gap, 90, 111–12
book modernization, 5, 87, 93, 96, 111–12, 114, 133, 140, 155
bookselling, 3, 68, 71, 107, 153
bookstores, 51, 53, 60, 66, 67, 68
book trade, 5, 7, 10, 18, 24, 26, 27, 47, 51, 93, 96, 125–26, 139
Bowen, Carroll (Curly), 141–42, 152
Bowker, 117
Brazil, 127, 128–29, 138–39, 151. *See also* Latin America
Brett, George P., 9, 35, 48–49, 133
British publishers, 28, 46, 47, 69, 113, 115, 117–121, 124–25
Buck, Byron, 95, 106, 115–16
Burdette, Franklin, 64, 83–84
Burma, 62, 69

Cameron, Don, 36, 37, 41, 50, 98

Index

Campaign of Truth, 19
Canfield, Cass, 9
Carnegie Endowment for International Peace, 13, 15, 35
censorship, 25, 28, 29, 38, 104, 108, 132, 138
Central Intelligence Agency (CIA), 37, 63, 65, 101, 130, 137–38, 152
children's books, 25, 64, 75, 104–5, 126, 128
Chile, 129, 151
China, 12, 15, 61, 104, 109
Clark, Alden, 116, 118–21, 124
Coffin, Frank, 110
Committee for Public Information (CPI), 12–13
Commonwealth Fund, 128, 136
communism, 15, 22–23, 25, 30, 40, 42–43, 54, 59, 61, 69, 72, 81, 85, 90, 101, 108, 133, 136. *See also* anti-communism
Conference on American Books Abroad, 27, 56, 73
Coombs, Philip, 127
copyright, 28, 43, 49, 142, 146
Council on Books in Wartime, 11, 16–18, 35, 130
Creel, George, 12–13
Cronkite, Walter, 135
Crowell, Robert L., 9, 24
cultural diplomacy, 4, 6–7, 11–12, 14–20, 22–23, 27, 39–40, 51, 58, 61, 65, 68–69, 72, 155

Daily, Jay E., 97
Dar al-Hilal, 46, 77
Dar al-Maaref, 46
Dawood, Samy, 52–54
development, 12, 14, 20–21, 57, 78, 89–90, 91–95, 100–101, 115, 131, 135–36, 147. *See also* modernization; United States Agency for International Development
Doubleday, 117, 133
Drum magazine, 116, 124, 180n21
D. Van Nostrand, 35. *See also* Johnson, Malcolm

East African Literature Bureau, 116
East-West Center, 143
education: development and, 21, 31, 90, 94–97, 99–101, 114–19, 128, 133, 135–36; Franklin's work in, 59–60, 64, 68, 88, 140, 141–42, 147, 151; U.S. faith in, 11, 14, 27, 72, 92; U.S. support for, 25–26, 93, 138. *See also* textbooks
Egypt: book distribution in, 51, 56, 77; book industry in, 43, 47, 51, 77, 143; booksellers in, 46, 47; Egyptian translation program, 45, 51; foreign policy of, 64, 144; Franklin's program in, 39–59, 143–44, 151, 153; literacy, 49; U.S. concern with, 40. *See also* Aroussy, Hassan Galal al-; Dar al-Hilal; Dar al-Maaref; translators
Eisenhower, Dwight D., 16, 21
Etudo, E. A., 118
Evans, Luther H., 9

Fafunwa, A. Babs, 117–18, 136
Farsi. *See* Persian
Florence Agreement, 30
Ford Foundation: establishment of, 13; Franklin, support for 100–102, 104, 117, 127–28, 133–34, 136; Indonesia, presence in, 68; Middle East, presence in, 47
Fox, Francis, 153
Franklin Publications (also known as Franklin Book Programs): authors, relationship with, 79–81; closure of, 153–54; corporate funding, 102, 135, 151; country surveys, 33, 41–43, 65, 67–68, 115, 126; establishment of, 9; founding aims, 32; Friends of Franklin, 136; leadership changes, 139–43; political views, 34, 37; protests against, 51–54, 143–44; reviewers, 74, 84; royalties, 45, 49, 79–80, 110; title selection principles, 32, 69, 83–85; training role, 95–96, 117, 128; U.S. publishing industry, relationship with, 34, 37, 79–81, 110. *See also* Afghanistan; Africa; Egypt; Ford Foundation; Indonesia; Iran; Latin America; Malaysia; Nigeria; Rockefeller Foundation; translators; United States Agency for International Development; United States Information Agency
Frase, Robert, 26, 36
Freedom House, 143
freedom to read, 27, 29–30
free enterprise, 11, 12, 47, 120
Fundacion Interamericana de Bibliotecologia Franklin (FIBF), 127–28

Gallup, George, 26
Griffith, Charles, 65, 67, 68–69, 79
Griswold, A. Whitney, 26
Guinzburg, Harold, 26, 28

Harris, Mike, 122, 134, 139–41, 145, 146, 148–49
Harris, Reed, 133
Harwood, Raymond, 142

Hausa, 108, 117, 130
Hawley, Claude, 84
Heaps, David, 124
Heinemann, 119
Hodge, Philip, 24, 41
Homayoun, Dariush, 73, 98, 145
Hong Kong, 61
Howe, Irving, ed., *The Radical Papers,* 133
human rights, 131–32

Igbo, 117, 130
India, 23, 60, 62, 64, 86, 95, 101, 110, 128, 139
Indonesia, 59–61, 67–70, 74, 93–94, 135, 140, 144–45. *See also* Bahasa Indonesia
Indo-Pakistani War, 145
Informational Media Guarantee Program, 27, 81
intellectual freedom, 19, 104. *See also* freedom to read
International Cooperation Administration (ICA), 94
International Information Administration, 20, 23
Iran: Afghanistan and, 98; censorship in, 104; Franklin, impact of, 155–56; Franklin program in, 61–64, 72, 73, 75–77, 99, 102–8, 147–50; literacy, 62, 103, 105, 149–50; nationalism, 105; paper, 107; printing plant, 106–7; technical missions to, 12; Tudeh party in, 63–64, 103. *See also* Pahlavi, (Princess) Ashraf; Pahlavi, (Shah) Mohammad Reza; Persian
Iraq, 40, 70–71, 75
Iroaganachi, John, 117
Islam, 43, 45, 46, 50, 54–56, 59, 67, 69, 72, 75–77
Israel, 40, 42, 43, 50, 55–56, 144

Jackson Committee, 21
Jahanshahi, Iraj, 136
JDR 3rd Fund, 136, 140
Jennison, Peter, 27
Johnson, Malcolm, 9, 35, 37, 42, 49, 61, 85, 87–88
Johnson, Joseph E., 35
Johnson, Robert L., 23
Johnson Wax Foundation, 151

Kenya, 110, 118, 120, 121. *See also* Africa
Kerr, Chester, 138
Kerr, W. P., 119
Khan, Ayub, 64, 89
Khan, N. M., 65–66

Knerr, Wilbur, 127
Knopf, Alfred A., 80–81, 110, 126–27, 138. *See also* Alfred A. Knopf, Inc.
Knopf, Blanche, 126
Koshland, William A., 50
Kraeling, Carl H., 9
Kurani, Habib Amin, 44
Kyle, Jack, 135–36, 142–43, 146, 151–52

Lacy, Dan, 26, 28, 29, 36, 115, 126
languages, 8, 10, 24, 49, 73–74, 80, 86, 116–18
Lasswell, Harold D., 9, 26
Latin America, 12–14, 115, 125–29, 135, 136, 151
Lebanon, 61, 70–71, 75, 108
Lederer, William J., and Eugene Burdick, *The Ugly American,* 81
Lerner, Daniel, 91, 93
Liberia, 62, 114
libraries: Carnegie, 15; community, 145, 147, 151; public, 14; school, 78, 97, 128, 145; UNESCO and, 30–31, 116; USIS, 16, 19, 23, 25, 29, 47, 68, 109, 134; village, 97. *See also* American Library Association
library development, 96, 97, 128–29
literacy, 6, 14, 28, 30–31, 43, 56, 72, 90, 92, 93, 94, 143
Little, Brown, 117
Longman, 117, 120
Lunt, Storer, 82

MacLeish, Archibald, 16
Macmillan Publishing (UK), 46, 120
Macmillan Publishing (US), 68, 95, 127. *See also* Brett, George P.
Mahmoud, Hassan, 44, 45
Malaya, 60–61, 71, 137, 145
Malaysia. *See* Malaya
Marriner, Robie D., 9
Mateen, A. T. M. Abdul, 65, 146
McCarthy, Joseph, 23, 29
McCarthy, R. M., 61
McGraw, Curtis W., 9
McGraw-Hill, 68, 69, 117, 139, 152
Metalious, Grace, *Peyton Place,* 111
Middle East, 37–43, 54–56, 59. *See also* Arabic; Egypt
Mitchell, Margaret, *Gone With the Wind,* 79–80
modernization: corporate, 47; efforts, 14, 27, 28, 40, 58, 94, 98–101, 103, 128; military, 90; theory, 91–93, 131. *See also* book modernization; development; Point Four program; technical assistance

Mohajer, Ali Asghar, 147–48, 151
Morpurgo, J. E., 119
Munger, Harold N., 36, 125
Murrow, Edward R., 85, 110; *This I Believe*, 69, 72–73, 75, 76–77

Naguib, Muhammad, 40, 46
Najm, Mohammed, 71, 156
Nasser, Gamal Abdel, 40, 51, 77
National Book Committee, 27, 88, 143
nationalism: Afghanistan, in, 98; Africa, in, 114; Iran, in, 73; Middle East and Egypt, in, 40, 42, 52, 54, 55, 58
National Science Foundation, 144
Nepal, 150
New American Library, 35, 117
Nigeria, 96, 101, 109, 113, 115–21, 123–25, 128, 135, 151. *See also* Africa
Nixon, Richard M., 1, 133, 138

O'Connor, John, 9, 26
Office of Educational Exchange, 18
Office of International Information, 18
Office of International Information and Cultural Affairs, 18
Office of International Information and Education Exchange, 18
Office of Strategic Services (OSS), 16
Office of the Coordinator for Inter-American Affairs (CIAA), 15
Office of War Information (OWI), 16, 18
Old Dominion Foundation, 136
Operations Coordinating Board, 22
Overseas Editions publishing program, 11, 17
Oxford University Press, 119, 121
Oyewole, 'Femi, 117

Pahlavi, (Princess) Ashraf, 75, 99, 104, 148
Pahlavi, (Shah) Mohammad Reza, 63, 75, 76, 88, 102–8, 132, 148–50
Pakistan, East, 7, 65–66, 97, 136, 139, 146–47, 152. *See also* Bengali
Pakistan, West, 40, 58, 60, 61, 64–65, 67, 69, 73, 75, 89, 95–96, 103, 145–46. *See also* Urdu
paper, 3, 70, 95, 97–98, 107
Pars Paper, 107
Pashto, 73, 98, 130
Pazhwak, Atiqullah, 98
Peace Corps, 92, 95, 115
Persian (language), 50, 61, 73, 75, 77–78, 87–88, 98, 100–101, 103–6, 108
Peyk magazine, 105, 150

Philippines, 12, 62, 69, 73, 95, 128, 152
piracy, 51, 80
PL480 program, 21, 70, 107
Pocket Books, 16, 109
Point Four program, 20–21, 64
Population Council, 128
Pratt, Dana J., 35, 71, 168n133
President's Committee on International Information Activities. *See* Jackson Committee
propaganda, 15–17, 19–22, 25, 32, 58, 65, 83, 109, 115, 126, 133, 143
psychological warfare, 16, 19, 21–22
Publishers for Peace, 138

Random House, 117
reading development, 26, 28, 35, 100
Rehman, M. K., 65
Rehman, S. A., 75
Reisman, David, 26
Richter, Anders, 142, 145, 152
Rockefeller Foundation, 13, 100–102, 128
Roshangar, Majid, 156

Sabine, George H., *A History of Political Theory*, 50, 56, 60
Said, Amina el, 104
Sanati, Homayoun, 63–64, 76, 107, 108, 147–49. *See also* Iran
Schumpeter Fund, 137
Shadily, Hassan, 69, 144–45
Shakespeare, Frank, 133–35
Sheeks, Robert, 145
Sherkat Sahami Offset, 106–8
Shimkin, Leon, 9
Shirer, William L., *The Rise and Fall of the Third Reich*, 78, 145
Simon and Schuster, 16
Silver Burdett, 65, 69
Six Day War, 144
Smith, Datus C.: biographical information, 31; Franklin, as chair of, 152; Franklin president, appointment as, 10; Franklin president, resignation as, 130; *A Guide to Book Publishing*, 100; *The Land and People of Indonesia*, 69. *See also* Franklin Publications
Smith, Dorothy Hunt, 122, 144, 174n149
Smith, Shirley, 118, 121, 133
Smith-Mundt Bill, 18
Snyder, Harry R., 41
Soviet Union: book publishing programs, 24, 27, 32, 51, 81, 87, 90, 108; foreign policy,

40–41, 62–63, 64, 98, 114; modernization model, 21, 91, 99; propaganda efforts, 13, 25
Spaulding, Bill, 60, 94, 96, 110, 115, 119
Spaulding, John, 105, 136
Spock, Benjamin, *Baby and Child Care*, 23, 75, 99
State Department (U.S.), 16, 18–25, 32, 34, 37, 41, 43, 61–62, 83, 124, 129. *See also* United States Information Agency
state-private network, 4, 11, 60, 102, 157
St. John, Francis R., 9, 36, 42, 49, 67, 68
Straus, Roger W., Jr., 138
Streibert, Theodore, 22–23, 84, 85
Suez crisis, 40, 58, 59, 107
Swahili, 108, 118, 130

Taiwan, 61
Taplinger, Robert, 66
technical assistance, 12, 20–21, 28, 50, 63, 78, 91–93, 94, 96–97, 100, 103, 115, 118, 140. *See also* modernization; Point Four program
Technical Cooperation Administration, 21, 28, 94
Tennessee Valley Authority (TVA), 14
textbooks: demand for, 68; editing and production of, 77, 98, 106, 108, 124, 146; medical, 128, 136; promotion and export of, 25–26; school, 68, 105, 145, 148–50; university, 25, 60, 68, 145. *See also* American Textbook Publishers Institute
Thailand, 60, 69
Thorp, Willard L., 24
Time, Inc., 117
translation: Franklin programs, 24, 27, 43, 48–49, 56, 60–61, 65, 67–68, 80, 84, 99, 105, 108–10, 118, 128–29, 134, 144, 146–47, 151; Franklin's procedures, 29, 33, 49; politics of, 72–79, 88; rights, 10, 44, 50, 61, 62, 69, 79–81, 112; USIA programs, 24, 45, 47, 86–87, 126; value of, 8, 19, 51, 140; World War II, in, 15, 17. *See also* Franklin Publications; Overseas Editions publishing program; translators
translators, 50, 64, 70, 73–75, 78, 104, 110
Triebe, Edward J., 150
Truman, Harry S., 19, 20. *See also* Campaign of Truth; Point Four program
Turkey, 40, 62, 128
Twentieth Century Fund, 136

United Nations Educational, Scientific, and Cultural Organization (UNESCO), 30–31, 73, 90, 116
United States Advisory Commission on Educational Exchange, 18, 19
United States Advisory Commission on Information, 18, 134
United States Advisory Committee on Cultural Information, 86
United States Agency for International Development (AID), 94–96, 115, 117, 121, 127, 129, 132, 135, 145, 150, 152
United States Government Advisory Committee on International Book Programs, 110, 123
United States Information Agency (USIA): book gift programs, 109; book translation and publishing programs 47, 51, 56, 61, 67–68, 72, 80, 85–87, 100, 108–10, 126, 134–35, 144; establishment of, 20, 21; Franklin, relationship with, 43, 51, 60, 82–86, 88, 99, 134–35, 144, 148, 151; Franklin programs, funding of, 34, 37, 64, 69, 87, 90, 106, 132–34. *See also* cultural diplomacy; Franklin Publications; libraries; propaganda
United States International Book Association, 18
United States International Information Administration, 20, 23
university presses, 25, 27, 32, 35–36, 101
Urdu, 60, 61, 65, 75, 76, 80, 88, 97, 109, 145

Vietnam War, 93, 131, 136, 138, 155

Wakefield, Rowan, 96
Waller, Theodore, 25, 26, 29, 35
Walls, Esther J., 122–24, 128–29
Weybright, Victor, 9, 32, 35, 79
Wilber, Donald, 62–63
Wilcox, Bruce, 139
Wiley, 117, 144
Wiley, W. Bradford, 94, 110, 138
Wilson, Donald M., 110
Wilson, Thomas J., 3, 35, 94, 110
W. K. Kellogg Foundation, 128, 136
World Bank, 152
World War I, information activities, 12–13
World War II, 11, 15–18, 62, 63, 101

Yoruba, 117, 130

Zaki, Ahmad, 44, 50

AMANDA LAUGESEN is a historian and lexicographer, and is currently Director of the Australian National Dictionary Centre, Australian National University. She is the author of a number of books and articles on US and Australian history.

www.ingramcontent.com/pod-product-compliance
Lightning Source LLC
Chambersburg PA
CBHW020737230426
43665CB00009B/465